STEVE EMANUEL'S
BOOTCAMP FOR THE MBE: CONSTITUTIONAL LAW

emanuel® BAR REVIEW

STEVE EMANUEL'S Bootcamp for the MBE

CONSTITUTIONAL LAW

STEVEN L. EMANUEL

Founder & Editor-in-Chief,
Emanuel Bar Review
Member, NY, CT, MD and VA bars

www.aspenlaw.com

Wolters Kluwer Law & Business | Aspen Publishers

Emanuel Bar Review is a division of Aspen Publishers, a Wolters Kluwer company.

Aspen Publishers
Attn: Permissions Department
76 Ninth Avenue, 7th Floor
New York, NY 10011-5201

For information about Emanuel Bar Review (including Emanuel Multistate Review), contact:

email: info@emanuelbarprep.com
phone: 1-888-MBE-PREP
fax: 781-207-5815
website: www.emanuelbarprep.com

Printed in the United States of America.

3 4 5 6 7 8 9 0

ISBN 978-0-7355-9738-9

TABLE OF CONTENTS

Preface vii

Constitutional Law Outline

Table of Contents to Outline 3

Outline 7

Constitutional MBE-Style Questions

Questions 117

Answers 135

PREFACE

Dear *Bootcamp* enrollee:

This book consists mainly of a short outline on Constitutional Law. I hope that you'll read the outline before you watch the online substantive lecture that's part of Steve Emanuel's Bootcamp for the MBE. If you can't read the outline before watching the online lecture, read it by way of review afterwards.

The outline section of this book does not contain any MBE-format questions — that's what we'll be doing in the 2-volume "*Emanuel's Essentials*" set of multi-choice questions and answers in context, which is part of your materials.

I have written the outline in an attempt to cover virtually all the substantive rules of law that the MBE examiners test in their Constitutional Law questions, and to highlight the traps they set. I've tried to omit any topic or rule of law that doesn't seem to pop up on the MBE, no matter how important that topic may have been in your law school Constitutional Law course.

The last part of the book consists of the 33 questions on Constitutional Law extracted from our 200-Question Self-Assessment Test, together with our model answers to those questions. I hope that you will first take the Self-Assessment Test on a stand-alone basis, and that you will only consult the Constitutional Law questions in this book as a means of reviewing after you've taken the Self Assessment Test.

Good luck, and see you online soon!

Steve Emanuel

Larchmont, NY

April 2010

CONSTITUTIONAL LAW OUTLINE

TABLE OF CONTENTS
CONSTITUTIONAL LAW OUTLINE

Chapter 1

THE SUPREME COURT'S AUTHORITY AND THE FEDERAL JUDICIAL POWER

I. THE SUPREME COURT'S AUTHORITY AND THE FEDERAL JUDICIAL POWER 7

II. CONGRESS'S CONTROL OF FEDERAL JUDICIAL POWER 9

Chapter 2

FEDERALISM AND FEDERAL POWER GENERALLY

I. THE CONCEPT OF FEDERALISM 9

Chapter 3

POWERS OF THE FEDERAL GOVERNMENT; THE SEPARATION OF POWERS

I. POWERS OF THE THREE FEDERAL BRANCHES 11

II. THE FEDERAL COMMERCE POWER 12

III. THE TAXING AND SPENDING POWERS 15

IV. THE SEPARATION OF POWERS 18

Chapter 4

TWO LIMITS ON STATE POWER: THE DORMANT COMMERCE CLAUSE AND CONGRESSIONAL ACTION

I. THE DORMANT COMMERCE CLAUSE 23

II. CONGRESSIONAL PRE-EMPTION AND CONSENT; THE SUPREMACY CLAUSE 27

Chapter 5

INTERGOVERNMENTAL IMMUNITIES; INTERSTATE RELATIONS

I. TAX AND REGULATORY IMMUNITIES 29

II. THE INTERSTATE PRIVILEGES AND IMMUNITIES CLAUSE 31

III. THE FULL FAITH AND CREDIT CLAUSE 32

Chapter 6

THE DUE PROCESS CLAUSE

I. INTRODUCTION 33

II. THE FOURTEENTH AMENDMENT GENERALLY 33

III. SUBSTANTIVE DUE PROCESS — ECONOMIC AND SOCIAL WELFARE REGULATION 34

IV. SUBSTANTIVE DUE PROCESS — REGULATIONS AFFECTING FUNDAMENTAL RIGHTS 37

V. PROCEDURAL DUE PROCESS 42

Chapter 7

EQUAL PROTECTION

I. EQUAL PROTECTION GENERALLY 46

II. ECONOMIC AND SOCIAL LAWS — THE "MERE RATIONALITY" TEST 49

III. SUSPECT CLASSIFICATIONS, ESPECIALLY RACE 51

IV. RACE-CONSCIOUS AFFIRMATIVE ACTION 53

V. MIDDLE-LEVEL REVIEW (GENDER, ILLEGITIMACY AND ALIENAGE) 56

VI. FUNDAMENTAL RIGHTS 59

Chapter 8

MISCELLANEOUS CLAUSES

I. FOURTEENTH AMENDMENT PRIVILEGES AND IMMUNITIES 62

II. THE "TAKING" CLAUSE 62

III. THE "CONTRACT" CLAUSE 65

IV. *EX POST FACTO* LAWS 66

V. BILLS OF ATTAINDER 66

Chapter 9

THE "STATE ACTION" REQUIREMENT; CONGRESS'S ENFORCEMENT OF THE CIVIL WAR AMENDMENTS

I. STATE ACTION 67

II. CONGRESSIONAL ENFORCEMENT OF CIVIL RIGHTS 70

Chapter 10

FREEDOM OF EXPRESSION

I. GENERAL THEMES 72

II. ADVOCACY OF ILLEGAL CONDUCT 76

III. TIME, PLACE AND MANNER REGULATIONS 76

IV. REGULATION OF SYMBOLIC EXPRESSION 83

V. DEFAMATION AND INVASION OF PRIVACY 83

VI. OBSCENITY 85

VII. COMMERCIAL SPEECH 86

VIII. SOME SPECIAL CONTEXTS 87

IX. FREEDOM OF ASSOCIATION, AND DENIAL OF PUBLIC BENEFITS OR JOBS 88

X. SPECIAL PROBLEMS OF THE MEDIA 92

Chapter 11

FREEDOM OF RELIGION

I. INTRODUCTION 94

II. THE ESTABLISHMENT CLAUSE 94

III. THE FREE EXERCISE CLAUSE 99

Chapter 12

JUSTICIABILITY

I. JUSTICIABILITY GENERALLY 103

II. ADVISORY OPINIONS 103

III. STANDING 103

IV. MOOTNESS 107

V. RIPENESS 109

VI. THE ELEVENTH AMENDMENT AND SUITS AGAINST THE STATES 110

VII. POLITICAL QUESTIONS 111

CONSTITUTIONAL LAW OUTLINE

This Outline attempts to limit its coverage to topics that have repeatedly occurred on actual MBE exams.

CHAPTER 1

THE SUPREME COURT'S AUTHORITY AND THE FEDERAL JUDICIAL POWER

I. THE SUPREME COURT'S AUTHORITY AND THE FEDERAL JUDICIAL POWER

A. Court's right to decide constitutionality: It is the Supreme Court, not Congress or the executive branch, that has the authority and duty to declare a congressional statute unconstitutional if the Court thinks it violates the Constitution.

B. Supreme Court review of state court decision: The Supreme Court may review state court opinions, but only to the extent that the decision was decided *based on federal law.*

1. "Independent and adequate state grounds": Even if there is a federal question in the state court case, the Supreme Court may not review the case if there is an "*independent and adequate*" state ground for the state court's decision. That is, if the same result would be reached even had the state court made a different decision on the federal question, the Supreme Court may not decide the case. This is because its opinion would in effect be an "advisory" one.

a. Violations of state and federal constitutions: If a state action violates the *same clause* of both state and federal constitutions (e.g., the Equal Protection Clause of each), the state court decision *may or may not be based on an "independent" state ground.*

[1] If the state court is saying, "This state action would violate our state constitution *whether or not* it violated the federal constitution," that's *"independent."*

[2] But if the state court is saying, "Based on our reading of the constitutional provision (which we think has the same meaning under both the state and federal constitutions), this state action violates *both* constitutions," this is *not "independent."* Therefore, if the Supreme Court thinks that the state court has misinterpreted the federal constitution, the Court may hear the case and reverse the federal aspect of the decision, because the state-law conclusion was not truly independent. (Normally, the Supreme Court should then remand to the state court for further proceedings on the state-constitutional claim, so that the state court can have a chance to change its mind about whether the two constitutions really have the same meaning.)

i. How to tell: One common way you can tell that the state ground is "independent" is that the state court mentions that the clauses of the state and federal constitutions have the same or nearly the same text, but the court then says something like "we have not interpreted the state version of this clause in a manner that is *coextensive* [or *"co-terminous"*] with the federal version, and in some instances have interpreted our state version *more broadly.*" If, after making such a statement, the state court concludes that there has been a violation of the state version of the clause, then you can be pretty confident that the state ground is independent and adequate, even if the state court concludes that the federal version has been violated as well.

Example: When Defendant is stopped in his car and arrested, the police open a small package they find on the passenger seat, discover that it contains drugs, and charge Defendant. He defends on the grounds that the search of the package violates both the Fourth Amendment of the federal constitution and a comparably-worded provision of the state constitution. He's convicted and appeals. The state's highest court holds that the search violates both the Fourth Amendment and the comparable state-constitutional provision, and orders that Defendant be given a new trial. In doing so, the court notes that "We have interpreted our own state constitutional ban on unreasonable searches and seizures to be broader than the Fourth Amendment. We would conclude that the search here violated our state provision even if we had concluded that it did not violate the Fourth Amendment." The prosecution petitions the U.S. Supreme Court for certiorari.

The U.S. Supreme Court may not hear the case. The state ground for reversing was independent and adequate, because the state court made it clear that the state defines the requirements of the state ban on unreasonable searches and seizures more broadly than the similarly-worded federal one.

C. **Federal judicial power:** Article III, Sec. 2, Clause 1, sets out the *federal judicial power.* This includes, among other things:

- ❑ cases arising under the *Constitution* or the *"laws of the U.S."* (i.e., cases posing a "federal question");
- ❑ cases of *admiralty*;
- ❑ cases between *two or more states*;
- ❑ cases between *citizens of different states*; and
- ❑ cases between a state or its citizens and a *foreign country or foreign citizen.*

Note: Notice from this list that the federal judicial power does *not* include cases where *both parties are citizens (i.e., residents) of the same state* and no federal question is raised.

1. **Supreme Court's jurisdiction:** Article III, Sec. 2, Clause 2, specifies the *Supreme Court's* jurisdiction.

- ❑ **Original jurisdiction of Court:** First, the Clause says that the Court shall have "*original* jurisdiction" in "all Cases affecting *Ambassadors*, other public Ministers and Consuls, and those in which a *State shall be a Party*." This means that in these few types of cases, the action can be *filed directly in the Supreme Court.*
- ❑ **Appellate jurisdiction of Court:** Second, the Clause says that "In all the other Cases before mentioned" (i.e., cases falling within the general federal judicial power as specified in Clause 1, and not falling within the Supreme Court's original jurisdiction), the Court shall have "*appellate* Jurisdiction, both as to Law and Fact, with such Exceptions, and under such Regulations as the Congress shall make." This means that Congress can control what categories of cases the Supreme Court can hear on appeal.

a. **Two types:** So the Supreme Court has very limited "original" jurisdiction over certain cases filed directly with the Court, and much broader "appellate" jurisdiction over all other federal cases, except if Congress has cut back that appellate jurisdiction.

II. CONGRESS'S CONTROL OF FEDERAL JUDICIAL POWER

A. Congress's power to decide: *Congress* has the general power to *decide what types of cases the Supreme Court may hear.* So Congress may dramatically limit the kinds of cases which the Supreme Court may hear on appeal.

1. **Limits by Congress:** But the Constitution imposes some important *limits* on the degree to which Congress can modify the Court's jurisdiction:

   - ❑ Congress cannot *expand* the Supreme Court's jurisdiction beyond the federal judicial power (as listed in Paragraph (C) on p. 8). [*Ex parte McCardle*]
   - ❑ Congress *can't take away* any category of cases falling within the Supreme Court's *original* jurisdiction.
   - ❑ Congress *can't add* categories to the Court's *original* jurisdiction. (That is, Article III, Sec. 2, Cl. 2 specifies that the Supreme Court's original jurisdiction applies only to cases "affecting Ambassadors, other public Ministers and Consuls, and those in which a State shall be a party," and Congress cannot add other categories to this very short list.)
   - ❑ With respect to limits on the Court's appellate jurisdiction, Congress must act on a *broad and neutral* basis, and may not try to *decide the substantive merits* of a particular controversy by depriving the Court of the jurisdiction to decide that controversy. [*U.S. v. Klein*]

     Example: Congress probably can't provide that the Supreme Court may not hear any case in which a party makes a challenge based on the Equal Protection Clause to a state or local government's decision to conduct school busing. This would likely be held to be a non-neutral attempt to decide the substantive merits (by making it impossible to challenge a race-based busing scheme).

B. Lower courts: Congress also may decide what *lower federal courts* there should be, and what cases they may hear. Again, the outer bound of this power is that Congress can't allow the federal courts to hear a case that is not within the federal judicial power.

> **Example 1:** Congress may cut back the jurisdiction of the lower federal courts pretty much whenever and however it wishes. Thus Congress could constitutionally *eliminate diversity jurisdiction* (i.e., suits between citizens of different states), even though such suits are clearly listed in the Constitution as being within the federal judicial power.
>
> **Example 2:** But Congress could not give the lower federal courts jurisdiction over cases between two citizens of the same state, where no federal issue is posed. The handling of such a case by the federal courts would simply go beyond the federal judicial power as recited in the Constitution.

CHAPTER 2

FEDERALISM AND FEDERAL POWER GENERALLY

I. THE CONCEPT OF FEDERALISM

A. The federalist system: We have a *"federalist"* system. In other words, the national government and the state governments co-exist. Therefore, you always have to watch whether some power being asserted by the federal government is in fact allowed under the Constitution, and you must also watch whether some power asserted by the states is limited in favor of federal power.

B. Federal government has limited powers: The most important principle in this whole area is that the federal government is one of *limited, enumerated powers*. In other words, the three federal branches (Congress, the executive branch, and the federal courts) can only assert powers *specifically granted* to them by the United States Constitution.

So any time Congress passes a statute, or the President issues, say, an Executive Order, or the federal courts decide a case, you've got to ask: What is the enumerated, specified power in the U.S. Constitution that gives the federal branch the right to do what it has just done? (This is very different from what our Constitution says about the powers of *state* governments: state governments can do whatever they want as far as the U.S. Constitution is concerned, unless what they are doing is *expressly forbidden* by the Constitution.)

1. **No general police power:** The most dramatic illustration of this state/federal difference is the general *"police power."* Each state has a general police power, i.e., the ability to regulate solely on the basis that the regulation would enhance the welfare of the citizenry. But there is *no general federal police power*, i.e., no right of the federal government to regulate for the health, safety or general welfare of the citizenry. Instead, each act of federal legislation or regulation must come within one of the very specific, enumerated powers (e.g., the Commerce Clause, the power to tax and spend, etc.).

   a. **Tax and spend for general welfare:** Congress *does* have the right to "*lay and collect taxes* ... to pay the debts and provide for the ... *general welfare* of the United States. ... " (Article I, Sec. 8.) But the phrase "provide for the ... general welfare" in this sentence modifies "lay and collect taxes ... to pay the debts. ... " In other words, the power to tax and spend is subject to the requirement that the general welfare be served; there is no *independent* federal power to provide for the general welfare. The MBE examiners love to try to mousetrap you with a choice that says a particular congressional statute is supported by Congress's power to "legislate for the general welfare."

   Exam Tip: Therefore, be extremely suspicious of any choice that seems to be saying that Congress has an independent power to regulate for the general welfare. Unless the facts make it clear that Congress is taxing and spending, *any choice relying on Congress's powers relating to general welfare is almost certainly wrong.*

C. "Necessary and Proper" Clause: In addition to the very specific powers given to Congress by the Constitution, Congress is given the power to "make all laws which shall be *necessary and proper* for carrying into execution" the specific powers. The "Necessary and Proper" Clause means that if Congress is seeking an *objective* that is within the specifically enumerated powers, then Congress can use *any means* that is: (1) *rationally related* to the objective Congress is trying to achieve; and (2) is not specifically forbidden by the Constitution.

1. **"Necessary and proper" mousetrap:** Often the MBE examiners will try to trick you by coupling the Necessary and Proper Clause with the supposed "general welfare" power (discussed *supra*). *Don't be fooled.* The Necessary and Proper Clause only works when Congress is using it to seek an objective that *falls within Congress's specifically enumerated powers.* Since as we saw above there is no general power to legislate to achieve the "general welfare," the availability of the Necessary and Proper Clause does not help Congress legislate to achieve the general welfare.

D. Can't violate specific constitutional provision: Even where congressional action appears to fall within a specific grant of power, the federal action may not, of course, violate some *other* specific constitutional guarantee. In other words, congressional (or other federal) action must satisfy *two* tests to be constitutional: (1) it must fall within some specific grant of power under the Constitution; and (2) it must not violate any specific constitutional provision.

CHAPTER 3

POWERS OF THE FEDERAL GOVERNMENT; THE SEPARATION OF POWERS

I. POWERS OF THE THREE FEDERAL BRANCHES

A. Powers of the three branches: Here is a summary of the powers of the *three branches* of the federal government:

1. **Congress:** Here are the main powers given to Congress:

   a. **Interstate commerce:** Congress has the power to *regulate interstate commerce*, as well as foreign commerce.

   b. **Taxing and spending:** Congress has the power to *tax* and the power to *spend.*

   c. **DC:** Congress can regulate the *District of Columbia.*

   d. **Federal property:** Congress has power to regulate and dispose of *federal property.*

   e. **War and defense:** Congress can *declare war,* and can establish and fund the armed forces.

   f. **Enforcement of Civil War amendments:** Congress can *enforce* the *post-Civil War amendments.* (For instance, under its power to enforce the Thirteenth Amendment's abolition of slavery, Congress can ban even private intrastate non-commercial conduct.)

   MBE Tip: When Congress properly acts under one of these powers, its action *takes precedence over an inconsistent act by a state,* on account of the Supremacy Clause. So, for instance, if there is a *federally-owned enclave* located within a state (e.g., a national park or military base), Congress's civil and criminal regulations are enforceable as to that enclave, and take precedence over any inconsistent state regulation.

2. **President:** Here are the main powers of the President:

   a. **Execution of laws:** The President holds the *"executive power."* That is, he *carries out* the laws made by Congress. It is his obligation to make sure the laws are "faithfully executed."

   b. **CEO of the U.S., and "Executive Orders":** The President's executive power makes him, in effect, the "Chief Executive Officer" of the U.S. government. This means that he has the inherent power to *supervise the conduct of the executive branch, including federal agencies.* The President will typically do this by issuing an *"executive order."* Such an order, if directed to executive-branch personnel, will be valid unless it is inconsistent with a congressional statute or some specific provision of the constitution itself.

      i. **MBE Tip:** You will often see questions in which the President issues an executive order that directs some part of the executive branch (typically a federal agency) to do something. If the facts tell you that there is no congressional statute on point, you should assume that the order is *constitutional.*

      ii. **Direction to private party:** Conversely, if the question involves an executive order in which the President directs someone *outside of the executive branch* (e.g., a *private party*) to do something, you should presume that the order is *unconstitutional* unless something in the facts suggests that Congress has at least tacitly granted the President authority in this area.

c. **Commander in Chief:** The President is *Commander in Chief* of the armed forces. So he directs and leads our armed forces (but he cannot declare war — only Congress can do this).

d. **Treaty and foreign affairs:** The President can make *treaties* with foreign nations (but only if two-thirds of the Senate approves). He appoints *ambassadors.* Also, he effectively controls our *foreign policy* — some of this power over foreign policy stems from his right to appoint ambassadors, but much is simply *implied* from the nation's need to speak with a single voice in foreign affairs (so that congressional involvement in the details of foreign affairs will generally not be appropriate).

e. **Appointment of federal officers:** The President appoints all *federal officers*. These include *Cabinet members*, *federal judges* and *ambassadors*. (But the Senate must approve all such federal officers by majority vote.) As to "*inferior* [federal] officers," it's up to Congress to decide whether these should be appointed by the President, by the judicial branch, or by the "heads of departments" (i.e., Cabinet members). (But Congress can't make these lower-level appointments itself; it may merely decide who *can* make these appointments. See *infra*, p. 21.)

f. **Pardons:** The President can issue *pardons*, but only for federal offenses. (Also, he can't pardon anyone who has been impeached and convicted.) The President's pardon power is plenary — his decision does not need the consent of, and cannot be overridden by, Congress or the judiciary.

3. **Judiciary:** The federal *judiciary* may decide "cases" or "controversies" that fall within the federal judicial power. See the section on "Federal Judicial Power" in Chapter 1 above.

II. THE FEDERAL COMMERCE POWER

A. **Summary:** Probably Congress's most important power is the power to "*regulate Commerce* … among the several states." (Article I, Sec. 8.) This is the "Commerce power."

> **Exam Tip:** Any time you have an MBE question in which Congress is doing something, first ask yourself, "Can what Congress is doing be justified as an exercise of the commerce power?" Most of the time the answer will be "yes."

B. **Summary of modern view:** There are *four broad categories* of activities which Congress can constitutionally regulate under the Commerce power:

1. **Channels:** First, Congress can regulate the use of the *"channels"* of interstate commerce. Thus Congress can regulate in a way that is reasonably related to highways, waterways, and air traffic. Congress can do so even though the activity in question in the particular case is completely intrastate.

2. **Instrumentalities:** Second, Congress can regulate the *"instrumentalities"* of interstate commerce, even though the particular activities being regulated are completely intrastate. This category refers to people, machines, and other "things" used in carrying out commerce.

   Example: Probably Congress could say that every truck must have a specific safety device, even if the particular truck in question was made and used exclusively within a single state.

3. **Articles moving in interstate commerce:** Third, Congress can regulate *articles moving* in interstate commerce.

   Example: The states and private parties keep information about the identities of drivers. Since this information gets exchanged across state lines (e.g., from states to companies that want to sell cars), the information is an article in interstate commerce and Congress may regulate how it's used. [*Reno v. Condon*]

4. **"Substantially affecting" commerce:** Finally, the biggest (and most interesting) category is that Congress may regulate those activities having a *"substantial effect"* on interstate commerce. [*U.S. v. Lopez*] As to this category, the following rules now seem to apply:

   a. **Activity is commercial:** If the activity itself is arguably *"commercial,"* then it doesn't seem to matter whether the *particular instance* of the activity directly affects interstate commerce, as long as the instance is part of a general class of activities that, *collectively*, substantially affect interstate commerce. So even purely intrastate activities can be regulated if they're directly "commercial." This is especially true where Congress regulates the intrastate commercial activities as part of a *broad scheme* to regulate interstate commerce in the same activity.

   Example: Congress makes it a crime to cultivate marijuana for one's personal medical use. *Held*, this statute is a valid exercise of the commerce power. Even though the activity barred in this scenario is totally intrastate, Congress could reasonably fear that if it exempted personal — and thus "intrastate" — cultivation and use of marijuana for medical purposes, some of the marijuana so cultivated would be illegally drawn into the interstate market, jeopardizing Congress's overall scheme of banning the drug. So even the private cultivation of marijuana for one's own personal use may be forbidden. [*Gonzales v. Raich*]

      i. **"Inseverable aggregates":** The drafters of the MBE will sometimes express this concept — that Congress can regulate individual intrastate-only activities if they are part of a broader category of activities that include interstate ones — by giving you a choice that says that the intrastate activity is one of many activities that *"in inseverable aggregates"* have a substantial effect on commerce. As long as Congress is directly regulating the activity (rather than forcing states to regulate it, which might be a Tenth amendment problem; see *infra*, p. 15), the choice containing the phrase "inseverable aggregates" is likely to be the correct answer.

      Example: Congress, relying on its Commerce power, requires that every commercial car wash in the country use only organic detergents, in order to reduce environmental damage. CarWash, a commercial car wash located in the middle of Texas, more than 100 miles from the border with any other state, challenges the constitutionality of the statute as applied to it. CarWash has only three employees, buys all of its supplies from in-state suppliers, and almost never washes the cars of individuals who reside more than a few miles away from its single location.

      The statute can constitutionally be applied to CarWash, because operation of even intrastate car washes has, in "inseverable aggregates," a substantial effect on commerce. That is, although CarWash's own activities may not substantially affect interstate commerce, the activities of *all commercial car washes in America taken together* definitely have a substantial affect on interstate commerce (e.g., by creating demand for commercial-strength car-wash detergent sold across state lines). Therefore, Congress can use its Commerce power to regulate CarWash as part of its regulation of the class of businesses of which CarWash is a part.

   b. **Activity is not commercial:** But if the activity itself is *not "commercial,"* then there will have to be a *pretty obvious connection* between the activity and interstate commerce, in order for Congress to be able to use its commerce power to regulate that activity.

   Example 1: Congress makes it a federal crime to possess a firearm in or near a school. The statute applies even if the particular gun never moved in (or affected) interstate commerce. *Held*, in enacting this statute Congress went beyond its Commerce power. To fall within the Commerce power, the activity being regulated must have a "substantial effect" on interstate commerce. The link between gun-possession in a school and interstate commerce is too tenuous to qualify as a "substantial effect," because if it did, there would be essentially no limit to Congress's Commerce power. [*U.S. v. Lopez*]

Example 2: Congress says that any woman who is the victim of a violent gender-based crime may bring a civil suit against the perpetrator in federal court. *Held*, Congress went beyond its Commerce power. Although it may be true that some women's fear of gender-based violence dissuades them from working or traveling interstate, gender-based violence is not itself a commercial activity, and the connection between gender-based violence and interstate commerce is too attenuated for the violence to have a "substantial effect" on commerce. [*U.S. v. Morrison*]

i. **Jurisdictional hook:** But where the congressional act applies only to particular activities each of which has a direct link to interstate commerce, then the act *will* probably be within the Commerce power. Thus the use of a *"jurisdictional hook"* will probably suffice.

   Example: Suppose Congress makes it a crime to possess a gun that has moved within interstate commerce in or near a school. Since the statute has a "jurisdiction hook" — it's limited to guns that have moved in interstate commerce — it's almost certainly a valid exercise of the Commerce power, notwithstanding *U.S. v. Lopez*, *supra*.

ii. **Detailed fact-finding by Congress:** Also, if Congress makes *detailed factual findings* justifying its conclusion that a particular activity being regulated by Congress has, in the aggregate, a substantial effect on commerce, the Court will give significant weight to this finding, and will likely agree that the regulation falls within Congress's commerce powers.

   Example: Congress makes it unlawful to use a metal bat in any organized youth-baseball game. Congress acts after holding hearings on the safety implications of metal bats, and after making detailed findings that several thousand young baseball players are injured each year by the greater velocity with which a ball comes off a metal bat than off a wooden bat. Congress also finds that these thousands of injuries have, in the aggregate, a substantial economic effect on health insurance premiums and on the productivity of parents who miss work to care for injured youngsters.

   The Supreme Court would almost certainly agree that the regulation falls within Congress's commerce powers: the detailed factual findings about the economic effect of the injuries that would be avoided with wooden bats, coupled with the fact that the product type being regulated is itself generally sold in commerce, would outweigh the fact that youth baseball games are generally not commercial in nature.

C. **The Tenth Amendment as a limit on Congress's power:** The *Tenth Amendment* provides that "the powers not delegated to the United States by the Constitution, nor prohibited by it to the States, are reserved to the States respectively, or to the People." This Amendment places a small but still significant limit on Congress's ability to use its commerce power to *regulate the states*.

1. **Generally-applicable law:** If Congress passes a *generally applicable law*, the fact that the regulation *affects the states* has virtually no practical significance, and the Tenth Amendment never comes into play. If the regulation would be valid if applied to a private party, it is also valid as to the state.

   Example: Congress passes minimum-wage and overtime provisions, which are made applicable to all businesses of a certain size. The statute contains no exemption for employees of state-owned mass transit systems. *Held*, the regulation even of state employees here is a constitutional exercise of the commerce power, and is not forbidden by the Tenth Amendment. [*Garcia v. San Antonio Metropolitan Transit Authority*]

2. **Use of state's law-making mechanisms:** But the Tenth Amendment *does* prevent Congress from interfering in certain ways with a state's *law-making processes*. Congress may not simply "commandeer the legislative processes of the states by directly *compelling them to enact and enforce a federal regulatory program.*" [*New York v. United States*]

   a. **Enactment of statute:** So Congress can't require a state to *pass a particular statute*, for instance.

      Example: To combat school violence, Congress passes a statute requiring each state legislature to enact a state law that makes it a state crime for any person to possess or sell a firearm within 1,000 feet of any school, if the firearm has moved in interstate commerce. This statute almost certainly violates the Tenth Amendment, because that amendment prevents the federal government from compelling a state to enact or enforce a particular law. [Cf. *N.Y. v. U.S.*]

   b. **Administrative actions:** Similarly, Congress may not compel a state or local government's *executive branch* to perform functions, even ones that are easy to do and involve no discretion.

      Example 1: Congress can't pass a statute requiring sheriffs employed by states or counties to perform background checks on applicants for handgun permits. [*Printz v. U.S.*]

      Example 2: Congress passes a statute requiring every employer of more than 10 employees to give a brief course in federal income-tax compliance to any new employee. The statute expressly applies to the states as employers. As applied to a state employer, the statute is unconstitutional, because it requires state executive officers to carry out a federal regulatory program, and thus violates the Tenth Amendment.

3. **Not a source of state authority:** The Tenth Amendment is not, as a practical matter, a source of affirmative state power — its only real function is to prevent Congress from interfering with state law-making as described above. Therefore, if a question involves the constitutionality of a state law (as opposed to a federal action), any choice that relies on the Tenth Amendment as the *reason the state law is constitutional* is probably *incorrect.*

III. THE TAXING AND SPENDING POWERS

A. **Taxing power:** Congress has the power to "*lay and collect taxes* ... to pay the Debts and provide for the Common Defence and *general Welfare* of the United States." (Article I, Sec. 8.)

This is an *independent source* of congressional power, so it can be used to reach conduct that might be beyond the other sources of congressional power, like the Commerce Clause. In other words, as long as Congress is raising revenue and using that revenue for the general welfare, the tax is a valid exercise of congressional power.

1. **Regulation:** This means that Congress can effectively *regulate* under the guise of taxing, so long as there's some real revenue produced. So the fact that the tax has a direct impact on areas ordinarily left to the states won't matter (and Congress doesn't have to be pursuing some specific objective supported by some other enumerated source of congressional power).

   Example: To raise revenue and to make public secondary education more attractive than private secondary education, Congress passes a tax on private schools, equal to $500 per student per year. Even though regulation of education is ordinarily left to the states, and even though Congress may have been more interested in regulation than in achieving tax revenue, the fact that the measure is cast as a tax and produces real revenue will be enough to make it a valid exercise of the plenary federal power to "lay and collect taxes ... to ... provide for the general welfare" of the U.S.

a. **Adverse economic consequences no problem:** When Congress taxes a particular product or activity, as long as the tax is rationally related to the raising of revenues, the fact that the tax will *produce adverse economic consequence* (e.g., *lower sales*) for the product or activity being taxed does not raise a constitutional problem.

b. **No relation needed between activity taxed and how funds are spent:** There does not have to be any particular relation between the activity being taxed and the use of the funds raised by the taxation. So as long as Congress can loosely be said to be pursuing the general welfare, Congress can tax activity *A* and spend the proceeds on activity *B*, where *A* and *B* have nothing to do with each other.

Example: Congress can place an excise tax on every new oil well, and spend the money on education. That's because there is no requirement that revenue raised by a tax on a particular activity be spent on a purpose that has something to do with that activity. Congress has plenary power to "tax and spend for the general welfare." And the Court will virtually never overturn Congress's determination that using the money from a tax on one activity, and spending it on a completely unrelated activity, somehow contributes to the nation's general welfare.

2. **Limits on taxing power:** There are a few *limits* which the Constitution places upon the taxing power. However, these limits will rarely be the source of the correct answer on the MBE — they're much more likely to be the source of a wrong "distractor" choice.

a. **Direct taxes:** "Direct taxes" must be allocated among the states in proportion to population. This provision is of little practical importance today. (See more about this *infra*, p. 17.)

b. **Customs duties and excise taxes must be uniform:** All *customs duties* and *excise taxes* must be *uniform* throughout the United States.

Example: Congress may not place a \$.10 per-gallon federal excise tax on gasoline sales that take place in New Jersey, and a \$.15 per-gallon tax on those that take place in Oklahoma.

i. **Meaning of "uniform":** The requirement of uniformity does *not* mean that the tax must have the same aggregate economic effect in one state as in another — all it means is that the tax rate on the particular item being taxed must be the same regardless of which state the item is produced or sold in.

c. **No export taxes:** Congress may *not* tax any *exports* from any state.

Example: Congress may not place a tax on all computers which are exported from any state to foreign countries.

B. **Spending power:** Congress also has the power to "pay the debts and provide for the common defense and general welfare of the United States." (Article I, Sec. 8.) This is the "*spending*" power.

1. **Independent power:** This is an independent power, just like the Commerce power. So Congress could spend to achieve a purely local benefit, even one that it couldn't achieve by regulating under the Commerce power. And the constitutional requirement that the spending be in furtherance of the "general welfare" has almost no significance (a point discussed further *infra*, p. 17).

2. **Special rule for "duties" and "excises":** There's a special rule for taxes that are *"duties"* or *"excises"*: Article I, Sec. 8 says that "all Duties, Imposts and Excises shall be *uniform* throughout the United Sates."

a. **Not usually significant:** This requirement of uniformity for duties or excise taxes merely means that Congress can't discriminate against one state in favor of another in setting them (e.g., by saying that residents of one state must pay a higher excise tax than residents of another). This clause will rarely if ever be violated in an MBE question — as long as the excise or duty is calculated the same way regardless of where the taxpayer lives, it's OK, and MBE questions will almost never violate this easy-to-satisfy principle.

3. **Special rule for "direct taxes":** Article I, Sec. 2, Clause 3 also has a special tax rule: *"direct"* taxes must be *"apportioned* among the several States which may be included within this Union, according to their respective Numbers[.]" (See also Article I, Sec. 9, Cl. 4, repeating this requirement.) This means that if a tax is a "direct" tax, it must be set in such a way that *the revenue produced by it comes from each state in proportion to that state's share of the nation's overall population.*

   a. **Very few taxes are "direct":** But *very few* taxes are deemed *"direct"* today. The only type of direct tax that would plausibly be introduced (or be mentioned on the MBE) would be a tax on *real property.*

      i. **Nearly all taxes are "indirect":** Apart from taxes on real property, virtually any other kind of tax — including pretty much any kind of "excise" tax or "duty" — would be deemed to be *indirect.* Therefore, virtually all taxes you'll see on the MBE would be indirect and would *not* have to produce from each state revenues proportionate to that state's population.

      Example: Congress imposes an excise tax of $10 on each new cell phone sold in the United States. It appropriates the entire proceeds of the tax to a special fund used to bring Internet service to poor rural school districts. Even if the tax yields much greater per capita revenue from some states than others, the tax won't violate the requirement that direct taxes be apportioned by population — that's because this tax, like virtually any non-real-estate tax, is an "indirect" tax, not a "direct" one.

4. **Use of conditions:** Congress may place *conditions* upon use of its spending power, even if the congressional purpose is in effect to regulate. Conditions placed upon the doling out of federal funds are usually justified under the "Necessary and Proper" Clause (which lets Congress use any means to seek an objective falling within the specifically-enumerated powers, as long as the means is rationally related to the objective, and is not specifically forbidden by the Constitution).

   Example: Congress makes available to the states certain funds that are to be used for improving the states' highway systems. Congress provides, however, that no state may receive any of these funds unless the state has by statute imposed a speed limit of no higher than 55 mph on all state roads. Even without reference to the Commerce Clause, this is a valid use of congressional power. That's because by the combination of the spending power and the "Necessary and Proper" Clause, Congress is permitted to impose conditions (even ones motivated solely by regulatory objectives) on the use of federal funds.

5. **General welfare:** When Congress spends, it must spend for the *"general welfare"* (since the constitutional grant of the power to tax and spend is Article I, Sec. 8's power to "pay the debts and *provide for* the common defense *and general welfare* of the United States"). But this requirement of general welfare has *very little bite* — as long as Congress *could rationally have believed* that the congressional spending would somehow contribute to the general welfare (and the spending doesn't violate some other specific constitutional prohibition), that's enough. So the fact that the Court might think the spending unwise or capricious won't make the spending scheme unconstitutional.

Example: Congress appropriates $1 million to be used as $10,000 grants to 100 students chosen on the basis of their responses to a "Why I want to Study Medieval Latin" essay contest, to permit each of the grantees to buy rare books to study medieval Latin at home. Even if the Supreme Court believes that this grant is so narrow that it does not really serve the "general welfare," and even though the activity being supported probably could not be supported by the commerce power, the court will almost certainly sustain the statute as a valid exercise of the spending power.

C. **"General Welfare" Clause:** Although, as noted above, Congress can "provide for the common defense and general welfare of the United States," remember that the reference to "general welfare" does *not* confer any independent source of congressional power. In other words, no statute is valid solely because Congress is trying to bring about the "general welfare." Instead, the phrase "for the general welfare" describes the circumstances under which Congress may use its "taxing and spending" power. So if Congress is *regulating* (rather than taxing and spending), it must find a specific grant of power (like the Commerce Clause), and it's not enough that the regulation will promote the general welfare.

IV. THE SEPARATION OF POWERS

A. **Separation of powers generally:** Let's now review some of the major practical consequences that come from the fact that each federal branch gets its own set of powers. These practical consequences are collectively referred to as *"separation of powers"* problems.

1. **President can't make the laws:** The most important single separation of powers principle to remember is that the *President cannot make the laws*. All he can do is to *carry out the laws* made by Congress.

Example: During the Korean War, President Truman wants to avert a strike in the nation's steel mills. He therefore issues an "executive order" directing the Secretary of Commerce to seize the mills and operate them under federal direction. The President does not ask Congress to approve the seizure. *Held*, the seizure order is an unconstitutional exercise of the lawmaking authority reserved to Congress. [*Youngstown Sheet & Tube v. Sawyer*]

a. **Line item veto:** The principle that the President can't make the laws means that the President can't be given a *"line item veto."* That is, if Congress tries to give the President the right to veto individual portions of a statute (e.g., particular expenditures), this will violate the Presentment Clause. (The Presentment Clause says that bills are enacted into law by being passed by both Houses, then being presented to the President and signed by him.) [*Clinton v. City of New York*]

b. **Congress's acquiescence:** But the scope of the President's powers may be at least somewhat expanded by *Congress's acquiescence* to his exercise of the power. This congressional acquiescence will never be *dispositive*, but in a close case, the fact that Congress acquiesced in the President's conduct may be enough to tip the balance, and to convince the Court that the President is merely carrying out the laws rather than making them.

c. **Implied powers:** Recall that Congress's powers are somewhat expanded by the "Necessary & Proper" clause — Congress can pass any laws reasonably related to the exercise of any enumerated power. There's no comparable "Necessary & Proper" clause for the President. But the effect is the same, because of the inherent vagueness of the phrase "shall take care that the laws be faithfully executed..." The Constitution does specifically enumerate some of the President's powers (e.g., the pardon power, the commander-in-chief power, etc.). But this specific list is not supposed to be exclusive. Instead of giving a complete list of the President's powers (as is done for Congress), the Constitution gives the President this general "executive" or "law carrying out" power.

i. **Consequence:** Consequently, so long as the President's act seems reasonably related to carrying out the laws made by Congress, the Court won't strike that act merely because it doesn't fall within any narrow, enumerated presidential power.

Example: Nothing in the Constitution expressly gives the President prosecutorial discretion (the power to decide whom to prosecute), yet he clearly has this power, because it's part of the broader job of "carrying out the law."

d. **Delegation:** Congress may *delegate* some of its power to the President or the executive branch. This is how federal agencies (which are usually part of the executive branch) get the right to formulate *regulations* for interpreting and enforcing congressional statutes.

i. **Requirements for delegation:** When Congress delegates some of its lawmaking power to the President or the executive branch, Congress must: (1) state reasonably concretely the *objectives* that the delegate (the recipient of the power) must try to achieve; and (2) specify *adequate criteria* by which the delegate should make its decision. If Congress doesn't satisfy these two requirements, the delegation can be struck down on separation-of-powers grounds.

ii. **Exam Tip:** These two requirements (concrete objectives and adequate criteria) are interpreted very *leniently*. Therefore, you should assume that the delegation in an MBE question is *valid* unless there's a very obvious problem.

[1] **Total lack of standards:** However, a *total lack of standards* by which a federal agency or other part of the executive branch is to carry out the delegated authority *would* make the delegation a violation of the separation of powers. And the MBE examiners will sometimes give you such a completely standardless delegation.

Example: Congress passes a statute creating a Federal Insurance Regulatory Commission, to be administered as part of the executive branch. Commissioners are to be appointed by the President. The statute authorizes the Commission to "regulate the insurance industry in America in any way the Commission shall decide is justified, in the sole discretion of a majority of the commissioners." Violation of any regulation enacted by the Commission is made a federal felony.

The statute clearly violates separation-of-powers principles, because Congress has not specified adequate criteria by which the agency (the delegate) is to make its decisions. Therefore, Congress has in effect delegated to the executive branch (the Commission) the law-making power.

2. **War powers:** Be alert for separation-of-powers issues when the President's *war-related powers* are at stake.

a. **Can't declare war:** The President is the Commander-in-Chief of the armed forces. But *only Congress, not the President, can declare war.* The President can commit our armed forces to repel a sudden attack, but he cannot fight a long-term engagement without a congressional declaration of war.

3. **The "legislative veto":** Be alert for separation-of-powers problems in a statutory scheme that looks like it may be a *"legislative veto."* In a legislative-veto scenario, Congress passes a statute delegating certain power to a federal agency, but also provides that if, after the agency acts (usually by issuing a regulation), both houses of Congress vote to cancel that agency action, the agency action is automatically nullified. This type of legislative veto effectively

deprives the President of his Article I, Sec. 7 right to veto any newly-passed statute (since the congressional undoing of the agency action is, in effect, a new statute), and thus violates separation-of-powers principles. [*I.N.S. v. Chadha*]

Example: A federal statute prohibits the operation of any radio station without a license from the Federal Communications Commission. The statute also provides that the FCC may issue a license allowing operation of a new radio station 30 days after the commission staff make a finding that such operation would be in the interests of the community to be served by the station. Another provision of the statute provides that Congress, by a simple majority of each House, may veto the issuance of a particular license by the Commission if the veto occurs within 30 days following the staff finding. After the FCC staff makes a finding that a radio station proposed to be licensed to the plaintiff would be in the interests of the community, and the Commission issues the license, both houses of Congress veto the issuance of the license.

In a suit by the plaintiff, the Court will hold that the statutory scheme is unconstitutional, because it is a legislative veto that deprives the President of his Article I, Sec. 7 right to veto any newly-passed statute. That is, the court will view Congress's undoing of the FCC action as a new statute, which must be subjected to the President's veto right.

4. **Treaties and executive agreements:** As noted, the President has the power to enter into a *treaty* with foreign nations, but only if two-thirds of the Senate approves. Additionally, the Court has held that the Constitution implicitly gives the President, as an adjunct of his foreign affairs power, the right to enter into an *"executive agreement"* with a foreign nation, without first getting express congressional consent.

5. **Presidential Commissions:** The President has the power to appoint a temporary *"Presidential Commission,"* as long as the powers given to the Commission are either advisory only, or are limited to those powers properly exercised by the executive branch (i.e., the Commission is to carry out the law rather than "make" the law). The President has this power to appoint a Presidential Commission even without the explicit authorization of the Congress, as long as the funds spent on the Commission's operations were properly appropriated by Congress (which may have occurred through a vague appropriation of funds to be used "as the President sees fit" or the like).

6. **Appointment and removal of executive personnel:** The President, not Congress, is given the power to *appoint federal executive officers*. This is the *"Appointments"* Clause.

   a. **General scheme:** More specifically, the scheme is that only the President, not Congress, may appoint "principal," i.e., *high-level* federal officers. Congress cannot appoint "inferior," i.e., *lower-level* federal officials either, but it may say which of three other entities — the President, the Courts, or the Cabinet — is to appoint these lower officials.

   b. **Congress can't appoint or remove federal executives:** The most important thing for you to remember about the appointment of federal officers on the MBE is that *Congress has no power to directly appoint or remove (except by impeachment) federal executive officers.* MBE questions often give you a fact pattern in which Congress reserves to itself the right to appoint, or remove by means other than impeachment, someone who in fact is a federal officer; it's then up to you to notice that by appointing or removing the officer, Congress has violated separation-of-powers principles.

      i. **What makes it hard:** These sorts of questions involving Congress's right to appoint or remove federal officers are trickier than you might think. That's mainly because the question will usually not *say* that the person being appointed or removed is a federal officer. Instead, the question will describe the powers of the post, and it's *up to you to notice that the holder of the post is a "federal officer"* as to whom the President must be the one who holds the power of appointment or removal.

[1] **Who is a "federal officer":** For MBE purposes, you will usually only have to worry about "principal" federal officers. This class consists basically of *Cabinet-level officials, members of panels or commissions that hold significant executive power, federal judges,* and *ambassadors.* So whenever you see Congress reserving to itself (or to a panel appointed by it) the power to either appoint or remove a Cabinet-level officer, a member of a federal commission with executive-type powers, or an ambassador, you will know that this is a separation-of-powers violation.

c. **Appointment:** Here is an example (drawn from a famous case) of Congress violating this principle by keeping to itself the power to *appoint* federal officers. Notice that if this fact pattern popped up on the MBE, the hardest part would be recognizing that members of the commission in question hold powers that are *primarily executive,* triggering the rule that only the President, not Congress, may appoint the members.

Example: Congress establishes the Federal Election Commission, which enforces federal campaign laws. The Commission has power to bring civil actions against violators. The statute establishing the Commission allows Congress to appoint a majority of the Commission's members. *Held,* the tasks performed by the Commission are primarily executive, and its members are "officers of the United States." Therefore, the members must be appointed by the President, not Congress. [*Buckley v. Valeo*]

d. **Removal of federal executives:** The power to *remove* federal executive officers, like the power to appoint them, basically *rests with the President, not with Congress.*

i. **President's power to remove with or without cause:** The President may as a general matter remove any executive appointee *without cause.* The only exceptions are that Congress may require the President to *have cause* in order to remove (1) an officer who is appointed pursuant to a statute specifying the length of the term of office; and (2) an officer who performs a *judicial* or *quasi-judicial* function, such as an administrative judge (putting aside the requirement of impeachment as the sole means of removing federal judges appointed for life under Article I).

Example: The President may remove an ambassador at any time, without cause.

ii. **Removal by Congress:** Conversely, *Congress* may *not* remove an executive officer. This is true whether the officer is a "principal" or "inferior" one. [*Bowsher v. Synar*] Furthermore, Congress may not even *indirectly* keep the power to remove an executive officer, by entrusting to a congressionally-appointed *panel or commission* the right to remove that officer.

Example: Congress creates the new Cabinet-level post of "Director of Vehicular Restructuring" to restructure the American auto industry. The Director is to be appointed by the President, with the advice and consent of the Senate. Simultaneously, Congress creates the "Auto Restructuring Commission," whose five members include the Speaker of the House, the Senate Majority Leader, the House Minority Leader and two presidential appointees. The Commission is given the right to remove the Director, but only for "cause." (Separately, Congress retains the power to remove the Director by standard impeachment proceedings.) After the newly-appointed Director fails to turn around the auto industry, the Commission, led by its three congressional members, votes to remove him for cause.

The removal is invalid, because it violates the principle that only the President may remove a federal officer. The facts tell you that the Director holds a "Cabinet-level" post, so that automatically makes him a principal federal officer. Only the President may remove such an officer. Since a majority of the Commission's members are picked by Congress, the Commission's action removal action is deemed to be by Congress rather than by the President (even though the President appointed a minority of the members). The fact that the removal is for cause does not make any difference.

[1] **Congress's right to limit President's removal powers:** However, Congress can to some extent *limit* the *power of the President* to remove an officer, if Congress specifies a term of office and then provides that removal is allowable only for cause.

Example: Congress may say that the Special Prosecutor — an executive officer — may only be removed by the executive branch for "good cause" or other inability to perform his duties.This limitation on the removal powers of the President is sufficiently modest that it does not violate separation-of-powers principles. [*Morrison v. Olson*]

iii. **Impeachment:** Separately, Congress may remove any executive officer by the process of *impeachment*, discussed below.

e. **Impeachment:** Congress can remove any "officer" of the U.S. (President, Vice President, Cabinet members, federal judges, ambassadors, etc.) by *impeachment.*

i. **House commences:** The House must vote by a *majority* to impeach (which is like an indictment).

ii. **Senate holds the trial:** Then, the Senate conducts the trial. A *two-thirds vote* of the Senators present is required to convict. Conviction can be for treason, bribery, or other "high crimes and misdemeanors." Probably only serious crimes, and serious non-criminal abuses of power, fall within the phrase "high crimes and misdemeanors."

7. **Removal of federal judges:** Federal *judges* cannot be removed by *either* Congress or the President. Article III provides that federal judges shall hold their office during "good behavior." This has been held to mean that so long as a judge does not act improperly, she may not be removed from office. The only way to remove a sitting federal judge is by formal *impeachment* proceedings, as noted above.

a. **Non-Article III judges:** However, the above "life tenure" rule applies only to garden-variety federal judges who hold their positions directly under Article III. Congress is always free to establish what are essentially *administrative* judgeships, and as to these, lifetime tenure is not constitutionally required.

B. Legislative and executive immunity:

1. **Speech or Debate Clause:** Members of Congress are given a quite broad *immunity* by the *"Speech or Debate" Clause:* "For any speech or debate in either house, [members of Congress] shall not be questioned in any other place." This clause shields members of Congress from: (1) *civil or criminal suits relating to their legislative actions*; and (2) *grand jury investigations* relating to those actions.

Example: Sen. Gravel, while at a U.S. Senate committee hearing, reads a classified Pentagon document (part of the "Pentagon Papers" concerning the Vietnam War) into the public record. The Speech or Debate clause would prevent a federal prosecutor from prosecuting Gravel for violating a national security statute by reading the document into the record, or from subpoenaing Gravel to appear at a grand jury hearing at which he is to be questioned on his motives for doing this reading. [Cf. *Gravel v. U.S.* (1972)]

a. **Covers assistants:** The Speech or Debate clause also covers *assistants* to members of Congress, to the extent that they perform acts that, if done by a member, would be protected by the clause, or acts that were designed to help a member's legislative activities. So, for instance, if an assistant does research for the purpose of helping the member to prepare for speech on the floor, or to help the member decide how to vote, the assistant is protected.

Example: In the *Gravel* case, *supra*, a grand jury is investigating the leaking of the Pentagon Papers. A prosecutor subpoenas Rodberg, an assistant to Sen. Gravel, to testify about why the Senator did the public reading. *Held*, Rodberg is immune from the subpoena if Sen. Gravel would be immune for the same conduct (which he would be). [*Gravel v. U.S., supra,* p. 22.]

b. **Not directly related to legislation:** But acts by a member of Congress (or an aide to a member) that relate solely to *non-legislative conduct* are not protected by the Speech or Debate clause. For instance, *press releases* issued to the public by a member of Congress or her aide are not protected, because they do not relate directly to conduct within Congress itself.

2. **Executive immunity:** There's *no executive branch immunity expressly written* into the Constitution. But courts have recognized an *implied* executive immunity based on separation of powers concepts.

   a. **Absolute for President:** The President has *absolute* immunity from civil liability for his *official* acts. [*Nixon v. Fitzgerald*] (There's *no* immunity for the President's *unofficial* acts, including those he committed before taking office. [*Clinton v. Jones*])

   b. **Qualified for others:** But all other federal officials, including presidential aides, receive only *qualified* immunity for their official acts. (They lose this immunity if they violate a "clearly established" right, whether intentionally or negligently.) [*Harlow v. Fitzgerald*]

3. **Executive privilege:** Presidents have a qualified right to refuse to disclose confidential information relating to their performance of their duties. This is called *"executive privilege."*

   a. **Outweighed:** Since the privilege is qualified, it may be outweighed by other compelling governmental interests. For instance, the need for the President's evidence in a *criminal trial* will generally outweigh the President's vague need to keep information confidential. [*U.S. v. Nixon*]

CHAPTER 4

TWO LIMITS ON STATE POWER: THE DORMANT COMMERCE CLAUSE AND CONGRESSIONAL ACTION

I. THE DORMANT COMMERCE CLAUSE

A. **Dormant Commerce Clause generally:** The *mere existence* of the federal commerce power *restricts the states* from *discriminating against*, or *unduly burdening*, interstate commerce. This principle is called the *"dormant Commerce Clause."* It's also sometimes referred to as the "negative implications of the Commerce Clause."

1. **Three part test:** A state regulation which affects interstate commerce must satisfy *each* of the following three requirements in order to avoid violating the dormant Commerce Clause:

   a. The regulation must pursue a *legitimate state end*;

   b. The regulation must be *rationally related* to that legitimate state end; and

c. The regulatory *burden* imposed by the state on interstate commerce must be *outweighed* by the state's interest in enforcing its regulation.

d. **Summary:** So to summarize this test, it's both a *"mere rationality"* test (in that the regulation must be rationally related to fulfilling a legitimate state end) plus a separate *balancing test* (in that the benefits to the state from the regulation must outweigh the burdens on interstate commerce).

e. **Congress may authorize:** But there's one very important *exception* to the above rules: even if a state regulation flunks either the "mere rationality" test or the "benefits/burdens balancing test," it will *still be constitutional* if *Congress has authorized* the states to engage in that type of regulation. In other words, Congress may *validate* what would otherwise be state violations of the dormant Commerce Clause. See *infra*, p. 27.

2. **Discrimination against out-of-staters:** Above all else, be on the lookout for *intentional discrimination against out-of-staters*. If the state is promoting its residents' *own economic interests*, this will not be a legitimate state objective, so the regulation will virtually automatically violate the Commerce Clause.

   Example: New York refuses to let a Massachusetts wholesaler set up a receiving station in New York, from which he can buy New York milk to sell it to Massachusetts residents. New York is worried that this will deprive New Yorkers of enough milk. *Held*, this restriction violates the dormant Commerce Clause — New York is protecting its own citizens' economic interests at the expense of out-of-staters, and this is an illegitimate objective. [*H.P. Hood & Sons v. DuMond*]

3. **Two things to look out for:** So combining the results of Pars. 1 and 2 above, there are two basic things to look out for in a dormant Commerce Clause problem; if *either one* exists, the measure is almost certainly unconstitutional:

   - ❑ The measure was *protectionist*; that is, it was motivated principally by a desire to *protect in-state economic interests at the expense of out-of-state interests*, and does so by *treating out-of-state interests less favorably*; or
   - ❑ The measure *unduly burdens* interstate commerce, in that the burdens the regulation imposes on interstate commerce are substantially greater than the in-state benefits produced by the regulation. (This can happen even though the measure treats in-staters and out-of-staters the same way.)

   a. **Protectionism:** If the facts tell you that the state is motivated by a desire to *protect the economic interests of in-state business,* and that these interests are being hurt by out-of-state competitors, the measure almost certainly violates the dormant Commerce Clause (by being *protectionist*), even if the state dresses up its measure in neutral "we're just protecting the public" rationale.

      Example: State A's legislature decides that its one in-state automobile manufacturer, Acme Motors, is being hurt by sales of cars manufactured in other states. The main problem is that Acme's cars can't run on ethanol, and cars made by Toyota in nearby state B can. For the purpose of boosting Acme's in-state sales, the state puts a cap on the number of ethanol-using cars that may be sold in the state each year.

      A court would certainly hold the State *A* ban violates the dormant Commerce Clause because it was an attempt to protect the economic interests of an in-state business at the expense of out-of-state producers. (Also, the statute would probably be found to violate the "undue burden" branch of the dormant Commerce Clause.)

4. **Lack of uniformity:** A measure that leads to a *lack of uniformity* is likely to constitute an unduly large burden on interstate commerce. For instance, if various states' regulations are *in conflict*, the Court will probably strike the minority regulation, on the grounds that it creates a lack of uniformity that substantially burdens commerce without a sufficiently great corresponding benefit to the state.

    a. **Converse:** Conversely, a regulation that does not produce a burdensome inconsistency with other states' regulations, and that treats in-staters and out-of-staters the same, is likely to be sustained. For instance, a state's regulation that applies only to *corporations incorporated in that state* probably won't pose inconsistency problems, because no corporation can be incorporated in more than one state; therefore, a state's regulation of its own corporations is unlikely to be found to be unduly burdensome to commerce.

5. **"Negative implications" phrasing on the MBE:** The MBE examiners usually will not use the phrase "dormant Commerce Clause." Instead, they will refer to the doctrine in a more formal way, usually by referring to the *"negative implications of the federal commerce power."*

6. **Import/export:** The most standard illustrations of forbidden protectionism are where the state says, *"You can't bring your goods into our state,"* or *"You can't take goods out of our state into your state."*

    a. **"Do the work in our state":** Statutes that pressure out-of-state businesses to *perform certain operations* within the state are likely to be found violative of the dormant Commerce Clause. Such statutes will probably be found to unduly burden interstate commerce.

    Example: Arizona, in order to raise the already-high reputation of Arizona cantaloupes, requires that all cantaloupes raised in Arizona be packed in Arizona. *Held*, the statute unduly burdens interstate commerce; the Court "view[s] with particular suspicion state statutes requiring business operations to be performed in the home State that could more efficiently be performed elsewhere. ... [T]his particular burden on commerce [is] virtually per se illegal." [*Pike v. Bruce Church, Inc.*]

7. **Discrimination by city or county against out-of-towners:** The dormant Commerce Clause also prevents a *city or county* from protecting its own local economic interests by discriminating against *both out-of-state and out-of-town (but in-state) producers.* [*Fort Gratiot Sanitary Landfill v. Mich. Dept. of Nat. Res.*]

    Example: A county located in state Blue puts a tax on any item purchased in the county from an out-of-county seller, but not on any item purchased in-county from an in-county seller. Even though the tax discriminates against out-of-county sellers located within the state just as much as it does against out-of-state sellers, it's still a violation of the dormant Commerce Clause because it's protectionist.

8. **Discrimination against foreign commerce:** The dormant Commerce Clause also prevents states (or local governments) from discriminating against *foreign commerce*, such as goods or services imported into the U.S. The actual text of the Commerce Clause (Article I, Sec. 8, Cl. 3) gives Congress the power to "regulate Commerce *with foreign Nations*, and among the several States," and the Supreme Court has interpreted the negative implications of the clause to apply essentially the same way to burdens on foreign commerce as it does to burdens on interstate commerce. Indeed, the need for the federal government to speak with "one voice" on foreign affairs means that the scrutiny of state burdens on imports or exports may even be harsher than in the interstate-commerce case.

    Example: State *A*, for the purpose of protecting its one in-state automobile manufacturer (which doesn't sell cars using ethanol), places a cap on the sale of cars using ethanol. The only affected manufacturer is a Japanese manufacturer with minimal U.S. operations. This discrimination against foreign commerce violates the dormant Commerce Clause.

9. **Market participant exception:** But there is one key *exception* to the dormant Commerce Clause rules: if the state is acting as a *market participant* — rather than as a regulator — it *may* favor local over out-of-state interests.

   a. **May favor local buyers or sellers:** This principle means that if a state (or local government) *owns or operates a business*, government may require that business to *prefer in-state buyers or sellers* over out-of-state ones. [*Reeves v. Stake*]

   Example: The State of Purple owns a steel mill. The state decides that in order to boost the local economy by creating more in-state steel-processing jobs, it will give a special 20% discount on any steel sold by the mill to any buyer who promises to process the steel into a manufactured product within the state. An out-of-state buyer of steel, who is not eligible for the discount, brings suit, challenging the discount's constitutionality.

   The plaintiff will lose — the discount is not a violation of the dormant Commerce Clause, because the state is acting as a market participant. Governments that are acting as market participants rather than as regulators may favor in-state buyers, even if the government is doing so for the sole reason of advancing the local economy at the expense of out-of-staters.

10. **Not a limit on Congress's powers:** The dormant Commerce Clause is *not* a *limit on what Congress may do,* only on what the states may do. The MBE examiners sometimes have Congress take an action (or fail to take an action) that arguably impedes interstate commerce, and then try to trick you into believing that this violates the dormant Commerce Clause (or else into believing that this violates Congress's commerce power). It doesn't — nothing Congress does can violate dormant Commerce Clause principles.

11. **Congress may consent:** If *Congress expressly consents* to a state's action that discriminates against commerce, this consent will prevent the state action from being a violation of the dormant Commerce Clause. We discuss the congressional-consent exception further *infra*, p. 27.

B. **State taxation of interstate commerce:** Just as state regulation may be found to unduly burden (or discriminate against) interstate commerce, so state *taxation* may be found to unduly burden or discriminate against interstate commerce, and thus violate the Commerce Clause. To strike a state tax as violative of the Commerce Clause, the challenger must generally show either a discrimination against interstate commerce, or an undue burden on interstate commerce.

   1. **Discrimination:** The dormant Commerce Clause will be violated if the tax *discriminates against* interstate commerce, by taxing in a way that unjustifiably benefits local commerce at the expense of out-of-state commerce.

      a. **Tax favoring local components:** Don't assume that a tax can't violate the dormant Commerce Clause simply because the tax is directly imposed only on in-staters. For instance, a tax that promotes the use of *locally-made components,* by taxing more heavily in-staters who use out-of-state components than in-staters who use in-state components, would violate the Clause.

   2. **Burdensome:** The dormant Commerce Clause will also be violated if the state's taxing scheme (perhaps taken in conjunction with other states' taxing schemes) unfairly *burdens* interstate commerce even though it doesn't discriminate on its face. One way this can happen is if the tax leads to *unfair cumulative taxation.* The test is whether, if every state applied the same tax, commerce would be unduly burdened.

      Example: The state of Alpha has a tax statute that provides that if a business operates a "facility" in Alpha employing more than 100 people, then all the profits earned by that business outside of Alpha attributable to the shipment of goods from any facility located within 1,000 miles of Alpha shall be subject to full taxation by Alpha. Corp, a business with only one facility in Alpha, having 120 employees, has 10 facilities located outside of Alpha but within 1,000 miles of it that make millions of dollars of profits by shipping goods to non-Alpha customers. Corp challenges the statute.

The statute violates the dormant Commerce Clause (or the "negative implications of the federal commerce power"), because it burdens Corp's out-of-state operations by charging a tax that is completely out of proportion to the in-state profits or operations of Corp. If every state taxed Corp's operations on the same basis, Corp would be subject to massively unfair overlapping cumulative taxation. [Cf. *Quill Corp. v. North Dakota*]

II. CONGRESSIONAL PRE-EMPTION AND CONSENT; THE SUPREMACY CLAUSE

A. Congressional pre-emption and consent: The discussion above relates only to the "dormant" Commerce Clause, i.e., the situation in which Congress has not attempted to *exercise* its commerce power in a particular area. Now, we consider what happens when Congress *does* take action in a particular area of commerce.

First, we'll look at where Congress's action limits the states' freedom to regulate (paragraph (B) below on Supremacy Clause and pre-emption); then we'll look at where Congress's action allows the states to regulate where otherwise they couldn't (paragraph (C) below on consent by Congress).

B. The Supremacy Clause and federal pre-emption: Article VI, Clause 2, states that "This Constitution, and the Laws of the United States which shall be made in Pursuance thereof … shall be the supreme Law of the Land. … " This is the *"Supremacy Clause."*

1. **Direct conflict:** The most natural application of the Supremacy Clause is that if a state law is *inconsistent with* a valid federal law covering the same subject matter, the state law is *invalid.*

   Example: Congress passes a statute stating that no person shall be required to retire earlier than the age of 65. State X passes a law stating that any university located in State X may require its tenured professors to retire at the age of 60. Assuming that the federal law is a constitutionally-valid exercise of congressional powers (which certainly seems to be the case), the law of State X is invalid under the Supremacy Clause — in the case of a conflict between a federal statute and a state law, the state law must give way.

   a. **Congress allows, state forbids:** One type of direct conflict arises when Congress gives a private party the express right to *do something*, and a state then *forbids* that party from doing the same thing. The party might in theory comply with both sets of regulations by not doing the thing, but the state prohibition thwarts the federal intent, and is therefore invalid under the Supremacy Clause.

   b. **Congress forbids, state allows:** Another type of direct conflict is where *Congress forbids* a particular action, and the *state allows* that action. Here, too, the Supremacy Clause means that the state action is invalid.

   c. **Conflict between aims:** Finally, there may be a direct conflict between the *objectives* of the federal government and the inconsistent objectives of a state; here, too, the Supremacy clause dictates that the state regulation must give way so as not to frustrate the objectives being sought by the federal regulation. So, for instance, if the objective of the federal government is to make it easy for a private party to do something, a state regulation that makes it hard for that party to do that thing may be found invalid under the Supremacy Clause.

2. **Congressional pre-emption:** Cases in which there is a direct conflict between a federal law and a state law (as in the above examples) are fairly easy to spot as violations of the Supremacy Clause. But the Supremacy Clause may also be violated if the state legislates or regulates in an area that has been *"pre-empted"* by federal regulation.

   a. **Federal occupation of field:** One way Congress may pre-empt state regulation is by making the decision to *occupy the entire field.* This is always a question of congressional *intent.*

      i. **State common law:** One commonly-tested scenario in which Congress is found to occupy the field is where Congress enacts a rule dealing with a particular subject, and simultaneously makes it clear that this federal rule is intended to *replace* (pre-empt) *state common-law* — such as state tort law — on the subject.

      Example: Congress requires a particular warning label on a product, and makes it clear that any product bearing the federally-required warning label may not be sued upon for violation of otherwise-applicable state tort law requiring additional or different warning labels. The congressional regulation will be interpreted to have pre-empted state tort law.

      ii. **Commerce Clause cases:** Another common area for finding a congressional intent to occupy the entire field and thus to pre-empt all state regulation is where Congress uses its affirmative Commerce power to *regulate an entire area.*

      Example: Suppose Congress uses its Commerce power to regulate the acceptability of a particular medical device (e.g., a heart stent). Manufacturers of federally-approved devices can make a strong argument that the states are pre-empted from adding on additional regulations of those devices, even if these are not directly inconsistent with the federal regulation — a court may well conclude that Congress *intended to completely occupy the field of regulation* of such medical devices.

3. **No conflict:** Conversely, where there is *no direct conflict* between the objectives and methods of the state and federal regulation, and there is no indication that the federal government intended to occupy the entire field, state regulation will *not* necessarily be pre-empted by federal regulation, even though both cover the same *subject area.*

   a. **More stringent state regulations:** One common MBE scenario in which there is *not* pre-emption is where the federal government regulates in an area, but the surrounding circumstances suggest that the feds *did not intend to displace more-rigorous state requirements.* As long as a person can *obey both regulations simultaneously* (i.e., obeying the more stringent state regulation does not prevent a person from simultaneously obeying the less-stringent federal one), the state regulation will probably not be pre-empted.

C. **Consent by Congress:** Congress may *consent* to state action that would otherwise violate the dormant Commerce Clause. Congress may even *allow a state to discriminate against out-of-staters.* Where Congress does this, the consent will be *effective*, turning what would otherwise be a violation of the dormant Commerce Clause into acceptable state regulation.

Example 1: Congress enacts a statute that says that any state may, by insurance regulations, prohibit the operation in the state of any insurance company not licensed in that state. The statute also provides that any state may deny a license to an insurer based outside the state even if the purpose is to promote the economic success of insurers based in the state.

The congressional statute will be valid, and state licensing procedures that discriminate against out-of-state insurance companies will therefore not violate the dormant Commerce Clause.

Example 2: The Green state legislature decides that the standard arrangement of tail lights on American trucks — one on each side, at the fender-level — causes accidents, because the lights are too far down relative to the road, and drivers in vehicles behind the truck don't see that the truck is braking. Therefore, the legislature passes a statute requiring every truck driven on any highway in Green to have a third tail light that is centered and is at the top of the truck. Federal regulation of truck tail lights requires only the two standard fender-level lights. An association of interstate truckers brings suit in federal court to have the regulation ruled a violation of the dormant Commerce Clause. While the action is pending, Congress enacts a statute that says, "Any state may impose additional tail light requirements for trucks driven on that state's highways."

The truckers association will lose. Even if a state regulation would otherwise be a dormant Commerce Clause violation because it unreasonably burdens interstate commerce, Congress is always free to change this result by explicitly allowing the state regulation. That's what happened here. So even if (as seems likely) the Green statute would otherwise be held to be a dormant Commerce Clause violation because it requires that trucks made for a national market be specially adapted for use on Green highways (thus constituting an unreasonable burden on commerce), the congressional statute negates the violation.

CHAPTER 5

INTERGOVERNMENTAL IMMUNITIES; INTERSTATE RELATIONS

I. TAX AND REGULATORY IMMUNITIES

A. Several types of immunities: There are several kinds of *immunities* produced by our federalist system:

1. Federal immunity from state taxation: The federal government is immune from being *taxed by the states.*

a. "Legal incidence" standard: This immunity applies only if the *"legal incidence"* of the tax — not just the practical or economic burden — falls on the federal government.

Example: In order to obtain a federal tax deduction, a number of landowners convey "conservation easements" to the U.S. Dept. of the Interior, in which the owner binds her heir to keep the land perpetually in an undeveloped state. In the state of Blue, such conservation easements are an interest in property, and are recorded in the real property records of the county where the land is located. Blue imposes a $50 tax on every deed that is to be recorded, which tax is to be paid by the grantee. The state refuses to grant an exemption to the Dept. of the Interior from being required to pay the $50 fee for each conservation easement in which the Dept. is the grantee.

The state's attempt to collect the tax directly from the Department violates the federal immunity from state taxation, and is therefore invalid. But the state *could* collect the money from the grant*or*, i.e., the private owner, because the immunity applies only where the "legal incidence" of the tax, not merely the economic impact, is on the federal government.

i. Tax on private contractors: Where a state taxes a *private contractor* who does work for the federal government under a cost-plus contract, the contractor will *not be immune* from the tax. The fact that the burden of this tax will be passed on to the federal government under the contract won't be enough to trigger the immunity. That's because on these facts, the *"legal incidence"* of the tax is not on the U.S. [*James v. Dravo Contracting* (1937)]

Example: Contractor has a fixed-price contract to clean an office building wholly owned by the U.S. government, and located in the state of Magenta. Magenta taxes the Contractor based on Contractor's gross revenues from all services performed within Magenta. Even though this tax may indirectly increase the U.S. government's costs of cleaning, the tax does not violate the federal government's immunity from state taxation, because the legal incidence of the tax falls on Contractor, not the federal government.

[1] Non-discriminatory: However, even where the legal incidence of the tax is on the contractor and not on the federal government, the tax must be *"non-discriminatory"* — if the state *singles out* contractors who do business with the federal government for higher taxes than those who do not, this probably *would* violate the federal government's immunity from state taxation.

Example: On the facts of the above Example, suppose that Magenta's tax was a special-purpose "federal contractor tax" that applied only to contracts for the provision of services to the federal government. Then, the tax on Contractor for its office-building janitorial contract *would* violate federal immunity from state taxation, because the tax singles out those who do business with the federal government for higher taxes than those who do not.

ii. **Employees:** A similar rule applies to federal government *employees* — a state may tax a federal employee without running afoul of the federal immunity from state taxation, as long as the state is not discriminating against such employees by taxing them more heavily than employees of other types of employers.

2. **State immunity from federal taxation:** The *states* have *partial immunity* from federal taxation. What this means is that the federal government can't tax property used in or income from a state's performance of its *basic governmental functions*

Example: The federal government probably can't put a property tax on a state's public parks.

3. **Federal immunity from state regulation:** The federal government is essentially free from *state regulatory interference*.

Example: A state cannot set the laws for conduct on a military post located within the state, unless Congress consents.

a. **Applies to generally-applicable rules:** This immunity from state regulation applies even where the state is merely trying to get the federal government to obey *generally-applicable rules* that are applied the same way to non-governmental persons, and it applies no matter how *reasonable* the state's regulation is.

Example: A state or city may not require a local U.S. Post Office to obey local environmental or building-code regulations, even if these regulations are the same ones that the state or city applies to non-governmental entities, and even if the regulations are perfectly reasonable.

b. **Federal contractors:** State regulation of a federal *contractor* (one performing a contract on behalf of the federal government) may also violate the federal immunity from state regulation. However, as in the state taxation context, the states have greater leeway to regulate federal contractors than to regulate the federal government directly.

i. **Federal purposes or policies:** In general, a state may regulate federal contractors as long as the regulation does not interfere with *federal purposes* or *policies*. For instance, a state regulation that has the effect of *substantially increasing the cost* borne by the federal government under the contract might be invalid as a violation of this immunity. But a state regulation that *does not discriminate* against the federal government in any way, and does not run afoul of any *clearly-stated federal interest*, would *not* violate the immunity.

Example: An office building located in the state of Red is wholly owned by the U.S. government. The U.S. hires JanitCo, a janitorial company, to clean the office building. The federal government's contract with JanitCo does not specify what cleaning chemicals may be used to clean the building. JanitCo uses carbon tetrachloride. There is no relevant federal policy on the use of carbon tetrachloride in the cleaning of federal buildings. A Red statute prohibits the use of carbon tetrachloride for cleaning applications. JanitCo Claims that the ban, as applied to this contract, violates the federal immunity from state regulation.

A court would almost certainly hold that the Red statute, as applied to JanitCo's contract, does not violate federal immunity from state regulation, because the lack of any mention in the contract of what chemicals may be used in the work, plus the absence of any other federal policy on the issue, means that no federal interest is being undermined.

4. **State immunity from federal regulation:** The converse immunity, immunity of the *states* from *federal* regulation, exists only in a very theoretical way. In general, federal regulation of the states is valid. However, if a federal regulatory scheme had the effect of preventing the states from exercising their *core functions*, this might be found to be a violation of the Tenth Amendment.

II. THE INTERSTATE PRIVILEGES AND IMMUNITIES CLAUSE

A. **Interstate Privileges and Immunities:** Article IV of the Constitution says that "the Citizens of each State shall be entitled to all Privileges and Immunities of Citizens in the several States." This is the *"interstate" Privileges and Immunities Clause.* (Be sure you distinguish this from the Privileges and Immunities Clause of the Fourteenth Amendment, which prevents a state from denying certain rights of "national citizenship" (like the right to travel).)

1. **Standard:** The interstate Privileges and Immunities Clause prevents a state from *discriminating against non-residents*. But it only operates with respect to rights that are *fundamental* to *national unity*.

   a. **What rights are fundamental:** The rights that are "fundamental in the national unity" are all related to *commerce*. Thus the right to *be employed*, the right to *practice one's profession*, and the right to *engage in business* are all fundamental, and are therefore protected by the interstate Privileges and Immunities Clause.

   Example: Alaska requires that Alaska residents be given an absolute preference over non-residents for all jobs on the Alaska oil pipeline. *Held*, since access to employment is a right fundamental to national unity, Alaska's decision to prefer its own citizens over out-of-staters impairs the out-of-staters' rights under the interstate Privileges and Immunities Clause, and is invalid. [*Hicklin v. Orbeck*, the "Alaska Hire" case]

2. **Only protects non-residents:** The Article IV P&I Clause only protects *non-residents of the state* that has taken the challenged action. So check your facts to make sure that the plaintiff is a non-resident — if she's a resident of the state that committed the act in question, she can't recover.

3. **Two-prong test:** Even if a state does impair an out-of-stater's exercise of a right fundamental to national unity, the state impairment is not necessarily invalid. But the state will lose unless it satisfies a two-pronged test:

   a. **"Peculiar source of evil":** First, the state must show that out-of-staters are a *"peculiar source of the evil"* the statute was enacted to rectify.

   b. **Substantial relation to state objective:** Second, the state must show that its solution (the discriminatory statute) is *"substantially related"* to this "peculiar evil" the out-of-staters represent. Generally, to meet this prong the state must show that there are no *less discriminatory alternatives* that would adequately address the problem. (For instance, in *Hicklin, supra*, p. 31, had Alaska been able to show that there was no other way to combat unemployment than to absolutely prefer in-staters, it would have met this prong.)

   MBE tip: If the state has impaired an out-of-stater's exercise of the right to be employed, to practice her profession, or to engage in business, you should *presume* that the P&I Clause has been *violated* — it's very hard for a state to jump over the "peculiar source of the evil" and "solution substantially related to the peculiar evil" hurdles.

4. **No "market participant" exception:** Recall that a state is immune from Commerce Clause violations if it's acting as a *market participant*. But there's *no* such market participant exception for the Privileges & Immunities Clause. (Thus even if, in *Hicklin*, *supra*, p. 31, Alaska had been hiring the workers itself, its absolute preference for residents would have violated the clause.)

5. **Distinguished from Equal Protection:** When a non-resident is discriminated against, he may also have an equal protection claim. But there are two key differences:

   a. **Aliens and corporations:** The Equal Protection Clause can apply to *corporations* and to *aliens*; the Privileges & Immunities Clause can't.

   b. **Rigorous scrutiny:** Conversely, the level of scrutiny given to the state's action is much tougher under Privileges & Immunities Clause than under Equal Protection Clause. Under equal protection analysis, non-residency isn't a suspect classification, and therefore the discrimination must just meet a standard of "mere rationality." Under the Privileges & Immunities Clause, by contrast, the statute must survive quite *rigorous scrutiny* — the non-residents must be a "peculiar source of the evil," and there must not be less-discriminatory alternatives available.

III. THE FULL FAITH AND CREDIT CLAUSE

A. **How tested on MBE:** The *Full Faith and Credit Clause* (Article IV, Sec. 1) is sometimes tested in MBE Con Law questions, even though in law school the subject is usually part of Civil Procedure rather than Con Law.

1. **Where FF&C Clause applies:** The FF&C Clause only applies when the courts of *two different states* are involved in the same controversy. (So you don't have to worry about the Clause if a federal court and a state court are hearing the same or related controversies.)

2. **Effect of Clause:** The FF&C Clause requires each state to give to the judgment of any other state *the same effect that that judgment would have in the state which rendered it.*

   a. **Collection of money judgments:** Most importantly, the FF&C Clause means that if State A renders a *money judgment* for X against Y, any other state (call it State B) is required to help X collect the judgment against Y the same way State B would help a person who had gotten a State B judgment to collect that judgment. As the idea is usually put, State B must *"enforce the judgment"* of the State A court.

b. First state's error of law: The second state must honor the first state's decision even if the second state is convinced that the first state *made an error of law*, applied the *wrong law* under conflict-of-laws principles, misinterpreted the second state's law while trying to apply it, or otherwise made a serious legal error. The idea is that the first state's judgment must be honored no matter what. (The sole exception comes in the very limited scenario in which the first court *did not properly have jurisdiction over the losing party* and the jurisdictional issue wasn't waived or litigated during the first proceeding.)

CHAPTER 6

THE DUE PROCESS CLAUSE

I. INTRODUCTION

A. Two major principles: Let's now turn to a discussion of rights guaranteed to individuals by the Constitution. Before we get into the individual rights, there are two general principles that are crucial to remember:

1. Protected against the government: First, practically all of the individual rights conferred by the Constitution upon individuals *protect only against government action.* They do *not* protect a person against acts by other private individuals.

Example: Suppose P is a woman who's two months pregnant, and none of the private hospitals in her state will perform an abortion. P's substantive due process right to an abortion has not been violated, because the government has not interfered with that right.

Note: The only exception to the "government action only" rule is the Thirteenth Amendment's ban on slavery, which *does* apply to private conduct.

2. Not directly applicable to states: The other general principle to remember is the central role of the Fourteenth Amendment's *Due Process* Clause. Many of the important individual guarantees are given by the Bill of Rights (the first ten amendments). For instance, the First Amendment rights of free expression and freedom of religion fall into this category. But the Bill of Rights does *not directly* apply to the states. However, the Fourteenth Amendment's Due Process Clause (which does apply to the states) has been interpreted to make nearly all of the Bill of Rights guarantees applicable to the states — these individual guarantees are "incorporated" into the Bill of Rights. "Incorporation" is discussed further below.

II. THE FOURTEENTH AMENDMENT GENERALLY

A. Text of Fourteenth Amendment: Section 1 of the Fourteenth Amendment provides, in full, that:

"All persons born or naturalized in the United States, and subject to the jurisdiction hereof, are citizens of the United States and of the State wherein they reside. No State shall make or enforce any law which shall abridge the *privileges and immunities* of citizens of the United States; nor shall any State *deprive any person of life, liberty, or property, without due process of law;* nor deny to any person within its jurisdiction the *equal protection of the laws.*"

1. Three rights: So in one sentence we have three major rights: (1) the right to due process; (2) the right to equal protection; and (3) the right to the privileges and immunities of national citizenship.

B. The Bill of Rights and the states: One of the major functions of the Fourteenth Amendment's Due Process Clause is to make the *Bill of Rights* — that is, the first ten amendments — applicable to the states.

1. **Not directly applicable to states:** The Bill of Rights is not *directly* applicable to the States.

2. **Effect of due process clause:** But the Fourteenth Amendment directly imposes on the states (and local governments as well) the requirement that they not deprive anyone of "life, liberty or property" without due process. Nearly all the guarantees of the Bill of Rights have been interpreted by the Supreme Court as being so important that if a state denies these rights, it has in effect taken away an aspect of "liberty."

3. **Application of Bill of Rights to states:** The Supreme Court has never said that due process requires the states to honor the Bill of Rights as a whole. Instead, the Court uses an approach called *"selective incorporation."* Under this approach, each right in the Bill of Rights is examined to see whether it is of *"fundamental"* importance. If so, that right is "selectively incorporated" into the meaning of "due process" under the Fourteenth Amendment, and is thus made binding on the states.

4. **Nearly all rights incorporated:** By now, nearly *all rights contained in the Bill of Rights* have been incorporated, one by one, into the meaning of "due process" (and thus made applicable to the states). The only major Bill of Rights guarantees *not* incorporated are:

   a. **Grand jury:** The Fifth Amendment's right not to be subject to a criminal trial without a *grand jury indictment* (so that a state may begin proceedings by an "information," as some states do); and

   b. **Right to jury in civil cases:** The Seventh Amendment's right to a *jury trial* in *civil* cases.

5. **"Jot-for-jot" incorporation:** Once a given Bill of Rights guarantee is made applicable to the states, the *scope* of that guarantee is interpreted the *same way* for the states as for the federal government.

   Example: The Fourth Amendment right not to be subject to an unreasonable search or seizure is interpreted the same way whether the case involves federal or state police — thus if on a given set of facts the FBI would be found to have violated the Fourth Amendment, so would local police.

C. The federal Due Process Clause: We'll generally be discussing the *Fourteenth* Amendment's Due Process Clause, which binds the states. But keep in mind that there is also a due process clause in the *Fifth* Amendment, that is binding on the *federal* government. Both clauses have been interpreted the same way, so that any state action that would be forbidden by the Fourteenth Amendment Due Process Clause is also forbidden to the federal government via the Fifth Amendment Due Process Clause. (For instance, exactly the same limits apply to federal and state regulations that impair the right to have an abortion.)

1. **MBE Tip:** So when the challenged action is being taken by the federal government, be sure to pick a choice that mentions the *Fifth* Amendment's Due Process Clause, not the *Fourteenth* Amendment's due process clause.

III. SUBSTANTIVE DUE PROCESS — ECONOMIC AND SOCIAL WELFARE REGULATION

A. Substantive due process generally: There are two quite different functions that the Due Process Clause serves. Most obviously, it imposes certain *procedural* requirements on governments when they impair life, liberty, or property. (We'll be talking about this "procedural due process" area below.) But the Due Process Clause also limits the *substantive power* of the states to regulate certain areas of human life. This "substantive" component of the Due Process Clause derives mainly from the interpretation of the term *"liberty"* — certain types of state limits on human conduct have been held to so unreasonably interfere with important human rights that they amount to an unreasonable (and unconstitutional) denial of "liberty."

> **MBE Tip:** Any time your fact pattern suggests that a state or federal government is *taking away* some thing or value that could be considered "life," "liberty," or "property," then entirely apart from the issue of whether the government has used proper procedures, you must ask the question: Has the government by carrying out this taking violated the individual's *substantive* interest in life, liberty, or property?

B. Fundamental and non-fundamental rights: There's an absolutely critical distinction that you must make right at the outset, when you're analyzing a substantive due process problem. That's the distinction between *fundamental* and *non-fundamental* rights.

1. **Non-fundamental rights:** If a right or value is found to be *"non-fundamental,"* then the state action that impairs that right only has to meet the easy *"mere rationality"* test. In other words, it just has to be the case that the state is pursuing a *legitimate governmental objective*, and is doing so with a means that is *rationally related* to that objective.

   a. **Economic regulation:** Nearly all *economic* regulation (and most *"social welfare"* regulation) will turn out to implicate *only non-fundamental rights*, and will almost certainly be *upheld* under this easy-to-satisfy mere-rationality standard. So anytime you can't find a fundamental right being impaired, you should presume that the measure does not violate substantive due process.

2. **Fundamental rights:** But if a state or federal government is impairing a *"fundamental"* right, then it's a different ball game entirely: here, the court uses *strict scrutiny*. Only if the governmental action is *"necessary"* to achieve a *"compelling"* governmental objective, will the government avoid violating substantive due process.

3. **Significance of distinction:** So 95% of the battle in analyzing a substantive due process problem is deciding whether the right in question is "fundamental" or not. Once you know that, you pretty much know how the case will come out — if the right is not "fundamental," there's almost certainly no substantive due process problem; if the right *is* fundamental, then strict scrutiny will almost certainly result in the measure being invalidated. So as you prepare for the MBE, it's worth devoting some significant mental effort to remembering which rights are fundamental.

   a. **Rights covered:** As we'll see below (p. 37), only rights related to *marriage, child-bearing* and *child-rearing* are deemed "fundamental" for substantive due process purposes.

C. Economic and social-welfare regulation: It is very easy for state *economic regulation* to survive substantive due process attacks. *Since 1937, the Court has not struck down an economic regulation for violating substantive due process.*

1. **Two requirements:** Today, an economic statute has to meet only two easily-satisfied requirements to be in conformity with substantive due process:

   a. **Legitimate state objective:** The state must be pursuing a *legitimate state objective*. But virtually any health, safety or "general welfare" goal comes within the state's *"police power"* and is thus "legitimate".

   b. **Minimally rationally related:** Second, there must be a *"minimally rational relation"* between the means chosen by the legislature and the state objective. To put it another way, the Court will presume that the statute is constitutional unless the legislature has acted in a completely *"arbitrary and irrational"* way.

2. **Easy to satisfy:** These two requirements are *very easy to satisfy* — it will be a rare MBE question that involves economic or social welfare legislation (and that does not involve a fundamental right) where the correct answer is that the regulation definitely violates a party's substantive due process rights.

   Example: The legislature of a state authorizes the insurance commissioner to regulate rates for life insurance. The insurance commissioner orders every insurer operating in the state to charge the same annual rate for all persons of any given age who are in good health, regardless of the person's gender. An insurer claims that the statute interferes with its substantive due process right to charge customers according to the risk they pose, and that the insurer should therefore be able to charge women less because they live longer.

   A court would hold that the statute does not violate the insurer's due process rights, because it meets the easy-to-satisfy requirements of being rationally related to one or more legitimate state objectives (e.g., making insurance affordable to all and combating inter-gender conflicts).

D. **Outside the economic area:** Outside the economic area, the same rule applies as long as no *fundamental right* is being affected: the state must merely be pursuing a legitimate state objective by rational means. So most *"social welfare"* legislation merely has to meet this very easy standard. We discuss below what rights are "fundamental" — in summary, those rights relate to sex, marriage, child-bearing and child-rearing, all components of the general "right to privacy." (By contrast, practically no economic rights are "fundamental" — the sole exception may be the right to practice a profession or calling, and even this is not certain.)

   Example: A state requires all motorcycle passengers to wear helmets conforming to certain standards, including having a face guard. The statute is enacted for safety purposes, after numerous studies showing that people who get in motorcycle accidents sustain fewer serious head injuries if they are wearing a helmet. A motorcyclist attacks the statute on the ground that it violates his substantive due process liberty interest in riding without a helmet, which he wants to do in order to feel the wind blowing against his face.

   The plaintiff probably does indeed have a liberty interest in riding helmetlessly. But that interest is not fundamental. Therefore, the statute will be sustained as long as it is rationally related to the achievement of a legitimate state objective. The statute here almost certainly qualifies — it's enacted for the purpose of pursuing the legitimate governmental objective of reducing serious head injuries, and the scientific research establishes that the statute is at least rationally related to the achievement of that objective.

1. **Regulation struck down even though right is non-fundamental:** Where the right being regulated is non-fundamental, and the review is therefore mere-rationality, the regulation will usually sustained, as in the above examples. But you may nonetheless occasionally see, on the MBE, an instance of a governmental regulation that is so clearly the product of unfair prejudice, and so irrational, that it nonetheless fails the easy mere-rationality test. Most dramatically, regulations that *interfere with sexual expression*, though given mere-rationality review, may be *struck down* as totally irrational.

   Example: Laws criminalizing sodomy, enforced principally against gays, have been struck down as failing the rational-relation test, on the theory that they demean homosexuals and interfere with their autonomy, in a way that the Supreme Court has deemed "illegitimate." [*Lawrence v. Texas*]

IV. SUBSTANTIVE DUE PROCESS — REGULATIONS AFFECTING FUNDAMENTAL RIGHTS

A. Fundamental rights generally: The rest of our discussion of substantive due process will be solely about *fundamental* rights.

1. Strict scrutiny: If a state or federal regulation is impairing a fundamental right, the court *strictly scrutinizes* the regulation. Here is what it means in practical terms for the Court to apply strict scrutiny to a state or federal regulation that impairs a fundamental right: (1) the objective being pursued by the state must be *"compelling"* (not just "legitimate" as for a non-fundamental right); and (2) the means chosen by the state must be *"necessary"* to achieve that compelling end. In other words, there must not be any *less restrictive means* that would do the job just as well (if there were, then the means actually chosen wouldn't be "necessary").

a. Burden of proof: When strict scrutiny is used, there is an important impact on *who bears the burden of persuasion.* In the usual case in which strict scrutiny is not being used, the *person attacking the statute has the burden* of showing that the state is pursuing an illegitimate objective, or that the state has chosen a means that is not rationally related to its objective. But if *strict scrutiny is used because a "fundamental" right is involved,* the *burden of proof shifts:* now, it's *up to the state to show that it's pursuing a compelling objective,* and that the *means it chose are "necessary"* to achieve that objective.

2. Rights governed: The only rights that have been recognized as "fundamental" for substantive due process purposes are ones related to the loose category *"right to privacy."* Sometimes this area is said to involve the "right to *personal autonomy*" — but what it really refers to is usually a person's right to *make his own decisions* about *highly personal matters*. This right of privacy or autonomy derives indirectly from several Bill of Rights guarantees, which collectively create a *"penumbra"* or *"zone"* of privacy.

a. List: The list of rights or interests falling within this "right to privacy" or "right to personal autonomy" include actually just a few related areas: *marriage*, *child-bearing*, and *child-rearing*. So anytime you're looking at a particularly narrow interest and you have to decide whether it's "fundamental," first ask yourself, "Does it fall within the areas of marriage, child-bearing, or child-rearing?" If not, it's probably not "fundamental."

i. Illustrations: So the "fundamental" rights for substantive due process purposes seem to consist mainly (maybe even solely) of these:

- ❑ the right to *use birth control*;
- ❑ the right to *live together with your family*;
- ❑ the right to *direct the upbringing* and *education* of your children;
- ❑ the right to *marry*.

ii. Non-illustrations: By contrast, an interest that does not fall within one of these areas probably is not fundamental — for instance, an adult's interest in having consensual sex outside of marriage seems not to be "fundamental." (The right to *abortion* used to be "fundamental," but now seems to be only "quasi-fundamental" after *Planned Parenthood v. Casey*, *infra*, p. 38.)

B. Birth control: Individuals' interest in *using birth control* is "fundamental." So whether a person is married or single, he or she has a fundamental interest in contraception, and the state cannot impair that interest without satisfying strict scrutiny.

Example: Planned Parenthood cannot be prohibited from supplying condoms or diaphragms to single or married adults who want them. [*Griswold v. Connecticut*]

C. Abortion: The right of *abortion* is the primary example of a right protected by substantive due process. But the right of abortion as it stood under *Roe v. Wade* has been largely overhauled — and *cut back* — by *Planned Parenthood of Southeastern Pennsylvania v. Casey* (1992).

1. **The right today:** In this post-*Casey* world, here is the status of abortion: A woman has a constitutionally-protected privacy interest in choosing to have an abortion *before viability*. However, the state has a somewhat countervailing interest in *protecting "potential life,"* even before viability. This conflict seems to yield the following results:

   a. **No right to ban:** The state does not have the right to *ban* all pre-viability abortions. Also, the state may not even forbid all pre-viability abortions except those necessary to save the life or health of the mother.

   b. **Regulation:** However, the state has a far greater ability to *regulate* the abortion process than it did before *Casey*. The state may regulate only if it does not place an *"undue burden"* on the woman's right to choose a pre-viability abortion. A regulation will constitute an "undue burden" if the regulation "has the purpose or effect of placing a *substantial obstacle* in the path of a woman" seeking a pre-viability abortion.

   c. **Not a fundamental right that will be strictly scrutinized:** Abortion is *no longer a fundamental right*, and restrictions on it are *no longer strictly scrutinized.*

2. **What constitutes "undue burden":** Most state regulation will probably *not* constitute an "undue burden," and will thus be sustained.

   Example 1 (informed consent): The state may impose an elaborate "informed consent" provision, whereby at least 24 hours before performing an abortion, the physician must inform the woman of the nature of the procedure, the health risks of both abortion and childbirth, the probable gestational age of the fetus, the availability of state-printed materials, etc. [*Casey*]

   Example 2 (parental consent): The state may require that an unemancipated woman under 18 not obtain an abortion unless she and one of her *parents* both provide informed consent (so long as the state allows for a "judicial bypass," as discussed below). [*Casey*]

3. **Consent:** Even after *Casey*, the state is limited in the extent to which it can require the *consent* of third parties before an abortion is performed.

   a. **Spousal consent:** The state may *not* give a pregnant woman's *spouse* a *veto right* over the woman's abortion decision. [*Planned Parenthood v. Danforth*] In fact, the state may not even require that the woman *notify* her spouse of her intent to get an abortion, even if the state exempts cases of spousal sexual assault or threatened bodily injury. [*Casey*]

   b. **Parental consent:** The state *may* require that an *unemancipated* woman under the age of 18 obtain *parental* consent. The state may also require that this parental consent be "informed," even if this requires an in-person visit by the parent to the facility, and even if it involves a 24-hour waiting period.

      i. **Judicial bypass:** But if the state does require parental consent, it must give the girl an *opportunity to persuade a judge that an abortion is in her best interests.* This is a *"judicial bypass."*

      ii. **Emancipation or maturity:** The state must also allow an individualized judicial hearing at which the girl may persuade the court that she is in fact sufficiently *mature* or *emancipated* that she is able to make this decision for herself. If the girl proves this, the abortion must be allowed even if the judge believes that the abortion is not in the girl's best interest.

4. **Public funding:** States may refuse to give *public funding* (e.g., Medicaid) for abortions even though they give such funding for other types of operations. Also, states may prohibit public hospitals from performing abortions, and may prohibit public employees from performing them while on the job. [*Webster v. Reproductive Health Svcs.*]

5. **Abortion counseling:** The government may, as a *condition of funding* family-planning clinics, insist that the doctor or other professional *not recommend abortion*, and not refer clinic patients to an abortion provider. [*Rust v. Sullivan*]

6. **Types of abortion:** The state probably has substantial freedom to place regulations on the *types* of abortions that may be performed.

   Example: The federal government may completely outlaw the "partial birth" abortion method, without giving an exception for cases in which the physician believes that the procedure may be needed to safeguard the woman's health. The ban on this procedure is rationally related to the achievement of several state goals, including safeguarding unborn life and making it less likely that a woman will later have profound regret over the particular abortion method she selected. Also, the ban does not constitute an undue burden on the woman's right to abort, because Congress has made a credible finding of fact that the partial-birth method is never necessary for the woman's health. [*Gonzales v. Carhart* (2007)]

   a. **Health of mother:** But when the state regulates the types of abortions that may be used, it must *protect the mother's life and health.*

   Example: The state can't ban a particular abortion method, unless it gives an exception for cases where that's in fact, as a medical matter, the method that is safest for the mother. [*Stenberg v. Carhart*] (This seems to remain a valid principle, despite the Court's 2007 decision in *Gonzales v. Carhart*, *supra*, that the partial-birth abortion method may be completely banned because it is never necessary to safeguard the mother's life or health.)

   b. **Ban on pre-viability abortions:** The legislature can't simply *ban* abortions taking place *before viability,* i.e., roughly, *before the start of the third trimester.* (The state can regulate fairly tightly here, but not ban.) And in fact, such a second-trimester ban will probably be invalid even if there's an exception for abortions necessary to protect the woman's life or health.

7. **Procedures surrounding abortion:** As the result of the 2007 decision in *Gonzales v. Carhart*, *supra*, the government *can impose procedures* that must be *followed prior to any abortion*, even if the effect and purpose of those procedures is to *induce some or many women to decide not to abort.* The procedures can't be an "undue burden" or a "substantial obstacle to the woman's exercise of the right to choose." But the procedures *can* "create a *structural mechanism* by which the State ... may *express profound respect for the life of the unborn."* [*Gonzales*] And that's true from the *early stages* of the pregnancy.

   a. **Informed consent:** In particular, the states can require particular detailed procedures in the interests of assuring that the woman has given *"informed consent"* to the abortion. For instance, rules that the physician must disclose certain possible *consequences* of abortion to the woman (e.g., that many women suffer from depression following the procedure), or that the physician must perform a *sonogram* and show the images to the woman, are likely *valid* post-*Gonzales*.

Example: The state of Violet passes a statute that before a physician may perform a second-trimester abortion, he or she must perform a sonogram, and must show the sonogram images to the woman. It is very likely that this requirement is constitutional under *Gonzales v. Carhart* — since the procedure is not difficult, time-consuming or expensive to perform, it probably does not constitute an "undue burden" on the woman's right to choose a second-trimester abortion. And even if the performing of the procedure will — by showing women images of the fetus — induce some to decide not to abort, that's permissible, since the state is entitled to "express profound respect for the life of the unborn," something that the sonogram requirement arguably does.

D. Family relations: Whenever the state interferes with a person's decision about how to live his *family life* and *raise his children*, you should be on the lookout to see whether a fundamental right is being interfered with.

1. Right to live together: For instance, *relatives* have a fundamental right to *live together.*

Example: A city may not enact a zoning ordinance that prevents first cousins from living together, because the right of members of a family — even a non-nuclear family — to live together is "fundamental," and any state interference with that right will be strictly scrutinized. [*Moore v. East Cleveland*]

a. No right for unrelated persons to co-habit: What the Court was protecting in *Moore* was clearly the right of *families* to live together, *not* the more general right to live with whomever one wants outside of ties of blood and marriage. The Court has held [*Belle Terre v. Borass*] that *unrelated people* have *no "fundamental right" to live together,* and in *Moore* the Court pointed out that families' right to live together was different, and much stronger.

Example: Two provisions of the Muni zoning ordinance deal with the rights of persons to live together in the same dwelling:

> *Section 1* provides that no more than 3 persons who are related, but who are not part of the same "nuclear family," may live together. "Nuclear family" is defined to include siblings, parents and children, but no other types of relatives (e.g., uncle/nephew, or first cousins).
>
> *Section 2* provides that no more than 3 persons who are unrelated, and who have no affectional ties, may live together. This section is designed to prevent the operation of "boarding houses" in which people with no pre-existing connection each rent a room in a house.

Appropriate persons challenge the constitutionality of these 2 provisions.

The court will *overturn* Section 1, because it infringes the fundamental right of relatives to live together, and is not necessary for the achievement of a compelling state interest (the strict scrutiny standard). But the court will *uphold* Section 2, because unrelated persons who have no pre-existing ties do not have a fundamental right to live together in a single dwelling. Therefore, the restriction imposed by Section 2 will be subject only to mere-rationality review. Since Muni could rationally believe that the operation of boarding houses causes social ills (e.g., a decline in property values from a transient population that has no incentive to maintain the houses properly), and could rationally believe that the no-groups-of-more-than-3-unrelated-persons was a reasonable way to prevent boarding houses, Section 2 will be found to satisfy this undemanding mere-rationality review standard.

2. Upbringing and education: Similarly, a parent's right to direct the *upbringing* and *education* of his children is "fundamental."

Example 1: The state may not require parents to send their children to public schools. Parents have a fundamental right to determine how their children will be educated. [*Pierce v. Soc. of Sisters*]

Example 2: A parent has a fundamental interest in deciding who will spend time with the child. Therefore, the state may not award visitation rights to a child's grandparents over the objection of the child's fit custodial parent, unless the state first gives "special weight" to the parent's wishes. [*Troxel v. Granville*]

a. **Right to continue parenting:** There's also probably a fundamental right to *continue parenting* — so the state can't take away your child just because it thinks a foster home would be "better" for the child. (Even if there's child abuse, the parent still has a fundamental right to parent, but here the state's interest in protecting the child would be "compelling," so putting the child in foster care would probably satisfy strict scrutiny.)

i. **No relationship:** But if a parent has *never married* the other parent, and has never *developed a relationship* with the child (e.g., they have never lived together), then there is probably *not* a fundamental right to continue to be a parent. So the state may, for instance, deny the non-custodial unwed parent who has never participated in the child's upbringing the right to block an adoption of the child. [*Quilloin v. Walcott*]

3. **Right to marry:** The *right to marry* is also fundamental, so again the state can only interfere with this right by passing strict scrutiny.

Example: A state may not forbid anyone from remarrying unless he is not current on all support payments from his prior marriage. [*Zablocki v. Redhail*]

E. **Adult sex:** There is no general fundamental right to engage in *adult consensual sexual activity*. Therefore, the Court will generally review restrictions on adult consensual sexual activity under the *mere-rationality* test.

1. **Rational-relation review "with bite":** However, although the Court will generally review restrictions on adult sexual activity under the mere-rationality test, the Court will sometimes *strike down* the regulation on the grounds that it interferes with people's sexual autonomy.

a. **Homosexual sodomy:** Most dramatically, the Court has *struck down* all state laws that *criminalize homosexual sodomy*, on the grounds that such laws "*demean the lives of homosexual persons*," and thus violate their substantive due process rights. Gays now have "the full right to engage in their [homosexual] conduct without intervention of the government." [*Lawrence v. Texas*]

2. **Other sexual conduct:** Notwithstanding *Lawrence v. Texas*, the state can almost certainly prohibit, and punish, such adult consensual sexual activities as *adultery, incest, bestiality and bigamy,* on the grounds that these activities are provably *harmful*, and their prohibition is therefore not merely an irrational expression of the majority's "moral disapproval."

3. **Married people's conduct:** But where the parties are *married* (to each other), there probably *is* a fundamental right to have even "deviant" sex, as long as it's not physically dangerous and is consensual. For instance, the state probably may not prohibit oral sex in marriage, since that would fall within the marriage area of the fundamental right to privacy.

F. **Right to freedom of bodily movement:** A person has a substantive due process right not to have his *physical liberty unreasonably restrained.* This principle is most commonly applied to *physical punishment such as imprisonment:* even if the government has the right to punish a person, a restraint on physical liberty that is grossly disproportionate to the offense will violate the prisoner's substantive due process rights.

1. **Mental institutions and schools:** On the MBE, this principle is most likely to be tested in *non-prison settings*. For instance, in such settings as *juvenile detention facilities, mental institutions* holding a person in civil commitment, and, especially, *public schools*, any restraints on physical freedom *must not be grossly disproportionate to the severity of the offense* and the circumstances in which it was committed.

   Example: Suppose that a public school decrees that any student caught whispering in class is to be subject to detention for four hours a day for the next five school days, no matter how quiet the whispering and no matter whether the student had previously committed an offense. A court would likely hold that imposing the full 20-hour-detention as punishment on a previously-well-behaved student who whispered very quietly was a violation of his substantive due process rights, because the punishment was grossly disproportionate to the severity of the offense.

G. **The "right to die," and the right to decline unwanted medical procedures:** Here is the state of the law of "right to die" and "right to pull the plug":

1. **Can't be forced to undergo unwanted procedures:** A competent adult has a Fourteenth Amendment liberty interest in *not being forced to undergo unwanted medical procedures*, including artificial life-sustaining measures. It's not clear whether this is a "fundamental" interest.

   Example: P, dying of stomach cancer, has a liberty interest in refusing to let the hospital feed him through a feeding tube.

2. **State's interest in preserving life:** The state has an important *countervailing interest in preserving life.*

3. **"Clear and convincing evidence" standard:** In the case of a now-incompetent patient, the state's interest in preserving life entitles it to say that it won't allow the "plug to be pulled" unless there is *"clear and convincing evidence"* that the patient would have voluntarily declined the life-sustaining measures. [*Cruzan v. Missouri*]

4. **No "right to commit suicide":** Terminally-ill patients do *not* have a general liberty interest in *"committing suicide."* Nor do they have the constitutional right to *recruit a third person* to help them commit suicide. [*Washington v. Glucksberg*]

   Example: A state may make it a felony for a physician to knowingly prescribe a fatal dose of drugs for the purpose of helping the patient commit suicide.

V. PROCEDURAL DUE PROCESS

A. **Introduction:** We turn now to the other main aspect of the Fourteenth Amendment's Due Process Clause: this is the requirement that the state act with adequate or fair *procedures* when it deprives a person of life, liberty or property. Here, the emphasis is on the particular case presented by the particular person — has the government handled his particular situation fairly? There are two main questions:

[1] Has the individual's life, liberty or property been *"taken"*?; and, if so,

[2] What *process was "due"* her prior to this taking?

1. **Life, liberty or property:** The most important single thing to remember about procedural due process is that there cannot be a procedural due process problem unless government is taking a person's *life*, *liberty* or *property*. In other words, there is *no general interest in having the government behave with fair procedures.*

   Example: A city hires for an opening on its police force. The city can be as arbitrary and random as it wants, because as we'll see, an applicant for a job has no liberty or property interest in obtaining the job. Therefore, the city doesn't have to give the applicant a hearing, a statement of reasons why she didn't get the job, a systematic test of her credentials, or any other aspect of procedural fairness.

2. **Distinction between substance and procedure:** Always distinguish between "substantive" due process and "procedural" due process. Procedural due process applies only where *individual determinations* are being made.

Example: Suppose a state passes a law that says that no person with unpaid child support may marry. This statute raises an issue of substantive due process — unless this means of enforcing child support payments is necessary to achieve a compelling state interest, the state may not use that method at all, against anyone. Separately, even if this "ban on marriage" could pass this substantive due process hurdle (which it apparently can't, based on past Supreme Court cases like *Zablocki v. Redhail*), the state still must use *adequate procedures* before enforcing the ban *against a particular person*. For instance, the state must probably provide a person with *notice* that the ban will be applied, and a *hearing* at which he can show that the ban shouldn't apply to him because (for instance) he's fully paid up. The obligation to use fair procedures always applies *"one case at a time,"* and governs the application of government action to a particular person in a particular situation.

a. **Often tested on the MBE:** The MBE examiners like to test you on this distinction between substantive and procedural due process. They do this by creating a government program that *gives benefits* to a certain class of persons, and then having the government *revoke the program as to that entire class.* You're then told that a person who has lost the benefits bring suit. In this kind of scenario, there is *no procedural due process problem*, since the government action is not based on whether the person falls within the class (a "one case at a time" problem, i.e., a procedural due process problem). Instead, the only issue is whether the government has a *substantive* due process obligation to maintain the program (which it will *not*, unless the affected persons have a fundamental right to continue receiving that particular benefit, which they generally will not have).

Example: In the face of a growing recession, the legislature of the state of Green enacts a program under which a person who becomes unemployed is guaranteed 40% of his or her former salary, up to a cap, for a period of one year. The regulations enacted pursuant to the statute say that the only grounds for terminating a person's eligibility are if the person becomes employed substantially full-time during the benefits period.

In January 2008, Rose loses her job and begins receiving benefits under the program. After six months, and at a time when Rose has not become re-employed, the Green legislature passes a new bill immediately suspending the entire unemployment-payment program for all recipients. The legislature acts because the costs of the program have been rising rapidly, and the legislature has concluded that the program is no longer reasonably affordable for Green taxpayers. Rose receives a letter telling her that her benefits have been discontinued "effective immediately." Rose challenges the termination on constitutional due process grounds.

Rose will *lose*. This is *not a procedural due process problem*, since government is not deciding that Rose doesn't fit into the category of persons entitled to receive benefits. Therefore, the fact that Rose got no advance notice of termination, and no form of hearing at which she could protest the end of benefits, doesn't matter. (If the program had not been terminated, and instead what happened was that the department in charge of administering it decided that Rose no longer *met the requirements* because, say, she had become substantially full-time employed, then this *would* be a procedural due process problem, and Rose would have at least some right to notice and a hearing. That's because now, the issue would be, does the claimant fit into the protected category?)

Since Rose has to make a substantive rather than procedural due process argument, she can win only if she can show that her substantive due process rights have been infringed. But since the receipt of unemployment benefits is not a fundamental right (receipt of monetary benefits from the government never is), Rose would have to show that the termination of the program was not rationally related to the achievement of a legitimate state objective. And Rose would not be able to make the showing — pursuit of fiscal stability is certainly a legitimate state objective, and the legislature could certainly have rationally believed that terminating this program was a reasonable means of pursuing that stability. (Remember that a social welfare measure that doesn't affect a fundamental right will almost never be struck down on substantive due process grounds; see *supra*, p. 35.)

B. Liberty: Remember that *"liberty"* is one of the things the government cannot take without procedural due process. What *is* "liberty" for due process purposes?

1. **Physical liberty:** First, we have the interest in "*physical*" liberty. This liberty interest is violated if you are *imprisoned*, or even if you are placed in some other situation where you *do not have physical freedom of movement* (e.g., juvenile and/or civil commitment).

2. **Intangible rights:** Also, a person has a liberty interest in being able to do certain intangible things not related to physical freedom of movement. There's no complete catalog of what interests fall within this "intangible" aspect of liberty. Here are some examples, however: (1) the right to drive; (2) the right to practice one's profession; (3) the right to raise one's family.

C. Property: The government also can't take *"property"* without procedural due process. Here are the things that may be "property" for procedural due process purposes:

1. **Conventional property:** First, of course, we have "conventional" property (i.e., personal and real property). Thus the government cannot impose a monetary fine against a person, or declare a person's car forfeited, without complying with procedural due process.

   a. **Debt collection:** Certain kinds of *debt collection* devices involve "property." For instance, if the state lets private creditors *attach* a person's bank account prior to trial (which means that the owner can't get at the funds), even that temporary blockage is a "taking" of property. Similarly, if the state lets a private creditor *garnish* a person's wages, that's a taking of property. On the other hand, if the state simply passes a law that lets creditors use *self-help* to repossess goods, there's no governmental taking of property when the creditor repossesses. (The due process requirement applies only where it is *government* that does, or at least is involved in, the taking of liberty or property.)

2. **Government benefits:** *Government benefits* may or may not constitute "property" rights. Generally, if one is just *applying* for benefits and hasn't yet been receiving them, one does *not* have a property interest in those benefits.

   Example: If P applies for welfare, and has never gotten it before, P does not have a property interest in receiving welfare. Therefore, the government does not have to comply with procedural due process when it turns P down. Thus the government doesn't have to give P a statement of reasons, a hearing, etc.

   a. **Already getting benefits:** But if a person has *already been getting the benefits*, it's probably the case that he's got a property interest in *continuing* to get them, so that the government cannot *terminate* those benefits without giving him procedural due process. [*Goldberg v. Kelly*]

      i. **State law can change:** But *state law can change even this* — for instance, if the state statute governing welfare benefits says that "benefits may be cut off at any time," a person probably *doesn't* have a property interest in continuing to get those benefits, so he has no claim to due process.

3. **Government employment:** A government *job* is similar to government benefits.

   a. **Applicant:** If a person is just *applying* for the job, he clearly does *not* have a property interest in it.

   b. **Already have job:** If a person already has the job, then the court looks to *state law* to determine whether the person had a property interest in the job.

      i. **Ordinarily at-will:** Ordinarily, under state law a job is *terminable at will*; if so, the jobholder has no property right to it, so he may be fired without due process.

      ii. **Legitimate claim of entitlement:** If either a statute or the public employer's *practices* give a person a *"legitimate claim of entitlement"* to keep the job, then she's got a property interest.

      Example: If a public university follows the publicized custom of never firing anybody from a non-tenured position without cause except on one year's notice, then a non-tenured teacher has a property right to hold his non-tenured job for a year following notice. [*Perry v. Sindermann*]

4. **Government licenses:** A *license* issued by the government, entitling the holder to pursue a *certain profession,* will typically constitute a property interest once bestowed. For instance, if the MBE fact pattern says that the license may only be revoked "for cause" or on account of the commission of a crime, this will typically mean that the license-holder has a property interest in the license.

   Example: A state grants a barber's license to any applicant of good character who passes a licensing exam. An administrative regulation says that the license shall be terminated only for "good cause." Once a person receives a barber's license, she has a property interest in it, so she is entitled to procedural due process before it can be revoked.

5. **Burden of proof on claimant:** Where a plaintiff claims to have a property interest in a government job or benefit, the plaintiff will normally have the *burden of persuasion* on that issue.

   Example: If P claims that she's entitled not to be fired by D without procedural due process because she has tenure in her job, P will have the burden of persuading the trier of fact that under state law, she has tenure and thus the right not to be fired without cause.

D. Process required: If a person's interest in property or liberty is being impaired, then she is entitled to due process. But *what procedures* does the person get? There is no simple answer.

1. **Court proceedings:** Where a person is a litigant in a formal *judicial proceeding*, a quite full panoply of procedural safeguards is constitutionally required for due process. The state is required to give the litigant the right to a *hearing*, the right to *call witnesses*, the right to *counsel*, the right to a *fair and objective trial*, and the right to an *appeal.*

2. **Non-judicial proceeding:** Where the property or liberty interest is being impaired in something *other* than a judicial proceeding, the state does *not* have to give the individual the full range of procedural safeguards that would be needed for a court proceeding. Instead, for any particular procedural safeguard that the plaintiff says she should get (e.g., the right to a hearing), the court conducts a *balancing* test: the strength of the plaintiff's interest in receiving the procedural safeguard is weighed against the government's interest in avoiding extra burdens. [*Mathews v. Eldridge*]

Examples: If *A* has been receiving welfare benefits, these benefits may not be terminated without giving *A* an evidentiary hearing, because a wrongful termination of welfare benefits, even temporarily, is likely to lead to extreme hardship, without a large countervailing benefit to the government. [*Goldberg v. Kelly*] By contrast, a tenured employee who is being fired from a government job gets fewer procedural safeguards — he gets notice of the charges and an opportunity to present some evidence, but not a full adversarial evidentiary hearing with right to counsel; this is so because the government's interest in being able to fire unsatisfactory employees quickly is factored into the balance. [*Cleveland Bd. of Ed. v. Loudermill*]

3. **Time for hearing:** Whatever right to a hearing the plaintiff has, that hearing must be held *before* the government deprives the plaintiff of any significant property interest. In the classic scenario in which the government wants to take away a person's job or stream of payments, the government must hold any required hearing *before cutting off the person's salary or payment stream.*

   Example: P is a tenured government employee who can only be dismissed for good cause. The government wants to fire P for unsatisfactory work. *Held*, whatever procedural protections P is entitled to (in this case, notice of the charges, an explanation of the evidence, and an opportunity to present P's side of the story), those protections must all be given *before* P is terminated or her salary cut off. [*Cleveland Bd. of Ed. v. Loudermill*]

4. **Embedded "standing" issue:** The MBE examiners will sometimes embed a *"standing"* issue into what seems to be solely a question about whether a person is entitled to particular due process procedures. As we'll see later (*infra*, p. 106), a person *won't* be entitled to a particular type of hearing if the providing of that hearing could not plausibly have *changed the outcome*, i.e., led to a *redressing* of the injuring for which the person is seeking redress.

   Example: A state requires that bar applicants graduate from an ABA-approved law school. The state refuses to give Applicant, who has passed the bar exam, a hearing to show why he should be admitted notwithstanding his having graduated from a non-ABA-approved law school. He claims that denial of such a hearing violates his procedural due process rights.

   The ABA requirement is constitutional, and therefore giving the hearing wouldn't make any difference to the outcome. Consequently, Applicant doesn't have federal-court standing to argue that he is constitutionally entitled to the hearing, because he hasn't suffered any "injury in fact" due to denial of a hearing. (The example is developed more fully on p. 106 *infra*.)

CHAPTER 7

EQUAL PROTECTION

I. EQUAL PROTECTION GENERALLY

A. **Text of clause:** The Equal Protection Clause is part of the Fourteenth Amendment. It provides that "[n]o state shall make or enforce any law which shall ... deny to any person within its jurisdiction the equal protection of the laws."

1. **General usage:** The Clause, like all parts of the Thirteenth, Fourteenth and Fifteenth Amendments, was enacted shortly after the Civil War, and its primary goal was to attain free and equal treatment for ex-slaves. But it has long been interpreted as imposing a *general* restraint on the governmental use of classifications, not just classifications based on race but also those based on sex, alienage, illegitimacy, wealth, or any other characteristic.

2. **State and federal:** The direct text of the Clause, of course, applies only to state governments. But the *federal* government is also bound by the same rules of equal protection — this happens by the indirect means of the Fifth Amendment's Due Process Clause. So if a given action would be a

violation of equal protection for a state, that same action would be unconstitutional if done by the federal government (though in this situation, strictly speaking this would be a violation of the Fifth Amendment's Due Process Clause, interpreted to guarantee equal protection of the laws against federal incursion).

a. **Government action only:** The Equal Protection Clause, and the Fifth Amendment's Due Process Clause, apply *only to government action*, not to action by private citizens. This is commonly referred to as the requirement of *"state action,"* and is discussed further below.

Example: D, a large private university, refuses to admit African American students. No government participates in this decision. The university's conduct cannot be a violation of the Equal Protection Clause, because there is no "state action."

3. **Making of classes:** The Equal Protection Clause is only implicated where the government *makes a classification*. It's not implicated where the government merely decides which of two classes a particular person falls into.

Example: If Congress says that a person can't receive Social Security if she works more than 1,000 hours per year, then it's made a classification that distinguishes between those who work more than 1,000 hours and those who work less — this classification can be attacked under the Equal Protection Clause. But an administrative determination that a particular person did or did not work 1,000 hours is not a classification, and cannot be attacked under the Equal Protection Clause, only the Due Process Clause.

4. **"As applied" vs. "facial":** Here is some nomenclature: If P attacks a classification that is clearly written into the statute or regulation, he is claiming that equal protection is violated by the statute or regulation *"on its face."* If P's claim is that the statute does not make a classification on its face, but is being *administered* in a purposefully discriminatory way, then he is claiming that the statute or regulation is a violation of equal protection *"as applied."*

Example: A statute that says "you must be a citizen to vote" creates a classification scheme "on its face" — citizens vs. non-citizens. But if P, who is black, claims that in actual administration, blacks are required to prove citizenship but whites are not, then his equal protection claim would be on the statute "as applied."

a. **Same standards for both:** Either kind of attack — facial or "as applied" — may be made. Both follow essentially the same principles. For instance, if no suspect classification or fundamental right is involved, the classification scheme will violate the Equal Protection Clause if it's not rationally related to a legitimate state objective, whether the scheme is on the face of the statute or merely in the way the statute is applied.

b. **Significance:** The distinction makes a large difference in who may bring suit. In a facial attack, P can win merely by showing that the clause could not constitutionally be applied to *some other persons not presently before the court.* If the court agrees, it will block the statute from being applied to anyone (including P). By contrast, in an as-applied attack, P must show that the statute is being unconstitutionally applied *as to him.* Outside of the First Amendment area, the court is increasingly requiring that an attack be as-applied instead of facial unless the plaintiff can show that statute would infringe the rights of a *substantial group* as opposed to a few people.

Example: A state requires anyone who wants to vote to present a picture ID. If the court allows a facial attack, P may attack the statute by showing that while P herself has never been turned away for lack of an ID (e.g., because she has one), there are other persons not before the court who do not have photo IDs, cannot reasonably get them, and have been or might be prevented from voting. (If P wins, the court will order that the statute not be applied against anyone.) If, on the other hand, the court insists on an as-applied attack, the suit cannot go forward until there is a plaintiff who can show that she herself does not have an ID, and that she has been prevented or reasonably fears that she would be prevented from voting on account of the ID requirement.

5. **What the Clause guarantees:** The Equal Protection Clause in essence guarantees that *people who are similarly situated will be treated similarly.*

   Example: Consider racial segregation in the public schools. Such segregation gives a different treatment to two groups that are similarly situated, African Americans and whites. Therefore, it violates the equal protection rights of African Americans. (Of course, this reflects a judgment that there are no meaningful differences between blacks and whites that relate to public education. If the issue were, say, compulsory medical screening for sickle cell anemia, blacks and whites might not be similarly situated.)

   a. **Dissimilar:** The Equal Protection Clause also guarantees that people who are *not* similarly situated will not be treated similarly. But this aspect is rarely of practical importance on the MBE.

6. **Three levels of review:** Recall that in our discussion of substantive due process, we saw that depending on the circumstances, one of two sharply different standards of review of governmental action was used, the easy "rational relation" test or the very demanding "strict scrutiny" standard. In the equal protection context, we have two tests that are virtually the same as these two, plus a third "middle level" of scrutiny. Let's consider each of the three types of review:

   a. **Ordinary "mere rationality" review:** The easiest-to-satisfy standard of review applies to statutes that: (1) are *not based on a "suspect classification"*; (2) do not involve a *"quasi-suspect"* category that the Court has implicitly recognized (principally gender and illegitimacy); and (3) don't impair a *"fundamental right."* This is the so-called *"mere rationality"* standard. Almost every *economic regulation* will be reviewed under this easy-to-satisfy standard. (This is similar to the ease with which economic regulation passes muster under the substantive due process clause.) Under this easiest "mere rationality" standard, the Court asks only "whether it is conceivable that the classification bears a rational relationship to an end of government which is not prohibited by the Constitution."

      i. **Standard summarized:** So where "mere rationality" review is applied, the classification must satisfy just two *easy tests*:

         [1] government must be pursuing a *legitimate governmental objective*; and

         [2] there must be a *rational relation* between the classification and that objective.

         Furthermore, it's not necessary that the court believe that these two requirements are satisfied; it's enough that the court concludes that it's *"conceivable"* that they're satisfied.

   b. **Strict scrutiny:** At the other end of the spectrum, the Court will give *"strict scrutiny"* to any statute which is based on a *"suspect classification"* or which impairs a *"fundamental right."* (We'll be discussing below the meaning of these two terms, "suspect classification" and "fundamental right.") A classification based on *race* is a classic example of a "suspect class"; the right to *vote* is an example of a fundamental right.

      i. **Standard:** Where strict scrutiny is invoked, the classification will be upheld only if it is *necessary* to promote a *compelling* governmental interest. Thus not only must the objective be an extremely important one, but the "fit" between the means and the end must be extremely tight. This strict scrutiny test is the same as for substantive due process when a "fundamental right" (e.g., the right to privacy) is involved.

c. **Middle-level review:** In a few contexts, the Court uses a *middle level* of scrutiny, more probing than "mere rationality" but less demanding than "strict scrutiny." This middle level is mainly used for cases involving classifications based on *gender* and *illegitimacy*.

i. **Standard:** This middle-level test is usually stated as follows: the means chosen by the legislature (i.e., the classification) must be *substantially related* to an *important governmental objective*. So the legislative objective must be *"important"* (but not necessarily "compelling," as for strict scrutiny), and means and end must be *"substantially related"* (easier to satisfy than the almost perfect "necessary" fit between means and end in strict scrutiny situations).

II. ECONOMIC AND SOCIAL LAWS — THE "MERE RATIONALITY" TEST

A. **Non-suspect, non-fundamental rights (economic and social legislation):** First, let's examine the treatment of classifications that do *not* involve either a *suspect class* or a *fundamental right*. Most *economic* and *social-welfare* legislation falls into this category.

1. **Mere rationality:** Here, as noted, courts use the "mere rationality" standard. In other words, as long as there is some *rational relation* between the classification drawn by the legislature and some *legitimate legislative objective*, the classification scheme will not violate the Equal Protection Clause.

MBE Tip: Where there is no suspect class or fundamental right at issue, be extremely skeptical of any choice that involves striking down a statute on equal protection grounds.

Example: A state insurance commissioner enacts a regulation requiring all health-care insurers in the state to charge the same medical insurance rates to any family, regardless of family size and regardless of the family members' health or sickness. Even though this regulation would cause some families (e.g., large ones or very sick ones) to get a bargain, and others (small ones and/or very healthy ones) to pay much more than they would under free-market conditions, a court would almost certainly *uphold* the regulatory scheme against equal protection attack. The court would so conclude on the grounds that the scheme is rationally related to achieving the legitimate governmental objective of helping larger unhealthy families not be priced out of the health insurance market.

a. **Need not be actual objective:** One thing this "mere rationality" standard means is that the "legitimate government objective" part of the test is satisfied even if the statute's defenders come up with merely a *"hypothetical"* objective that the legislature "might have" been pursuing. The government does not have to show that the objective it's pointing to was the one that *actually motivated* the legislature.

b. **No empirical link:** Also, there does not have to in fact be even a "rational relation" between the means chosen and the end — all that's required is that the legislature *"could have rationally believed"* that there was a link between the means and the end.

c. **Loose fit:** Finally, a very *loose fit* between means and end will still be acceptable.

2. **Conclusion:** Therefore, if you decide that a particular government classification does *not involve a suspect category or a fundamental right,* and should thus be subjected to "mere rationality" review, *be extremely skeptical of any choice that involves striking down the classification on equal protection grounds.*

3. **"Grandfather clause" as rational classification:** One illustration of the extreme deference given by courts to economic regulations that do not involve a suspect class or fundamental right is that *"grandfather"* schemes are almost always *upheld.* That is, when government decides to ban some economic or land-use activity that it used to permit, but it allows people who have been pursuing that activity for a long time to continue (i.e., to be "grandfathered in"), this distinction or classification will almost always be found rational and thus valid.

   Example: City bans all vendors of food products from operating carts on City streets, because City has determined, by means of traffic studies, that such vendors clog City streets. The ordinance gives a permanent exemption, however, to any individual who, as of the effective date of the ordinance, has been selling food products from a cart on City streets on a substantially full-time basis for at least 10 years.

   This "grandfathering" of those who have sold for ten years is clearly a classification, so a vendor who has been selling for four years, and who loses his rights, could launch an equal protection attack. But the court would almost certainly conclude that the 10-year cutoff was enacted in pursuit of a legitimate governmental objective (traffic amelioration), and that it was not irrational (since City could reasonably have believed that partially rather than completely stopping such vending would nonetheless improve the traffic problem, and that doing so based on length-of-tenure was a fair way to draw the line).

4. **Other (non-economic) non-fundamental rights:**

   a. **"Equal protection" can sometimes be correct choice:** Usually, a claim that a particular economic regulation (which does not involve a suspect class or fundamental right) violates equal protection will fail, because it's hard to concoct fact patterns in which the legislation clearly fails to meet the easy-to-satisfy rational-relation-to-a-legitimate-state-objective standard. But the MBE examiners often create economic-regulation fact patterns in which "equal protection" is the *correct answer*, not because the claimant will *necessarily* win, but because the equal protection claim *might possibly win* whereas all the other claims cannot possibly succeed. So when you're given a set of clauses on which the claimant might rely, and the state seems to be acting illogically, don't be scared to choose "equal protection" as the *best available basis* for the claim, even in a non-suspect-class/non-fundamental-right scenario.

5. **Non-suspect classes:** Here are some classifications that have been held (or would likely be held) *not* to involve a suspect or quasi-suspect class:

   a. **Age:** Classifications based on *age.*

   Example: Suppose that a state requires all state troopers over 50 to retire, in order preserve a physically fit police force. Because age is not a suspect or quasi-suspect classification, the "mere rationality" test will be used. Because there is some slight overall relation between age and fitness, this requirement is satisfied, so the retirement rule does not violate equal protection. [*Mass. Board of Retirement v. Murgia*]

   b. **Wealth:** Classifications based upon *wealth.*

   Example: Suppose that a state provides that no low-income housing project may be built in any community unless a majority of the voters approve it in a popular referendum. A resident who would like to live in the low-income housing that would be built if allowed challenges the statute on equal protection grounds. Even if P shows that the statute was motivated by a desire to discriminate against the poor, P's constitutional challenge will probably fail. Because wealth is not a suspect or quasi-suspect class, the court will use "mere rationality" review, and will uphold the statute if it finds that the legislature could reasonably have believed that its statute might help achieve some legitimate state objective, perhaps letting communities avoid the greater governmental cost that arguably accompanies concentrations of low-income residents.

c. **Status as convicted criminal:** Classification based on having been *convicted of a crime*. Thus states that treat convicted criminals less favorably than non-convicts face only mere-rationality review.

III. SUSPECT CLASSIFICATIONS, ESPECIALLY RACE

A. **Suspect classifications:** At the other end of the spectrum, we apply *strict scrutiny* for any classification that involves a *"suspect class."*

1. **Race and national origin:** There are only three suspect classes generally recognized by the Supreme Court:

[1] *race*;

[2] *national origin* (or *"ethnicity"*); and

[3] for some purposes, *alienage*.

So be on the lookout for a classification based on race, national origin, or alienage. For other classifications, you can safely assume that these are not suspect.

2. **Purposeful:** On the MBE, probably the most important single thing to remember about strict scrutiny of suspect classifications is that this strict scrutiny will only be applied where the differential treatment of the class is *intentional* on the part of the government. If the government enacts a statute or regulation that merely has the unintended incidental *effect* of burdening, say, African Americans more than whites, the court will *not* use strict scrutiny. [*Washington v. Davis*]

This rule that "unintended disparate effects on one racial or ethnic group don't trigger strict scrutiny" seems to be the most frequently-tested aspect of suspect classifications on the MBE.

Example 1: City gives a standardized test to all applicants for the local police force. City and the test designers do not intend to make it harder for African Americans than for whites to pass the test. But it turns out that a lot fewer African Americans pass than whites, even though the applicant pools otherwise seem identical. This differential *will not trigger strict scrutiny*, because the government did not intend to treat African Americans differently from whites.

Example 2: U.S. Customs officials notice that when random searches of incoming passengers at airports are performed, a higher percentage of passengers entering through major airports in Miami and Houston are found smuggling narcotics than in other U.S. international airports. Therefore, federal authorities triple the number of federal Drug Enforcement Agency officials at these airports to perform searches. A group of U.S. citizen of Latin American ancestry asserts (correctly) in a class action that the increased scrutiny means that American citizens of Latin American origin are more likely to be searched than those of European origin, because the former are disproportionately likely to enter through Miami and Houston. The group therefore claims that the government's practice of increased DEA staffing in Miami and Houston must be strictly scrutinized under the Equal Protection Clause as a discrimination based on national origin.

The group will lose. Assuming that the DEA did not intend to examine incoming U.S. citizens of Latin American ancestry more closely than other citizens — and merely intended, in a race-and-ethnicity-neutral way, to put resources in those airports where drug smuggling had been seen to be most likely — the disparate impact on Latin American U.S. citizens will *not trigger strict scrutiny* of the DEA's staffing practices. (Instead, the staffing decision will be upheld as long as it is rationally related to a legitimate governmental objective, which it clearly is, since it's rational for drug-interdiction authorities to use heavier staffing at entry points with high smuggling rates, and legitimate to try to reduce drug smuggling.)

3. **Strict equals fatal:** Once the court does decide that a suspect classification is involved, and that strict scrutiny must be used, that scrutiny is almost always *fatal* to the classification scheme.

   a. **"Necessary" prong:** Sometimes, this is because the state cannot show that it is pursuing a "compelling" objective. But more often, it's because the means chosen is not shown to be *"necessary"* to achieve that compelling objective. A means is only "necessary" for achieving the particular objective if there are *no less discriminatory alternatives* that will accomplish the goal as well, or almost as well.

   Example: Suppose that, following the 9/11 attacks, the U.S. government put all Islamic Arabic-speaking U.S. citizens into internment camps. Presumably — even in an America frightened by terrorism — the Supreme Court would not find this to be a "necessary" means of dealing with the danger of terrorism, because less discriminatory alternatives like frequent document inspections and/or loyalty oaths would be almost as effective as virtual imprisonment.

4. **Some examples:** Here are two contexts in which claims have been made (and in most instances accepted) that a suspect class has been intentionally discriminated against in violation of equal protection:

   a. **Child custody and adoption:** Some notion of "racial compatibility" or "racial purity" may motivate state officials to differentiate based on race in *child custody* and *adoption* proceedings. In general, the practical rule is that the state may not impose flat rules that handle child custody and adoption differently based solely on the race of the child and parents.

   Example: Mother and Father are divorced, and Mother is given custody of Child. All are white. Mother then marries Husband, who is African American. The family court transfers custody to Father, on the grounds that Child will be socially stigmatized if she grows up in an interracial family. *Held*, this custody decision can't survive strict scrutiny — government may not bow to private racial prejudices. [*Palmore v. Sidoti*]

   b. **Political process:** Actions taken by government that relate to the *political process*, and that are intended to disadvantage racial or ethnic minorities, often run afoul of equal protection.

   Example: A state requires that in every election, each candidate's race must appear on the ballot. *Held*, this violates the Equal Protection Clause because it was motivated by a desire to keep African Americans out of office. [*Anderson v. Martin*]

5. **Segregation:** The clearest example of a classification involving a suspect class and thus requiring strict scrutiny is *segregation*, the maintenance of physical separation between the races.

   a. **General rule:** Official, intentional segregation based on race or national origin is a violation of the Equal Protection Clause. As the result of *Brown v. Board of Education*, even if the government were to maintain truly "separate but equal" facilities (in the sense that, say, a school for blacks had as nice a building, as qualified teachers, etc., as a school for whites), the intentional maintenance of separate facilities *per se* violates the Equal Protection Clause.

   b. **Education and housing:** The two areas where official segregation is most often found are *education* and *housing*.

i. **Education:** Thus if a school board establishes attendance zones for the purpose of making one school heavily African American and/or Hispanic, and another school heavily white, this would violate equal protection.

ii. **Housing:** Similarly, government may not intentionally segregate in housing. For example, it's a violation of equal protection for a city to do its *zoning* in such a way that all *government-subsidized housing* is built in the heavily black part of town, if the intent of this zoning practice is to maintain racial segregation.

c. **Must be *de jure*:** But it's critical to remember that there is a violation of equal protection only where the segregation is the result of *intentional government action.* In other words, the segregation must be *"de jure,"* not merely *"de facto."*

Example: School district lines are drawn by officials who have no desire to separate students based on race. Over time, due to housing choices made by private individuals, one district becomes fully African American, and the other all-white. Even though the schools are no longer racially balanced, there has been no equal protection violation, because there was no act of intentional separation on the part of the government. [*Cf. Bd. of Ed. v. Dowell.*]

d. **Wide remedies:** If a court finds that there has been intentional segregation, it has a wide range of *remedies* to choose from. For instance, it can bus students to a non-neighborhood school, or order the redrawing of district boundaries. But whatever remedy the court chooses, the remedy must *stop* once the effects of the original intentional discrimination have been eradicated. (Then, if because of housing patterns or other non-government action, the schools become resegregated, the court may *not* reinstitute its remedies.)

IV. RACE-CONSCIOUS AFFIRMATIVE ACTION

A. **Race-conscious affirmative action:** You may get an MBE question about race-conscious *affirmative action* as distinguished from official discrimination against racial minorities. If you see a question in which government is trying to help racial or ethnic minorities by giving them some sort of preference, you should immediately think "equal protection" and you should think "strict scrutiny."

1. **Public entity:** Remember that there can only be a violation of equal protection if there's *state action*, that is, action by the federal government or by a state or municipality. In general, the use of affirmative action by private entities does *not* raise any constitutional issue (except perhaps where a judge orders a private employer to implement a race-conscious plan). But any time you have a fact pattern in which a police department, school district, public university, or other governmental entity seems to be intentionally preferring one racial group over another, that's when you know you have a potential equal protection problem.

2. **Strict scrutiny:** *Any affirmative action program that classifies on the basis of race will be strictly scrutinized.* [*Richmond v. Croson*] So a race-conscious affirmative action plan, whether it's in the area of employment, college admissions, voting rights or anywhere else, must be adopted for the purpose of furthering some "compelling" governmental interest, and the racial classification must be "necessary" to achieve that compelling governmental interest.

a. **Past discrimination:** Since a race-conscious affirmative action plan will have to be in pursuit of a "compelling" governmental interest, probably the only interests that are likely to qualify are: (1) the government's interest in *redressing past discrimination*; and (2) a *university's* interest in *student-body diversity*. So if the government is merely trying to get a *racially-balanced work force*, to make African Americans *more economically success-*

ful, or any other objective that is not closely tied to one of these two objectives, you should immediately be able to say, "The government interest is not compelling, and the measure flunks the strict scrutiny test."

b. **Clear evidence:** Even if the government's trying to redress past discrimination, there's got to be *clear evidence* that this discrimination in fact occurred.

   i. **Societal discrimination:** Redressing past discrimination "*by society* as a whole" will *not* suffice. There must be past discrimination closely related to the problem, typically discrimination *by government.*

c. **Quotas:** One device that is especially vulnerable to equal protection attack is the racially-based *quota.* A racially-based quota is an inflexible number of admissions slots, dollar amounts, or other "goodies" set aside for minorities. For instance, it's a quota if the state says that one-half of all new hires in the police department must be African American, or if it says that 20% of all seats in the public university's law school class will be set aside for African Americans and Hispanics. Probably *virtually all racially-based quotas will be struck down even where the government is trying to eradicate the effects of past discrimination* — the Court will probably say that a quota is not "necessary" to remedy discrimination, because more flexible "goals" can do the job.

d. **Congress:** It doesn't make any (or at least much) difference that the affirmative action program was enacted by *Congress* rather than by a state or local government. Here, too, the Court will apply strict scrutiny if the program is race-conscious. [*Adarand Constructors, Inc. v. Pena*]

B. Some contexts:

1. **Preferential admissions:** Any scheme that gives a preference to one racial group for *admission* to a public university has to be strictly scrutinized. However, such preferences will not necessarily be invalidated as the result of this strict scrutiny. Here are what seem to be the main rules governing affirmative action in public-university admissions, as the result of the twin 2003 cases of *Grutter v. Bollinger* and *Gratz v. Bollinger*:

   [a] Race-conscious admissions measures will *receive strict scrutiny*, and thus must be narrowly-tailored to achieve a compelling objective;

   [b] The pursuit of *diversity in the student body* can be a *compelling objective*;

   [c] A *one-student-at-a-time evaluation* in which the student's race is merely one factor among various ones considered is *sufficiently narrowly-tailored*; but

   [d] Mechanical approaches resembling *quotas*, such as automatically awarding an applicant a fixed number of *points* towards admission based on his race, are *not narrowly-tailored* and therefore violate equal protection.

   Example 1 (valid): The University of Michigan Law School evaluates each applicant's entire file, weighing such variables as undergraduate GPA, LSAT scores, and the contribution the applicant will make to diversity in the student body. The school treats as a major "plus" factor an applicant's membership in one of three historically-discriminated-against groups, blacks, Hispanics and Native Americans. The school does so to create a "critical mass" of these minority students, so that they will participate without feeling isolated.

   Held (by a 5-4 vote), this form of affirmative-action is constitutional. The interest in a diverse student body is a compelling one, and the approach here — in that it relies on an individualized, non-mechanical evaluation of each applicant — is narrowly tailored to achieve that interest. [*Grutter v. Bollinger*]

Example 2 (invalid): The Univ. of Michigan undergraduate college awards pre-measured "points" to applicants for various attributes (e.g., up to 5 points for being an outstanding artist or student leader). Every black or Hispanic applicant automatically gets 20 points for diversity. 100 points are needed for admission. The extra 20 points for minority-group status has the effect that virtually every minimally-qualified black or Hispanic applicant is admitted, whereas many well-qualified non-minority applicants are rejected.

Held (by 6-3), this form of affirmative action is unconstitutional, because it is not narrowly-tailored to the achievement of the compelling interest in student-body diversity. The scheme here is a mechanical one that is equivalent to a quota, not an individualized-evaluation scheme like the one approved in *Grutter*. And the fact that "near-misses" can be flagged for individualized review does not save the scheme. [*Gratz v. Bollinger*]

2. **Minority set-asides:** *Minority set-asides*, by which some percentage of publicly-funded contracts are reserved for minority-owned businesses, will be subjected to scrutiny and generally struck down. That's true whether the set-aside is enacted by Congress or by a state/local government.

3. **Employment:** Any time a public *employer* gives an intentional preference to one racial group, strict scrutiny will probably be called for.

   a. **Layoffs:** If the employer intentionally prefers blacks over whites when it administers *layoffs*, that preference will almost certainly be unconstitutional. [*Wygant v. Jackson Bd. of Ed.*]

   b. **Hiring:** A racial preference in *hiring* is almost as hard to justify (though it might pass muster if that particular public employer had clearly discriminated against African Americans in the past, and there seemed to be no way short of a racial preference in hiring to redress that past discrimination).

   c. **Promotions:** A race-based scheme of awarding *promotions* to cure past discrimination (so that African Americans eventually get promoted to the levels that they would have been at had there not been any discrimination in the first place) is the easiest to justify, since it damages the expectations of whites the least. But even this will have to satisfy strict scrutiny.

4. **Drawing of election districts:** A *voter* who thinks she has been disadvantaged by the drawing of *electoral districts* in a race-conscious (or other "group-conscious") way may bring an equal protection suit against the government body that drew the district lines. But the plaintiff must show either: (1) that the lines were drawn with the *purpose* and *effect* of *disadvantaging the group* of which P is a part; or (2) that *race* was the *"predominant factor"* in how the district lines were drawn.

   a. **"Partisan gerrymander" claims almost impossible to win:** The first of these types of claims — "my group has been systematically disadvantaged" — is used to attack *"partisan gerrymanders,"* gerrymanders based on political factors rather than racial factors. These claims are *almost impossible to win.* [*Vieth v. Jubelirer; League of United Latin Amer. Citizens v. Perry*]

   Example: A state legislature controlled by Democrats enacts a redistricting plan that, by the way boundaries are drawn, is intended to make it easier for Democrats to get elected to the U.S. Congress than for Republicans. As long as no race-based or ethnicity-based criteria are used (just "political party" criteria), the plan will probably not violate the Equal Protection Clause.

b. **Race as predominant factor:** But the second type of attack — "race was the predominant factor in drawing district lines" — has a *much better chance of success.* If the court concludes that *race* was indeed the *predominant factor* in how the electoral district lines were drawn, the court will *strictly scrutinize* the lines, and probably strike them down. Legislatures may "take account" of race in drawing district lines (just as they take account of ethnic groups, precinct lines, and many other factors), but they *may not make race the predominant factor,* unless they can show that using race in this way is necessary to achieve a compelling governmental interest (e.g., eradication of prior official voting-rights discrimination). The desire to create the maximum number of "majority black" districts will not by itself be a "compelling" interest. [*Miller v. Johnson*]

V. MIDDLE-LEVEL REVIEW (GENDER, ILLEGITIMACY AND ALIENAGE)

A. **Middle-level review generally:** A few types of classifications are subjected to "middle-level" review, easier to satisfy than strict scrutiny but tougher than "mere rationality."

1. **Standard:** Where we apply the middle-level standard, the government objective must be *"important,"* and the means must be *"substantially related"* to that objective.

2. **Classes that receive:** There are two main types of classifications that get middle-level review: (1) *gender*; and (2) *illegitimacy*. We also consider *alienage* here, because it has aspects of both strict scrutiny and mere rationality, so it's kind of a hybrid.

B. **Gender:** The most important single rule to remember in the entire area of middle-level scrutiny is that *sex-based classifications get middle-level review.* [*Craig v. Boren*] So if government intentionally classifies on the basis of sex, it's got to show that it's pursuing an *important* objective, and that the sex-based classification scheme is *substantially related* to that objective. Usually the classification will fail this mid-level review.

> **Example 1:** City sets the mandatory retirement age for male public school teachers at 65, and for female teachers at 62. Because this classification is based upon gender, it must satisfy middle-level review: City must show that its sex-based classification is substantially related to the achievement of an important governmental objective. In this case, it is unlikely that City can make this showing.

> **Example 2:** The state of Orange bans the sale of "near beer" (supposedly non-intoxicating beer with a relatively small but non-zero alcohol content) to males under the age of 21, but not to females under 21. The state reasons that young males are more likely to drive and speed while slightly intoxicated than are young females.
>
> If a 20-year-old male attacks the statute's constitutionality, the state will be required to demonstrate that its scheme is "substantially related" to the achievement of an "important" governmental objective. (In *Craig v. Boren, supra*, the Court concluded that a comparable statute failed this mid-level review.)

1. **Benign as well as invidious:** The same standard of review is used whether the sex-based classification is *"invidious"* (intended to harm women) or *"benign"* (intended to help women, or even intended to redress past discrimination against them).

2. **Male or female plaintiff:** This means that where government classifies based on sex, the scheme can be attacked either by a *male* or by a *female*, and either gender will get the benefit of mid-level review.

Example: In Example 2 above, a 20-year-old woman could attack the constitutionality of the near-beer statute — and get the benefit of mid-level review — even though the woman is theoretically advantaged by the statute's favoring young woman over young men.

3. **Purpose:** Sex-based classifications will only be subjected to middle-level review if the legislature has *intentionally* discriminated against one sex in favor of the other. (This is similar to the requirement for strict scrutiny in race-based cases.) If, as the result of some governmental act, one sex happens to suffer an *unintended burden* greater than the other sex suffers, that's not enough for mid-level review.

   Example: Massachusetts gives an absolute preference to veterans for civil service jobs. It happens that 98% of veterans are male. *Held*, this preference does not have to satisfy mid-level review because the unfavorable impact on women was not intended by the legislature. Therefore, the preference does not violate equal protection, since it satisfies the easier "mere rationality" standard. [*Personnel Admin. of Mass. v. Feeney*]

4. **Stereotypes:** Be on the lookout for *stereotypes*: if the legislature has made a sex-based classification that seems to reinforce stereotypes about the "proper place" of women, it probably cannot survive mid-level review.

   Example 1: Virginia maintains Virginia Military Institute as an all-male college, because of the state's view that only men can handle the school's harsh, militaristic method of producing "citizen soldiers." *Held*, this sex-based scheme does not satisfy mid-level review, because it stems from traditional ways of thinking about gender roles; there are clearly some women who are qualified for and would benefit from the VMI approach, and these women may not be deprived of the opportunity to attend VMI. [*U.S. v. Virginia*]

   Example 2: P, a woman, brings a civil suit against D, the city who employs her. The suit alleges that D permitted P's superior to sexually harass her. The attorney defending D uses all six of his peremptory jury challenges to eliminate all female jurors from the jury panel. The lawyer does so because he believes that female jurors will likely be biased in favor of another woman who is claiming sexual harassment. The resulting all-male jury finds for D, and P appeals.

   An appellate court would apply mid-level review to the lawyer's use of the peremptory challenges (and would likely reverse the verdict on constitutional grounds). D's lawyer's reasoning reinforced the stereotypical assumption about women's attitudes, and therefore constituted a gender-based classification that was not substantially related to any important governmental objective.

C. **Illegitimacy:** Classifications disadvantaging *illegitimate children* also get middle-level review.

1. **Claims can't be flatly barred:** Therefore, the state can't simply bar unacknowledged illegitimate children from bringing wrongful death actions, from having any chance to inherit, etc. Such children must be given at least *some reasonable opportunity* to obtain a *judicial declaration of paternity* (e.g., in a suit brought by their mother). Once they obtain such a declaration, they must be *treated equivalently to children born legitimate.*

   Example: Pennsylvania passes a statute of limitations saying that no action for child support may be brought on behalf of an out-of-wedlock child unless the action is brought before the child turns 6. *Held*, the statute violates the child's equal protection rights. Since the classification is based on out-of-wedlock status, it will be upheld only if it is substantially related to an important governmental objective. Concededly, Pennsylvania has an interest in avoiding the litigation of stale or fraudulent claims. But the 6-year statute of limitations is not "substantially related" to the achievement of that interest. [*Clark v. Jeter*]

D. Alienage: Alienage might be thought of as a "semi-suspect" category. In fact, however, alienage classifications, depending on the circumstances, will be subjected either to *strict scrutiny* or to *mere rationality* review (so there's only middle-level review as a kind of "average").

1. **Distinguished from national origin:** Be careful to distinguish "alienage" from "national origin": if a person is discriminated against because he is *not yet a United States citizen,* that's "alienage" discrimination. If, on the other hand, he's discriminated against because he is a naturalized citizen who originally came from Mexico (or whose ancestors came from Mexico), that's discrimination based on "national origin." Remember that national origin always triggers strict scrutiny, whereas alienage does not necessarily do so.

2. **General rule:** Subject to one large exception covered below, discrimination against aliens is subject to *strict scrutiny.*

   Example 1: A state cannot deny welfare benefits to aliens, because such a classification based on alienage cannot be shown to be necessary to the achievement of a compelling state interest. [*Graham v. Richardson*]

   Example 2: A state cannot prevent resident aliens from practicing law, because such a classification cannot survive strict scrutiny. [*In re Griffiths*]

3. **"Representative government" exception:** But the major exception is that strict scrutiny for alienage classifications does not apply where the discrimination against aliens relates to a *"functions that go to the heart of representative government."* Thus persons who "hold[] state *elective* or *important nonelective executive, legislative, and judicial positions,*" and those who are government "officers" who "participate directly in the *formulation, execution, or review of broad public policy*" may be required to be citizens. [*Cabell v. Chavez-Salido*; *Ambach v. Norwick*]

   a. **Illustrations:** Basically, this means that if the alien is applying for an important *government job or official position*, and the performance of this job is *closely tied in with politics, justice or public policy*, we use only *"mere rationality"* review. So government may discriminate against aliens with respect to posts like the following:

      ❑ *state trooper*;

      ❑ *public school teacher*;

      ❑ *juror*;

      ❑ *"deputy probation officer"* (though this represents probably the least-important post as to which the Supreme Court has found the "heart of representative government" exception applicable. See *Cabell, supra*).

   b. **Low-level government jobs:** But don't make the mistake of thinking that because what's involved is a government job, strict scrutiny automatically fails to apply. If the job is *not* closely tied in with politics, justice or public policy — something that is true of most *low-level rank-and-file jobs* — then *strict scrutiny applies.*

      Examples: Strict scrutiny would almost certainly be applied to a city ordinance that said that no resident alien may work for the city government as a *sanitation worker*, or as a *clerk* in the motor vehicle bureau having no policy-related authority.

4. **Education of illegal aliens:** A last special-case rule in the area of alienage is that if a state denies *free public education* to *illegal aliens*, this will be subjected to intermediate-level review, and probably struck down. [*Plyler v. Doe*] (But this comes from a combination of the fact that the plaintiffs were aliens and also that they were children. If a state discriminates against *adult* illegal aliens, we don't know whether something higher than middle-level review will be applied.)

VI. FUNDAMENTAL RIGHTS

A. Fundamental rights generally: Now, let's look at the second way strict scrutiny can be triggered in equal protection cases: there will be strict scrutiny not only when a "suspect classification" is used, but also when a *"fundamental right"* is burdened by the classification the government has selected. Whenever a classification burdens a "fundamental right" or "fundamental interest," the classification will be subjected to strict scrutiny *even though the people who are burdened are not members of a suspect class.*

1. **"Fundamental" defined:** "Fundamental" means something absolutely different in this equal protection context than it means in the substantive due process context. Remember that in due process, the fundamental rights are ones related to privacy. Here, the fundamental rights are related to a variety of other interests protected by the Constitution, but generally having nothing to do with privacy.

2. **List:** The *short list* of rights that are "fundamental" for equal protection strict scrutiny purposes is as follows:

   [1] the right to *vote*;

   [2] (possibly) the right to be a *political candidate*;

   [3] the right to have access to the *courts* for certain kinds of proceedings; and

   [4] the right to *migrate interstate.*

B. Voting rights: The right to *vote* in state and local elections is "fundamental," so any classification that burdens that right to vote will be strictly scrutinized.

> **Example 1:** A *poll tax* will be strictly scrutinized and almost certainly invalidated. [*Harper v. Virginia Bd. of Elect.*]

> **Example 2:** A requirement that the voter *own property* or otherwise have some "special interest" in order to vote will normally burden the fundamental right to vote and thus be struck down. [*Kramer v. Union Free School Dist.*]

> **Example 3:** The requirement that a voter have *resided* within the state for more than a certain time prior to election day burdens the right to vote and will be strictly scrutinized. [*Dunn v. Blumstein*].

1. **Exception for special-purpose districts:** The one exception to the rule that voting rights are fundamental and abridgements of them will be strictly scrutinized is *special-purpose districts* like water districts. These may restrict the vote to landowners. [*Ball v. James*]

   > **Example:** A special-purpose district is formed to furnish water to all farmers in a particular area. The enabling legislation for the district says that only landowners in the region being served can vote for the five-member governing board of the district. Although the right to vote in elections is generally fundamental, the landowner-only restriction here will not be strictly scrutinized, because of the special-purpose nature of the district.

   a. **MBE trap:** But the MBE examiners may try to trick you, by using a special-purpose district in a problem that *does not involve voting rights,* but some other kind of potential equal protection violation. Don't be misled — special-purpose districts have to *obey* the usual Fourteenth Amendment rules outside the voting context.

   > **Example:** A special agricultural district is set up solely to aid farmers in a particular geographic region. The elected governing board of the district gives a preference in obtaining district-funded chemical-supply contracts to minority-owned businesses.

This minority set-aside program will be strictly scrutinized and almost surely struck down. That's because, although the district is a special-purpose district, only the *right to vote for the governing body* of the district, not such non-voting aspects as government contracts, will be subjected to the easy mere-rationality review rather than to strict scrutiny.

2. **Limiting of voter's choices:** If the state regulation of voting merely has the effect of *"burdening"* the right to vote, instead of preventing the voter from voting at all, the Court does *not* strictly scrutinize the regulation. Instead, the Court balances the degree of the burden against the magnitude of the state's interest. This is true, for instance, of regulations that *limit the voter's choices.*

   Example: A state may completely ban all write-in votes, as long as it gives candidates reasonable access to the ballot. [*Burdick v. Takushi*]

3. **Fifteenth Amendment:** When you analyze a governmental action that arguably restricts of the right to vote, do not overlook the *Fifteenth Amendment,* which in Sec. 1 says that "The right of citizens of the United States to *vote* shall not be denied or abridged by the United States or by any State on account of *race, color, or previous condition of servitude."* As we have already seen, most restrictions on the right to vote are given Fourteenth Amendment due process/fundamental rights analysis. But occasionally, a direct limit on the right to vote on racial grounds will be found to violate the Fifteenth Amendment.

   Example: If a state required black voters to pass a literacy test but not white voters, this would be a Fifteenth Amendment violation.

   a. **Ballot access:** But the Fifteenth Amendment does not apply to *"ballot access"* problems — restrictions that make it hard for a candidate to get on the ballot, or for new political parties to succeed, even if imposed on racial grounds, are given Fourteenth, not Fifteenth, Amendment scrutiny.

C. **Ballot access:** The right to be a *political candidate*, and to have your name on the ballot, seems to be "quasi-fundamental."

1. **Two invalid restrictions:** There are two kinds of ballot restrictions to which the Supreme Court does seem to give strict or almost-strict scrutiny: (1) restrictions that substantially and unfairly limit the ballot access of minor parties or independent candidates; and (2) restrictions that are based on wealth. Let's consider each.

   a. **Unfair to new parties:** The Court strictly scrutinizes restrictions that are unfair to *new, not-yet-established political parties*, or to *independent candidates*. More particularly, ballot restrictions that are so severe that *minor-party* and independent candidates have *no realistic opportunity to get on the ballot* are given strict scrutiny, under *both* the *Equal Protection Clause* and the *First Amendment's freedom of association.* Where the new party consists mainly of *racial or ethnic minorities* that have traditionally not had much success locally getting their preferred candidates nominated by the two traditional parties, strict scrutiny is especially likely.

   Example: A state statute provides that a minor party can get its candidate on the ballot only if it presents signatures from 15% of the voters, holds a formal primary, and has an elaborate party structure. *Held*, the statute is such an interference with the right of minor parties to get their candidates on the ballot, and so favors the two major established parties, that it must be strictly scrutinized. The statute cannot survive this scrutiny, and violates both equal protection and the First Amendment's freedom of association. [*Williams v. Rhodes*]

   b. **Based on wealth:** The Court strictly scrutinizes ballot access limits that are based on *wealth,* and that represent a real impediment to candidacy.

   Example: California imposes a $700 candidate filing fee (in the early 1970s), which the state refuses to waive for an indigent candidate. *Held*, the unwaivable fee violates equal protection. [*Lubin v. Panish*]

2. **Candidate eligibility rules:** But reasonable rules concerning the eligibility of the individual candidate, that don't fall into either of these two categories — unfair to new parties / independent candidates, or based on wealth — are generally *upheld* by the Court. Thus a state may set a *minimum age*, or may require that the candidate have *resided for a certain period of time* in the state or district where he is seeking office.

D. **Court access:** Access to the *courts* is sometimes a "fundamental right," so that if the right is burdened by a state-imposed classification, that classification will sometimes be closely scrutinized. Basically, what it comes down to is that if the state imposes a *fee* that the rich can pay but the poor cannot, and the access relates to a *criminal* case, strict scrutiny will be used.

Examples: The state cannot charge an indigent for his trial transcript in a criminal case. [*Griffin v. Illinois*] Similarly, the state must provide an indigent with free counsel on appeal.

1. **Civil litigation:** When *civil* litigation is involved, access to the courts is usually *not* fundamental. Only for various family-law proceedings (e.g., *divorce, paternity suits, termination of parental rights*) is the state barred from charging fees. [*Boddie v. Connecticut*]

E. **Right to travel:** The so-called *"right to travel"* is generally a "fundamental" right. This term "right to travel" is misleading — it's really the right to *change one's state of residence or employment.* So any time the state imposes a classification that burdens one's right to change her state of residence or employment, that classification will be strictly scrutinized.

1. **Duration of residence:** This mainly means that if the state imposes a substantial *waiting period* on newly-arrived residents, before they can receive some *vital governmental benefit*, this will be strictly scrutinized.

Example: Pennsylvania denies welfare benefits to any resident who has not resided in the state for at least a year. *Held*, this one-year waiting period impairs the "fundamental right of interstate movement" so it must be strictly scrutinized, and in fact invalidated. [*Shapiro v. Thompson*]

2. **Vital government benefit:** But the key phrase here is *"vital government benefit"* — if the benefit is *not* vital, then the state may impose a substantial waiting period.

Example: A one-year waiting period before a student can qualify for low in-state tuition at the public university probably does not burden a fundamental right, and thus does not need to be strictly scrutinized.

F. **Necessities:** The right to *"necessities"* is *not* fundamental. So if the state distributes necessities in a way that treats different people differently (or if it distributes the money to be used to buy these things differentially), there will be no strict scrutiny because there is no fundamental right.

1. **Education:** For instance, one does not have a fundamental right to a *public school education*. Therefore, the state may allow or even foster inequalities in the distribution of that public school education, without violating any fundamental right, and thus without having to pass strict scrutiny. [*San Antonio School Dist. v. Rodriguez*]

Example: The Ps claim that Texas' system of financing public education violates equal protection, because districts with a high property tax base per pupil consistently spend more on education than those with a low base are able to do.

Held, education is not a fundamental right. Therefore, Texas' scheme merely has to undergo "rational relation" review. Because the use of property taxes to finance education is a rational way of achieving the legitimate state goal of giving each local school district a large measure of control over the education its residents get, this "mere rationality" standard is satisfied. [*San Antonio School Dist. v. Rodriguez*, *supra*, p. 61.]

a. **Complete deprivation:** Actually, it's still possible that a *complete deprivation* of public education might be held to be a violation of a "fundamental" right. If a state simply refused to give any public education *at all* to some groups of residents, this might be such a large deprivation that it would amount to a violation of a fundamental right, and thus be subject to strict scrutiny.

2. **Food, shelter:** There is no fundamental right to the material *"necessities of life."* Thus *food*, *shelter*, and *medical care* are not "fundamental" for equal protection purposes. Therefore, the state may distribute these things unevenly. Similarly, the state may give some people but not others money for these things without having to survive strict scrutiny.

Example: The state can give a smaller per capita welfare payment to big families than small families, without having the scheme subjected to strict scrutiny. This is because the food and shelter for which the payments are used are not "fundamental rights." [*Dandridge v. Williams*]

CHAPTER 8

MISCELLANEOUS CLAUSES

I. FOURTEENTH AMENDMENT PRIVILEGES AND IMMUNITIES

A. **Privileges and Immunities Clause (P&I) Generally:** The Fourteenth Amendment has its own "Privileges and Immunities" Clause: "No state shall make or enforce any law which shall abridge the privileges or immunities of citizens of the United States."

1. **National rights only:** But this clause is very narrowly interpreted: it only protects the individual from state interference with his rights of *"national"* citizenship. The most important of these rights of "national" citizenship are: (1) the right to *travel from state to state* (which as we saw is also protected by the Equal Protection Clause); and (2) the right to *vote in national elections*.

2. **Right to change state of residence:** The clause is most relevant where a state treats *newly-arrived residents less favorably* than those who have resided in-state for a longer time: this violates the "right to travel," protected by the clause.

Example: If a state gives newly-arrived residents lower welfare payments than ones who have been residents longer, this is a violation of the "right to travel" protected by the Fourteenth Amendment P&I clause. [*Saenz v. Roe*]

3. **Strict scrutiny:** The Court gives *strict scrutiny* to state laws that interfere with the rights of national citizenship. [*Saenz v. Roe*]

II. THE "TAKING" CLAUSE

A. **The "Taking" Clause Generally:** The Fifth Amendment contains the "Taking" Clause: "*[N]or shall private property be taken for public use, without just compensation.*"

1. **General meaning:** The gist of the Taking Clause is that the government may take private property under its "power of eminent domain," but if it does take private property, it must *pay a fair price*. This is true even if the property is taken to serve a compelling governmental interest.

2. **Taking vs. regulation:** The government (whether it's federal or state) must pay for any property that it "takes." On the other hand, if it merely *"regulates"* property under its police power, then it

does not need to pay (even if the owner's use of his property, or its value, is substantially diminished).

a. **Land use regulations:** Usually the problem of distinguishing between a compensable "taking" and a non-compensable "regulation" occurs in the context of *land-use regulation.*

b. **Guidelines:** Here are some guidelines about when a land-use regulation will avoid being a taking:

   i. **No denial of economically viable use:** A land-use regulation must not "deny an owner *all economically viable use* of his land," or it will be considered a taking. However, few land use regulations are likely to be found to deny the owner all economically viable use of his land. For instance, if a particular 3-story building is made a landmark, the fact that the owner can't tear down the building to build a skyscraper doesn't deprive him of "all economically viable use." But if the state were to *permanently* deny the owner the right to *build any dwelling* on the land, this *would* probably constitute a denial of all economically viable use.

   Example: The state of South Carolina, in order to protect against coastal erosion, prohibits landowners from building any permanent habitable structure at all on certain parcels. P owns 2 vacant parcels (for which he paid $1 million), on which the building ban applies. *Held*, by the Supreme Court, if this regulation indeed prevents P from making any "economically viable use" of the parcels (something for the state court to decide on remand), there has been a "taking" for which the state must pay compensation, even if the state was just trying to protect the health and safety of its citizens. [*Lucas v. South Carolina Coastal Council*]

   Note: Most zoning, environmental laws and landmark-preservation laws will satisfy this don't-deny-all-economically-viable-uses rule, and will thus *not* be takings, but merely non-compensable regulations.

   [1] **Temporary but near-total land-use restrictions:** If a land-use law merely *temporarily* prevents all economically viable use of a parcel, this will *not necessarily* constitute a taking — *all surrounding circumstances* must be considered to determine whether the interference with use is significant enough to constitute a taking. For instance, a 2- or 3-year *moratorium on development* of a particular parcel, until a permanent land-use scheme can be enacted by government, might well *not* constitute a taking even though for that period an affected owner can't make any economically viable use of her parcel. [*Tahoe-Sierra Preservation Council v. Tahoe Regional Planning Agency*]

   Example: The City of Purple is alarmed by soil erosion from parcels surrounding Lake Purple, erosion that is filling the lake with sediment and damaging wildlife. Therefore, the City institutes a two-year moratorium on the issuance of any building permit for construction of any dwelling or structure on any parcel within 200 feet of the lake's shoreline. The city regulation announcing the moratorium says that during the moratorium period, the city will study the problem further and, it hopes, adopt permanent regulations to deal with it. During the moratorium period, existing uses of any parcel along the lake, including recreational, hunting and agricultural, may be continued. A lakeside landowner who wishes to build a house on his vacant parcel (which he brought pre-moratorium solely to build a house on it) sues the city, arguing that the moratorium requires that he be compensated for the fact that his property has lost all economically-viable use during the two-year period.

The landowner will likely lose. Under *Tahoe-Sierra*, *supra*, a regulation that temporarily, though completely, restricts all development will not constitute a *per-se* taking, and instead must be evaluated by considering all surrounding circumstances. Here, the limited geographical coverage, the seriousness of the sediment/erosion problem, the relatively short-term duration of the moratorium, and the need for time to study the problem before formulating a permanent regulatory solution, all suggest that the interference with the owner's use is not so major as to constitute a taking.

ii. **Permanent physical occupation:** If the government makes or authorizes a *permanent physical occupation* of the property, this will *automatically* be found to constitute a taking, no matter how minor the interference with the owner's use and no matter how important the countervailing governmental interests.

Example: The state requires landlords to permit cable TV companies to install their cable facilities in the landlord's buildings. *Held*, this compulsory cabling was a taking because it was a permanent physical occupation, even though it didn't really restrict the owner's use of his property or reduce its value. [*Loretto v. Teleprompter*]

iii. **Diminution in value:** The more drastic the *reduction in value* of the owner's property, the more likely a taking is to be found. But a very drastic diminution in value (almost certainly much more than 50%) is required.

iv. **Landmark:** *Landmark preservation schemes*, just like zoning and environmental regulations, will *rarely* be found to constitute a taking. This is especially true where the designation of a particular building to landmark status occurs as part of a *comprehensive* city-wide preservation scheme.

Example: New York City didn't carry out a taking when it designated Grand Central Station as a landmark; this was true even though this designation prevented the owner from constructing a 55-story office building above the Terminal. [*Penn Central v. New York City*]

v. **"Give-backs":** When a government conditions a building permit on some *"give-back"* by the owner, two major requirements must be met, or else the give-back will be held to be a taking:

- ❑ the means chosen by the government (the give-back) must *"substantially advance"* the governmental objective being pursued [*Nollan v. Cal. Coastal Comm.*]; and
- ❑ there must be a *"rough proportionality"* between the burdens on the public that the building permit would bring about, and the benefit to the public from the give back. [*Dolan v. City of Tigard*]

Example: P is a property owner who wants to enlarge the plumbing and electric supply store she runs on the property. D, a city, issues her a permit to do this, but conditions the permit on P's willingness to convey a 15-foot strip of land on her property (about 10% of the total property) to the city, to be used as a bicycle pathway. P claims that this exaction is a taking.

Held, for P. There must be a "rough proportionality" between the trade-off demanded by D and the burden to the public from P's proposed development. Here, D did not satisfy this requirement. For example, although D calculated the number of additional car trips per day that would be caused by P's expansion, it did not show that the reduction in traffic from the bike path would be roughly proportional to the increase in traffic from the store expansion. [*Dolan v. City of Tigard, supra*, p. 64.]

3. **Requirement of "public" use:** The Taking Clause says that private property shall not be taken *"for public use"* unless just compensation is paid. This language has been interpreted by the Supreme Court as prohibiting the taking of private property for *private use, even if just compensation is made*. Thus the government cannot simply take private property from one person, and give it to another, without any public purpose.

   a. **"Public use" construed broadly:** However, the Supreme Court has construed the requirement of a "public use" quite *broadly*. Here are two principles illustrating just how broadly the Court stretches the phrase:

   ❑ So long as the state's use of its eminent domain power is "*rationally related* to a *conceivable public purpose*," the public use requirement is satisfied. [*Hawaii Housing Authority v. Midkiff*]

   ❑ The property *need not be open to the general public after the taking*. Therefore, the fact that the property is *turned over to some private user* does not prevent the use from being a public one as long as the public can be expected to derive some benefit (e.g., economic development) from the use.

   Example: The City of New London, as part of an economic-development plan for the City's waterfront area, condemns 15 houses owned by the Ps. The properties are not blighted. The plan contemplates turning the properties over to private developers. The Ps claim that this is not a "public use," and thus violates their rights under the Fifth Amendment even if "just compensation" is paid.

   Held, for the City. Even though the properties are being turned over to private developers (not made available to the public), and even though the properties were not blighted, this is still a "public use" as the term is used in the Fifth Amendment. [*Kelo v. New London*]

III. THE "CONTRACT" CLAUSE

A. **The "Contract" Clause:** The so-called "Contract" Clause (Article I, Sec. 10) provides that "no state shall ... pass any ... law *impairing the obligation of contracts.*" The Clause effectively applies to *both federal and state governments*. The Clause has a different meaning depending on whether the government is impairing its own contracts or contracts between private parties.

1. **Public contracts:** If the state is trying to escape from its *own financial obligations*, then the Court will *closely scrutinize* this attempt. Here, the state attempt to "weasel" will be struck down unless the modification is "*reasonable* and *necessary* to support an *important* public purpose" (basically *middle-level review*).

2. **Private contracts:** But when the state is re-writing contracts made by *private parties*, the judicial review is not so stringent. Here, even a *substantial* modification to contracts between private parties will be allowed so long as the state is acting "*reasonably*" in pursuit of a "legitimate public purpose." So we apply what is basically "mere rationality" review in this situation.

   Example: If a state's economy is in shambles with widespread home mortgage foreclosures, the state probably may temporarily order a lower interest rate on home mortgages, or impose a moratorium on mortgage repayments, without violating the Contract Clause.

i. **Identify Clause on the MBE:** On the MBE, you will sometimes see a scenario in which government interferes with an existing private-sector contract, and you are asked not to say how the Contracts Clause challenge would be decided, but merely to identify what constitutional provision represents the plaintiff's best chance of attacking the government action. The Contracts Clause will typically be the answer (as opposed to, say, the Ex Post Facto Clauses or the Bill of Attainder Clause).

Example: In early 2007, a farmer contracts to sell his entire output of wheat for the next two years to a grain elevator. In late 2007, the legislature of the state where the elevator is located passes a statute abrogating all wheat-supply agreements between farmers and grain elevators that last more than two years. If the grain elevator wants to attack the constitutionality of the statute, the provision offering it the greatest chance of success will be the Contracts clause.

IV. *EX POST FACTO* LAWS

A. Constitutional prohibition: Article I, in §§ 9 and 10, prohibits both state and federal governments from passing any *"ex post facto"* law. (These are together the "Ex Post Facto" Clauses.) An *ex post facto* law is a law which has a *retroactive punitive effect.* So government may not *impose a punishment* for conduct which, at the time it occurred, was *not punishable.* Also, government may not *increase* the punishment for an offense over what was on the books at the time of the act.

Example: On June 1, Joe smokes a cigarette in a public building. On June 10, the state legislature makes it a crime, for the first time, to smoke in a public building. Because of the ban on *ex post facto* laws, Joe cannot be convicted of the June 1 smoking, since it was not a crime at the time he did it. The same would be true if the legislature on June 15 increased the penalty for such smoking over what it was on June 1.

1. Criminal only: The ban on *ex post facto* laws applies only to measures that are *"criminal"* or *"penal,"* not to those that are civil. Basically, this means that only measures calling for *imprisonment* will come within the *ex post facto* ban (so a measure that imposes, say, *disbarment*, or one that imposes *deportation*, can be made retroactive, since these sanctions are civil). (See, e.g., *Galvan v. Press.*)

a. Significance: The fact that *ex post facto* laws must be criminal or penal means that where government merely *takes away some right* that a person has had for years — but doesn't do so for the purpose of punishing that person — this won't be an *ex post facto* violation. The MBE examiners will often try to trick you by having the legislature *take some professional or economic right away* from a person that she's had for a long time — this won't be an *ex post facto* violation if there's no punitive intent.

V. BILLS OF ATTAINDER

A. Generally: Article I prohibits both the federal government and the states from passing any *"bill of attainder."* A bill of attainder is a legislative act which "applies either to named individuals or to easily ascertainable members of a group in such a way as to *punish* them without a *judicial trial.*"

Example: Congress prohibits the payment of salaries to three named federal agency employees, on the grounds that they are engaged in subversive activities. This is an invalid bill of attainder, since it applies to named or easily-identified individuals, and punishes them without a judicial trial. [*U.S. v. Lovett*]

B. Definition of "punishment": The Bill of Attainder Clause applies only to legislative *"punishment"* of specific individuals or narrowly-defined groups. But cases have defined "punishment" somewhat broadly, to include measures having not only a "retributive" function, but also measures whose purpose is "rehabilitative," "deterrent" or "preventative." Thus a ban on union participation by Communist Party members was deemed "punishment" (and was thus a bill of attainder) even though the ban's purpose was to prevent strikes. [*U.S. v. Brown* (1965)]

1. **Pure regulation not covered:** However, measures that are taken solely for the purpose of *regulation*, and which have *no substantial stigmatizing element*, are *not* prohibited by the Bill of Attainder Clause, even though they may contain aspects that are unfavorable to certain individuals.

   a. **Significance:** So, as in the case of *ex post facto* laws, don't be fooled into thinking that an essentially regulatory action by government is a bill of attainder, even if it singles out named persons or a group whose members can be easily-ascertained.

   Example: A state hospital changes its policy, and requires any physician who wishes to have the right to admit patients to the hospital to be a resident of the state. P, who lives just over the border in the next state, and who has had admitting rights for years, attacks the change on constitutional grounds. Assume that the hospital has acted out of the belief that state funds are being expended to run the hospital, and that those physicians who derive economic benefit from the change should therefore be required to be state residents.

   This new policy is not a bill of attainder. Because the hospital has merely changed the residency requirement for practicing medicine at the hospital, and wasn't trying to punish or stigmatize anyone, the regulation was not a bill of attainder even though the affected doctors were members of a small and easily-ascertained class. (Instead, the policy can be successfully attacked on the grounds that it violates the Article IV Privileges and Immunities Clause.)

CHAPTER 9

THE "STATE ACTION" REQUIREMENT; CONGRESS'S ENFORCEMENT OF THE CIVIL WAR AMENDMENTS

I. STATE ACTION

A. State action generally: Virtually all of the rights and liberties guaranteed by the Constitution to individuals are protected only against interference by the government. We summarize this rule by referring to the requirement of *"state action."*

1. **Key principle:** This general principle is key for the MBE: *Unless government is somehow involved with the challenged action, and that government involvement is sufficient to constitute "state action," the action cannot violate constitutional rights and liberties* (due process, equal protection and free speech and association, to mention the most commonly-invoked rights).

   Example: City owns an auditorium that it will rent to any person or group who pays a uniformly-applied hourly fee and also posts a security deposit. City rents the auditorium on these terms to Org, a local civic organization that restricts its membership to persons descended from white protestants who came to this country from England. P, who unsuccessfully sought to join Org but was rejected because he is of Latin American ancestry, sues City on the grounds that it has violated the Fourteenth Amendment Equal Protection Clause by renting to an organization that discriminates on the basis of national origin.

P will lose because of the state-action requirement: City's involvement with Org's private conduct here is so limited, and so independent of the discrimination, that no state action will be found. City will rent to anyone, and charges the same hourly rate to everyone. So the fact that the government is renting to an organization practicing national-origin-based discrimination does not constitute any kind of endorsement or encouragement by the government of (or unusual benefit to the government from) the discrimination.

2. **Two doctrines:** But sometimes, even a *private individual's act* will be found to be "state action" that must comply with the Constitution. There are two main doctrines that may lead a private act to be classified as state action; if *either* of these doctrines applies, then the private action is "state action" even if the other doctrine would not apply. The two doctrines are the *"public function"* doctrine and the *"state involvement"* doctrine. The rest of our discussion concerns these two doctrines.

B. "Public function" doctrine: Under the *"public function"* approach to state action, if a private individual (or group) is entrusted by the state to perform functions that are *governmental in nature*, the private individual becomes an *agent of the state*, and his acts constitute state action.

1. **Political system:** The *electoral process* is a "public function," and is thus state action. Therefore, the carrying out of *primary elections* is state action, even if the acts are directly carried out by "private" political parties.

Example: A state convention of Democrats (in essence, a "private" political party) rules that only whites may vote in the Texas Democratic Primary. *Held*, this racial restriction is "state action," and therefore violates the Fifteenth Amendment. The primary is an integral part of the election scheme, and the running of elections is traditionally a "public function," so the running of the primary is state action even though it is directly carried out by private groups. [*Smith v. Allwright*]

a. **Company town:** Similarly, operation of a *"company town"* is a "public function," and thus is state action, because towns are usually operated by the government.

i. **Shopping centers not a public function:** But operation of a *shopping center* is *not* the equivalent of operating a company town, so a person does not have any First Amendment rights in the shopping center. [*Hudgens v. NLRB*]

b. **Parks:** Operation of a *park* is usually deemed a governmental function, so generally the operation of a park will constitute "state action" under the "public function" doctrine. Therefore, even if the park is being operated by private persons, it must still obey constitutional constraints (e.g., it can't be operated for whites only). [*Evans v. Newton*]

c. **Prisons:** Operation of a *prison* is almost certainly a public function, so if government delegates to a private corporation the job of running a prison, the corporation must furnish due process.

Example: PrisonCorp. gets a contract to operate the prisons for the state of Green. The warden of a prison operated by the company requires P, a prisoner, to spend one week in solitary confinement based solely upon a written report by Guard, an employee of the company, that Guard saw P hit another prisoner. P sues PrisonCorp, asserting that he is entitled to a hearing before this punishment is imposed. The company defends on the grounds that it is not a governmental actor and therefore need not furnish due process before imposing this punishment.

PrisonCorp would almost certainly lose with this "no due process required" argument — operating a prison is a public function, so an otherwise-private actor that operates in prison must furnish the same due process as a government would have to furnish.

d. **Municipal corporation:** If the entity is a *"municipal district"* or *"municipal corporation,"* its actions will *automatically* be deemed state action.

C. **"State involvement" doctrine:** Even if the private individual is not doing something that's traditionally a "public function," his conduct may constitute state action if the state is *heavily involved* in his activities. This is the *"state involvement"* branch of state-action doctrine. Here are some of the ways in which the state and private actor can be so closely involved that the private person's acts become state action:

1. **Commandment:** The state may become responsible for the private party's actions because it *commanded*, i.e., required, the private party to act in that way.

Example: The state enforces a private agreement among neighbors that none will sell his house to a black. Because the state has lent its state judicial enforcement mechanism to this otherwise private contract, the combination of enforcement and private discrimination violates equal protection. [*Shelley v. Kraemer*]

2. **Encouragement:** If the state *"encourages"* the private party's actions, then the private action may be converted into state action.

3. **Symbiosis:** There is state action if there exists between the state and private actor a *"symbiotic"* relationship, i.e., a relation between the two that is *mutually beneficial.*

Example: A Wilmington, Delaware, city agency owns and runs a parking garage complex. The agency gives a 20 year lease to a privately-operated restaurant located in the complex. The restaurant refuses to serve African Americans. *Held*, African Americans who are refused service have had their equal protection rights violated. The relation between the restaurant and the publicly-run garage was so close and symbiotic — the garage wouldn't have been able to operate viably without rents from the restaurant — that the restaurant's actions must be imputed to the state, and therefore constitute state action. [*Burton v. Wilmington Parking Authority*]

a. **Contrast:** But contrast the symbiotic relationship in *Burton* with the situation in the Example on p. 67 involving the auditorium. There, the state was willing to rent to anyone, and charged the same hourly rate to everyone. So the fact that the state was renting to the ethnically-discriminatory organization here did not constitute any kind of endorsement or encouragement by the state of (or unusual benefit to the state from) the discrimination. Consequently, there was no state action, and the organization's conduct wasn't subject to the Fourteenth Amendment.

4. **Entanglement or entwinement:** State action may arise from the fact that the state is so *"entangled"* or *"entwined"* with a private actor that even though the state might not directly benefit from the private actor's conduct, the conduct will still be treated as state action. This is true where the state and the private party *act together* to carry out the action being challenged.

Example 1: A state allows a private litigant — either a civil litigant or a defendant in a criminal case — to use peremptory challenges to exclude jurors on racial grounds. This conduct constitutes state action, and therefore violates the Equal Protection Clause. [*Edmondson v. Leesville Concrete Co.*; *Georgia v. McCollum*]

Example 2: A state recognizes a private association of high schools as being the regulator of high school interscholastic sports. Most members of the association are public high schools within the state, and these schools are active in the association affairs as part of the schools' official business of running athletic programs. Because the association's activities are deeply entwined with state affairs, the association's conduct is state action. [*Brentwood Academy v. Tenn. Secondary School Athl. Assoc.*]

a. **Mere acquiescence not enough:** But if the state merely *acquiesces* in the private party's discrimination, this won't be enough of a state involvement to convert the private actor's conduct into state action.

Example: The state regulates all utilities. A private utility cuts off plaintiff's service without notice or a hearing, and this fact is known to the state, which does not object. *Held*, the utility's conduct was not state action, because the state merely acquiesced in that conduct, rather than actively participating in it. [*Jackson v. Metropolitan Edison Co.*]

b. **Licensing:** Similarly, the fact that the state has *licensed* a private person, or somehow *regulates* the person's activities, is generally *not* enough to convert the private person's conduct into state action.

Example: A private club refuses to serve African Americans. Even though the state has given the club one of a limited number of liquor licenses, this act of licensing is not enough to turn the club's action into state action. [*Moose Lodge v. Irvis*]

c. **Supplying of money:** Again similarly, the mere fact that the state *spends public funds* to help the private person carry out activities usually *won't* be enough to make those activities state action, if the state does not get involved in the details of how those activities are conducted (e.g., by encouraging the private person to discriminate).

II. CONGRESSIONAL ENFORCEMENT OF CIVIL RIGHTS

A. **Post-Civil War Amendments generally:** Congress has special powers to enforce the post-Civil War amendments, i.e., the Thirteenth, Fourteenth, and Fifteenth Amendments. First, let's quickly review what each of these amendments does:

1. **Thirteenth Amendment:** The Thirteenth Amendment *abolishes "slavery"* and *"involuntary servitude."*

2. **Fourteenth Amendment:** The Fourteenth Amendment requires the states to give *"due process," "equal protection,"* and *"privileges and immunities."*

3. **Fifteenth Amendment:** The Fifteenth Amendment bars the states from denying *voting rights* on the basis of race, color or previous condition of servitude.

B. **Congress's power to enforce:** Each of these three amendments contains a *special provision entitling Congress to enforce it.* Thus Section 2 of both the Thirteenth and Fifteenth Amendments, and Section 5 of the Fourteenth, all say that Congress *"shall have the power to enforce,"* by "*appropriate legislation,"* the provisions of the Amendment.

1. **Independent source:** This is an *independent source* of congressional power, and will sometimes let Congress forbid conduct (especially state governmental conduct) that Congress would not otherwise be able to forbid, such as conduct not reachable by the Commerce power.

a. **Voting:** On the MBE, be on the lookout especially for a congressional statute that prohibits states or cities from doing something that may impair the *voting rights* of citizens — Congress's enforcement powers under both the Fourteenth and Fifteenth Amendment may well allow Congress to make such a prohibition, even if it couldn't reach that conduct under any other power such as the Commerce power.

Example: Congress concludes that states have sometimes used literacy tests and poll taxes to restrict the rights of blacks to vote in state elections. It therefore forbids any state or subdivision thereof from using any literacy test or poll tax, regardless of the race of the voter in question, and regardless of whether the governmental unit has ever previously used such a device to abridge voting rights.

So long as Congress has a reasonable belief (not necessarily even a belief that the Supreme Court agrees with) that such devices may impair the voting rights guaranteed by the Fourteenth Amendment due process clause and/or the Fifteenth Amendment, the congressional statute will be within Congress's powers. And that fact may be important, because quite possibly no other source of congressional power — including the Commerce power — may authorize the statute. [Cf. *Katzenbach v. Morgan* (1966)]

C. **Congress's power to reach private conduct:** These special post-Civil-War-Amendment enforcement powers let Congress reach a lot of *private conduct* that it could not reach by means of any other congressional power.

1. **Fourteenth and Fifteenth Amendments:** When Congress enforces the Fourteenth and Fifteenth Amendments, it has some, but not unlimited, power to reach private conduct. So Congress could, for instance, make it a crime for a private citizen to *interfere with a state official* who is trying to guarantee another person's equal protection rights or voting rights.

   Example: Congress can make it a crime for D, a private citizen, to prevent a school principal from allowing African Americans to enroll in an all white school.

   a. **Can't reach purely private discrimination:** But Congress under the Fourteenth Amendment *cannot* simply make it a crime for *one private person to practice ordinary racial discrimination against another.* (Congress would instead have to use its power to regulate interstate commerce; this is the basis on which the 1964 Civil Rights Act, forbidding racial discrimination in places of public accommodation, was upheld. [*Katzenbach v. McClung*])

2. **Thirteenth Amendment:** But the *Thirteenth* Amendment is *different.* Section 1 of the Thirteenth Amendment provides that "neither slavery nor involuntary servitude, except as a punishment for crime ... shall exist within the United States." Section 2 gives Congress the power to "enforce this [amendment] by appropriate legislation." The Thirteenth Amendment, unlike the Fourteenth and Fifteenth, is *not explicitly limited to governmental action.* Indeed, that's the most important thing to remember about the Thirteenth Amendment, and its principal use today — it's practically the only clause in the entire Constitution that prevents one private citizen from doing something to another. So the Thirteenth Amendment gives Congress important authority to reach certain private conduct that it couldn't reach through the Fourteenth and Fifteenth Amendments.

   a. **"Badges of slavery":** If the Thirteenth Amendment only meant that Congress could take special action to ensure that slavery itself, in its most literal sense, shall be wiped out, the Amendment wouldn't be of much practical use today. But instead, the Supreme Court has held that the Amendment allows Congress also to stamp out the *"badges and incidents"* of slavery. In fact, Congress has the power to determine what the "badges and incidents of slavery" are, so long as it acts rationally — once Congress defines these "badges and incidents," it can then forbid them.

   Example: Congress can prohibit private citizens from racially discriminating when they sell their own houses. That's because Congress could have rationally concluded that barriers to enjoyment of real estate, and discrimination in housing, are relics of slavery. [*Jones v. Alfred H. Mayer Co.*]

b. **Ancestry, ethnic discrimination:** As we've just seen, the Thirteenth Amendment clearly lets Congress prevent private discrimination against African Americans, on the grounds that it's a "badge or incident" of slavery. *All other racial minorities are also protected* — Congress could probably even bar private racial discrimination against *whites* based on the Thirteenth Amendment (although the Court has never explicitly decided this).

c. **Non-racial grounds:** But it's doubtful whether private discrimination based on *non-racial grounds* (e.g., *ancestry, ethnic background,* religion, sex, etc.) can be barred by Congress acting pursuant to the Thirteenth Amendment — the Court has certainly never held that non-racial discrimination can be covered.

d. **Statute must exist:** The application of the Thirteenth Amendment to a broad range of "badges and incidents of slavery" applies only where Congress has used its *enforcement* powers by passing a *statute* that relies on the Amendment. If private citizen *A* discriminates against *B* on the basis of race, but the type of discrimination is not one that Congress has outlawed, then the Thirteenth Amendment's "naked" or "self-executing" scope *won't* be enough to reach that discrimination. Probably actual *peonage* — the keeping of a person as a slave — is the only type of private racial discrimination that is directly barred by the Thirteenth Amendment in the absence of a congressional statute.

CHAPTER 10

FREEDOM OF EXPRESSION

I. GENERAL THEMES

A. **Text of First Amendment:** The First Amendment provides, in part, that "Congress shall make no law ... abridging the *freedom of speech,* or of the press; or the right of the people peaceably to assemble, and to petition the Government for a redress of grievances."

1. **Related rights:** There are thus several distinct rights which may be grouped under the category "freedom of expression": freedom of *speech,* of the *press,* of *assembly,* and of *petition.* Additionally, there is a well-recognized "freedom of *association*" which, although it is not specifically mentioned in the First Amendment, is derived from individuals' rights of speech and assembly.

B. **Two broad classes:** Whenever you consider governmental action that seems to infringe upon the freedom of expression, there's one key question that you must always ask before you ask anything else. That question is, "Is this governmental action '*content-based*' or '*content-neutral*'?" If the action is "content-based," the government's action will generally be subjected to strict scrutiny, and the action will rarely be sustained. On the other hand, if the action is "content-neutral", the government's action is subjected to a much less demanding standard, and is thus much more likely to be upheld.

1. **Classifying:** A governmental action that burdens a person's expression is "content-based" if the government is aiming at the *"communicative impact"* of the expression. By contrast, if the government is aiming at something other than the communicative impact of the expression, the government action is "content-neutral," even though it may have the *effect* of burdening the expression.

Example 1 (content-based): Virginia forbids pharmacists to advertise the prices of prescription drugs, because it's afraid that the public will buy drugs at the lowest available price and will therefore receive low-quality goods and services. This government ban is "content-based," since the speech is being regulated because of the government's fears about how consumers will respond to its *communicative impact.* Therefore, the government's ban will be strictly scrutinized, and is in fact violative of the First Amendment. [*Virginia Pharmacy Bd. v. Virginia Consumer Council*]

Example 2 (content-neutral): A city forbids the distribution of all leaflets, because it wishes to prevent littering. This ban is "content neutral" — the government is banning all leaflets, regardless of their content, and the harm sought to be avoided (littering) would exist to the same extent regardless of the message in the leaflets. Therefore, the government action is subject to less rigid review — more or less "intermediate level review" (although it was still struck down on these facts). [*Schneider v. State*]

a. **Tip:** Here's a tip to help you decide whether a given governmental action is content-based or not: Would the harm the government is trying to prevent exist to the same degree if the listeners/readers *didn't understand English*? If the answer is "no," the action is probably content-based.

Example: Suppose a consumer in the prescription-drug case above didn't speak English. He wouldn't suffer the harm the state was trying to prevent — being induced to buy bad drugs or bad service for a cheap price — even if he saw or read the advertising, so it's clearly the content of the communication that the state is objecting to. But in the case of the ban on littering, even a whole city of non-English-speakers would suffer the same harm — littered streets — so the ban is content-neutral.

b. **Motive counts:** When a court decides whether a regulation is content-based or content-neutral, *motives* count for everything — the question is what the state really *intends* to do. If the court believes that the state intends to inhibit certain speech because of its message, the court will treat the statute as content-based (and strictly scrutinize it) even though it is neutral on its face.

C. **Analysis of content-based government action:** Once we've determined that a particular government action impairing expression is "content-based," we then have to determine whether the expression falls within a category that is *protected* by the First Amendment.

1. **Unprotected category:** If the speech falls into certain pre-defined *unprotected* categories, then the government can basically ban that expression completely based on its content, without any interference at all from the First Amendment.

a. **Listing:** The main "unprotected" categories are: (1) *obscenity*; (2) *fraudulent misrepresentation*; (3) *defamation*; (4) *advocacy of imminent lawless behavior*; and (5) *"fighting words."*

b. **Not totally unprotected:** But even speech falling within an "unprotected category" receives one small First Amendment protection: government must regulate in a basically *content-neutral* way.

Example: The state may ban all "fighting words." But it may not choose to ban just those fighting words directed at the listener's race, religion, or other enumerated traits. [*R.A.V. v. City of St. Paul*]

2. **Protected category:** All expression not falling into one of these five pre-defined categories is "protected." If expression is protected, then any government ban or restriction on it based on its content will be *presumed to be unconstitutional.* The Court will subject any content-based regulation of protected speech to *strict scrutiny* — the regulation will be sustained only if it (1) serves a *compelling governmental objective*; and (2) is *"necessary,"* i.e., drawn as *narrowly as possible* to achieve that objective (since a broader-than-needed restriction wouldn't be a "necessary" means).

Example: A District of Columbia statute bans the display of any sign within 500 feet of a foreign embassy, if the sign would bring the foreign government into "public disrepute." *Held*, this regulation is content-based, since a sign is prohibited or not prohibited based on what the sign says. Therefore, the regulation must be strictly scrutinized, and cannot be upheld. Even if the government's interest in protecting the dignity of foreign diplomats is compelling — which it may or may not be — the statute is not "necessary" to achieve that interest, since a narrower statute that only banned the intimidation, coercion or threatening of diplomats would do the trick. [*Boos v. Barry*].

a. **"Viewpoint neutrality" not enough:** A regulation will be deemed to be "content-based," and thus subject to strict scrutiny, even if it merely puts *an entire subject off limits.* In other words, the fact that government is prohibiting or restricting debate on a particular topic — regardless of which side of the debate the speaker takes — in a particular forum will generally be enough to trigger strict scrutiny of the restriction. That's especially true of speech in traditional public forums like streets, sidewalks and parks (see *infra*, p. 81).

Example: The City of Redville, after dealing with physical altercations growing out of the protesting of abortion clinics in the city, passes an ordinance stating that "No person shall be permitted to picket or demonstrate within 500 feet of any abortion clinic located in the city." The ordinance applies both to pro-choice and pro-life demonstrators, and applies even when the demonstration is on city-owned streets, parks, or other traditional "public forums" (see *infra*, p. 81). This ordinance will be deemed to be content-based rather than content-neutral, because it puts an entire subject-matter category (but only that category) off-limits. So it's content-based even though it applies equally regardless of which side of the abortion debate the demonstrator is taking.

b. **Religious speech gets equal protection:** The requirement of content-neutrality is now so strong that it seems to take precedence over the *Establishment Clause* (which protects separation of church and state). Thus if the government allows private speech in a particular forum, it may not treat *religiously-oriented* speech *less favorably* than non-religiously-oriented speech.

Example: If a public university gives funding for student publications on various topics, the requirement of content-neutrality means that the university must give the same funding to a student publication whose mission is to proselytize for Christianity. [*Rosenberger v. Univ. of Virginia*]

D. **Analyzing content-neutral regulations:** Now, let's go back to the beginning and assume that the government restriction is *content-neutral.*

1. **Three-part test:** Here, we have a *three-part test* that the government must satisfy before its regulation will be sustained if that regulation substantially impairs expression:

a. **Significant governmental interest:** First, the regulation must serve a *significant governmental interest.*

b. **Narrowly tailored:** Second, the regulation must be *narrowly tailored* to serve that governmental interest. So if there's a somewhat *less restrictive* way to accomplish the same result, the government must use that less-intrusive way.

Example: Preventing littering is a significant governmental interest. But the government can't completely ban the distribution of handbills to avoid littering, because the littering problem could be solved by the less restrictive method of simply punishing those who drop a handbill on the street. [*Schneider v. State*]

c. **Alternative channels:** Finally, the state must *"leave open alternative channels"* for communicating the information.

Example: Suppose a city wants to ban all billboards. If a political advertiser can show that there's no other low-cost way to get his message across to local motorists, this billboard ban might run afoul of the "alternative channels" requirement.

2. **Mid-level review:** This three-part test basically boils down to *mid-level* review for content-neutral restrictions that significantly impair expression (as opposed to strict scrutiny for content-based restrictions).

3. **Time, place and manner regulations:** The three-part test applies to time, place and manner regulations applicable to public forums — see p. 76.

E. **Overbreadth:** The doctrine of *overbreadth* is very important in determining whether a governmental regulation of speech violates the First Amendment. A statute is "overbroad" if it bans speech that could constitutionally be forbidden but *also* bans speech that is protected by the First Amendment.

1. **Means of avoiding standing problem:** Overbreadth helps with *standing* problems in First Amendment cases. *Outside* the First Amendment area, a litigant can only get a statute declared unconstitutional if he can show that it's unconstitutional in its *application to him.* But the overbreadth doctrine lets a litigant prevail if he can show that the statute, applied according to its terms, would violate the First Amendment rights of *persons not now before the court.* So overbreadth is really an exception to the usual rule of "standing" — under the usual standing rules, a person is not normally allowed to assert the constitutional rights of others, only his own.

Example: A state statute prohibits any retailer from selling "any printed book or magazine whose contents would be harmful to minors because of the violent or sexually explicit content of the materials." Store, a local stationery store, sues to have the statute ruled unconstitutional as applied to a particular non-obscene but sexually-explicit magazine that Store wishes to carry.

Store will win if it can show that enforcement of the statute against it would cause the First Amendment rights of its adult customers (even ones who are not parties to the litigation) to be violated — Store doesn't have to show that it had its own independent First Amendment right to sell these materials.

2. **"Substantial" overbreadth:** In cases where the statute is aimed at *conduct* that has expressive content (rather than aimed against pure speech), the overbreadth doctrine will only be applied if the overbreadth would be *"substantial."* In other words, the potential unconstitutional applications of the statute must be *reasonably numerous* compared with the constitutional applications.

F. **Vagueness:** There is a second important First Amendment doctrine: *vagueness.* A statute is unconstitutionally vague if the conduct forbidden by it is so *unclearly defined* that a reasonable person would have to *guess at its meaning.*

1. **Distinguish from overbreadth:** Be careful to *distinguish vagueness from overbreadth:* they both leave the citizen uncertain about which applications of a statute may constitutionally be imposed. But in overbreadth, the uncertainty is hidden or "latent," and in vagueness the uncertainty is easily apparent.

Example: Consider the same statute as in the preceding Example, prohibiting any retailer of books or magazines from selling "any printed book or magazine whose contents would be harmful to minors because of the violent or sexually explicit content of the materials."

The statute is unconstitutionally *vague* because it would leave a reasonable person unsure about what conduct is forbidden. For instance, how would a retailer know just how "violent" a publication would have to be to be "harmful" to minors? What's the meaning of "harmful" here? The text of the statute simply leaves the reader wondering what's forbidden and what's not (and this lack of clarity is readily apparent, even to one who knows nothing about Con Law).

Now, consider why the statute is also *overbroad.* As we saw above, that's because the statute forbids a substantial amount of constitutionally-protected conduct (e.g., the right of adult reader to read non-obscene material). That defect is latent — you have to know something about the First Amendment to know that some protected conduct is being forbidden.

II. ADVOCACY OF ILLEGAL CONDUCT

A. Advocacy of illegal conduct: Remember that one of our "unprotected categories" is the *advocacy of imminent illegal conduct.* The government can ban speech that advocates crime or the use of force if (but only if) it shows that two requirements are met:

1. **Intent:** The advocacy must be *intended* to incite or produce "imminent lawless action"; and

2. **Likelihood:** The advocacy must in fact be *likely* to incite or produce that imminent lawless action.

III. TIME, PLACE AND MANNER REGULATIONS

A. Time, place and manner generally: Let's now focus on regulations covering the *"time, place and manner"* of expression. This is the area of Freedom of Expression on which you are most likely to be tested on the MBE. The statement below of the rules for analyzing "time, place and manner" restrictions assumes that the speech that is being restricted is taking place in a *public forum.* (If it's not, then the government has a somewhat easier time of getting its regulation sustained; we'll be talking about these non-public forum situations later.)

1. **Three-part test:** A "time, place and manner" regulation of public-forum speech has to pass a *three-part test* to avoid being a violation of the First Amendment:

- ❑ It must be *content-neutral*;
- ❑ It must be *narrowly tailored* to serve a *significant governmental interest*; and
- ❑ It must leave *open alternative channels* for communicating the information.

Let's consider these one at a time.

a. **Content-neutral:** First, the time, place and manner regulation has to be *content-neutral.* In other words, the government can't really be trying to regulate content under the guise of regulating "time, place and manner."

Example: City enacts an ordinance allowing parades or demonstrations "to protest governmental policies" to be conducted only between 10 a.m. and 4 p.m. No such restrictions are placed on other kinds of parades or demonstrations. Even though this restriction is ostensibly merely a "time, place and manner" restriction, it violates the requirement of content-neutrality, because the restriction applies to some expressive conduct but not others, based on the content of the speech.

b. **Narrowly tailored for significant governmental interest:** Second, the regulation has to be *narrowly tailored* to serve a *significant governmental interest.* This basically means that not only must the government be pursuing an important interest, but there must not be some significantly *less intrusive* way that government could achieve its objective.

Example: Suppose the government wants to prevent littering on the streets. Even though prevention of littering is an important governmental objective, the government may not simply ban all distribution of handbills, because there is a significantly less restrictive means of achieving this objective — a direct ban on littering — so the ban on handbills is not "narrowly tailored" to achieving the anti-littering objective.

c. **Alternative channels:** Finally, the state must "leave open *alternative channels*" for communicating the information.

Example: City is a medium-sized city, with six public parks and many streets. City enacts an ordinance stating that any parade or demonstration, no matter what the content of the message, shall take place only in Central Park or on Main Street. City argues that its limited budget for police security, and the greater ease of handling crowds in these two places than in other places, justify the ordinance. Even though this time, place and manner restriction is apparently content-neutral and is arguably narrowly tailored for a significant governmental interest, it probably violates the "leave open alternative channels" requirement because it puts off-limits for parades and demonstrations the vast majority of locations within City.

2. **Application to conduct:** These rules on when the state may regulate the "time, place and manner" of expression apply where what is being regulated is pure speech. But much more importantly, these rules apply where the state is regulating *"conduct"* that has an expressive component. *So the state can never defend on the grounds that "We're not regulating speech, we're just regulating conduct."*

Example: It's "conduct" to hand out handbills, or to form a crowd that marches down the street as part of a political demonstration. But since both of these activities have a major expressive component, the state cannot restrict the conduct unless its satisfies the three-part test described above, i.e., the restriction is content-neutral, it's narrowly tailored to achieve a significant governmental interest, and it leaves open alternative channels.

3. **"Facial" vs. "as applied":** A "time, place and manner" regulation, like any other regulation impinging upon First Amendment rights, may be attacked as being either "facially" invalid or invalid "as applied." (See p. 47 for the distinction.) Thus even a time, place and manner restriction that has been very carefully worded so as to satisfy all three requirements listed above may become unconstitutional *as applied to a particular plaintiff.*

Example: A City ordinance provides that any parade or demonstration participated in by more than five people shall be held only after the purchase of a permit, which shall be issued by the City Manager for free to any applicant upon two days notice. The City Manager normally issues such permits without inquiring into the nature of the demonstration planned by the applicant. P, who is known locally as an agitator who opposes the current city government, applies for a permit. The City Manager denies the permit, saying, "I don't like the rabble-rousing you've been doing." Even though the ordinance on its face is probably a valid time, place and manner restriction, the application of the ordinance to P's own permit request violates P's First Amendment rights, because that application is not being carried out in a content-neutral manner.

B. **Licensing:** Be especially skeptical of governmental attempts to require a *license* or *permit* before expressive conduct takes place.

1. **Content-neutral:** Obviously, any permit requirement must be applied in a *content-neutral* way.

Example: Local officials give permits for speeches made for purposes of raising money for non-controversial charities, but decline to give permits for demonstrations to protest the racism of local officials. The requirement of content neutrality in the licensing scheme is not being satisfied, and the scheme will be automatically struck down.

2. **No excess discretion:** Also, the licensing scheme must set forth the grounds for denying a permit *narrowly* and *specifically*, so that the *discretion of local officials* will be *curtailed.*

Example: A municipal ordinance cannot require a permit for every newspaper vending machine where the permit is to be granted on "terms and conditions deemed necessary by the mayor" — the grounds for denying a permit must be set forth much more specifically, to curb the official's discretion. [*Lakewood v. Plain Dealer Publ. Co.*]

3. **Narrow means-end tailoring:** Finally, the permit *mechanism* must be *closely tailored* to the *objective* that the government is trying to achieve.

Example: A village bans any "canvasser" from going onto residential property for the purpose of promoting any "cause" without first getting a Solicitation Permit from the mayor. The village defends the ordinance on the grounds that it helps prevent fraud, and protects residents' privacy. *Held*, this ordinance is invalid on its face, because it's not tailored to the village's stated interests. For instance, the ordinance applies even to religious and political proselytizing unaccompanied by fund-raising, which poses little risk of fraud. Conversely, the interest in protecting residents' privacy could be just as well achieved by letting residents post No Solicitation signs that it would be an offense to ignore. [*Watchtower Bible and Tract Soc. v. Stratton*]

4. **Reasonable means of maintaining order:** But if these three requirements — content-neutral application, limited administrative discretion and close means-end fit — are satisfied, the permit requirement will be *upheld* if it is a *reasonable means of ensuring that public order is maintained.*

Example 1: A requirement that a permit be obtained before a large group of people may march would probably be upheld as a reasonable way of maintaining order, if the requirement is applied in a content-neutral way and is drafted so as to apply without exception to *all* large marches.

Example 2: A city has two consistently-applied rules: (1) that no demonstrations of more than 100 people will be allowed without a permit in a particular city park; and (2) that no permit will be issued for such a demonstration to occur after 10 P.M. in that park, because it adjoins a quiet residential neighborhood. A group that wishes to protest a U.S. war in the Middle East asks for a permit for a midnight candlelight vigil, asserting (and believing) that this method of protest will be more dramatic and effective than a daytime or early-evening vigil.

The court will apply the 3-part test from p. 76, and will likely conclude that the denial of the permit satisfies these requirements. In particular, it will likely hold that the no-permits-after-10-P.M. rule is narrowly tailored to the significant governmental interest in safeguarding the quiet of adjacent residences.

C. **Right to be left alone:** People have no strong *right to be left alone*, and the government therefore can't regulate broadly to protect that right. As a general rule, it's *up to the unwilling listener* (or viewer) *to avoid the undesired expression.*

Example: A city can't make it a misdemeanor to walk up and down the street handing advertising brochures to people without the recipient's express consent. (It's up to the recipient to decline the handbill.)

1. **Captive audience:** But if the audience is *"captive"* (unable to avert their eyes and ears), this makes it *more likely* that a fair degree of content-neutral regulation *will be allowed.* (However, the fact that the audience is captive is just one factor in measuring the strength of the state interest in regulating.)

   Example: A state may make it a crime to approach close to a woman who is entering an abortion clinic, if the approacher's purpose is to orally "counsel or educate" the woman and the woman does not consent to the approach. [*Hill v. Colorado*].

D. **Canvassing:** A speaker's right to *canvass*, that is, to go around ringing doorbells or giving out handbills, receives substantial protection.

1. **Homeowner can say "no":** The individual listener (e.g., the homeowner), is always free to say, "No, I don't want to speak to you about becoming (say) a Jehovah's Witness." The city can then make it a crime for the speaker to persist.

2. **City can't give blanket prohibition:** But the *government* cannot say "No" *in advance* on behalf of its homeowners or other listeners.

   Example: A city passes an ordinance providing that "All doorbell ringing for the purpose of handing out handbills is hereby forbidden." *Held*, such an ordinance violates the First Amendment, even if (as the city claims) it is a content-neutral ordinance designed to protect unwilling listeners, such as those who work nights and sleep days. The most the city can do is to provide that once the individual homeowner makes it clear he doesn't want to be spoken to, the speaker must honor that request. [*Martin v. Struthers*]

3. **Time, place and manner:** But the authorities may impose "time, place and manner" limits on canvassing, if these limits: (1) are content-neutral; (2) serve a significant governmental interest; and (3) leave open adequate other channels for communication.

   Example: A town might prohibit canvassing after 6:00 P.M., if its policy is truly content-neutral (e.g., it wasn't enacted for the purpose of silencing Jehovah's Witnesses), is enacted to protect homeowners' night-time tranquility, and allows solicitation to take place at other times.

E. **Fighting words:** One of our other "unprotected categories" consists of *"fighting words."* "Fighting words" are words which are likely to make the person to whom they are addressed commit an *act of violence*, probably against the speaker. Expression that falls within the "fighting words" category can be flatly banned or punished by the state. [*Chaplinsky v. New Hampshire*]

   Example: D picks out one member of his audience and calls him a liar, racist and crook. D can be arrested for this speech, because these are words that might well provoke a reasonable person to whom they are addressed into physically attacking D.

1. **Limits:** But the "fighting words" doctrine is tightly limited:

   a. **Anger not enough:** It's not enough that the speaker has made the crowd angry; they must be so angry that they are *likely to fight.*

   b. **Crowd control:** The police must *control* the angry crowd instead of arresting the speaker if they've got the physical ability to do so. (In other words, the police can't grant the hostile crowd a "heckler's veto.")

   c. **Dislike of speaker's identity:** The doctrine doesn't apply where it's the mere *identity* or *lawful acts* of the speaker, rather than his threatening words, that moves the crowd to anger.

F. Offensive language: Language that is *"offensive"* is nonetheless protected by the First Amendment.

1. **Profanity:** This means that even language that is *profane* may not be banned from public places.

   Example: D wears a jacket saying "Fuck the Draft" in the L.A. County Courthouse. D cannot be convicted for breaching the peace. The state may not ban language merely because it is "offensive," even if profane. [*Cohen v. Calif.*]

2. **Racial or religious hatred:** Similarly, this means that messages preaching *racial or religious hatred* are protected (at least if they don't incite imminent violence or come within the "fighting words" doctrine).

   Example: A member of the American Nazi Party tells a predominantly-Jewish audience, "Jews are the scum of the earth and should be eliminated." D cannot be punished for, or even restricted from, saying these words.

3. **Limits:** But offensive language *can* be prohibited or punished if: (1) the audience is a *"captive"* one (e.g., the speech occurs on a city bus or subway); or (2) the language is *"obscene,"* under the formal legal definition of this term (lewd and without socially redeeming value).

G. Regulation of "hate speech": Government efforts to regulate *"hate speech"* — for instance, speech attacking racial minorities, women, homosexuals, or other traditionally disfavored groups — may run afoul of the First Amendment for being content-based.

1. **General rules:** Here are the general rules about how a state may go about banning hate speech:

   ❑ **Ban on "true threats":** A state may ban *"true threats,"* that is, words or acts that communicate the speaker's *intent to commit unlawful violence* to a particular individual or group. (However, as we'll see below, a state may probably not single out certain types of threats for banning based on their content, like banning only race-based threats.) So if a state has banned all threats of imminent violence, this ban can be used to punch, say, a threat to lynch someone on account of his race. [Cf. *Va. v. Black.*]

   ❑ **Ban based on listed topics or motives:** A ban on speech or conduct intended or likely to incite anger or violence based solely on *particular listed topics or motives* — such as race, color, religion or gender hatred — is *impermissibly content-based.* That's true even if all the speech/conduct banned falls within an *"unprotected"* category such as, here, *"fighting words."* [*R.A.V. v. St. Paul*]

   Example: City bans only those "fighting words" that evoke hatred or conflict based on race, ethnicity or gender (not fighting words based on, say, the listeners' political affiliation). This enactment is content-based, in that it selects speech for proscription based on its content. Therefore, the statute will be strictly scrutinized, and struck down for not being sufficiently narrowly-tailored to achieve the compelling state interest in avoiding dangerous physical conflict. (However, a state could ban *all* fighting words — it just can't select fighting words based only on certain types of hatred.) [*R.A.V.*]

   ❑ **Worst examples:** However, a state *may* impose a content-based ban on *particular instances* of unprotected speech if the ban forbids *only the very worst examples* illustrating *the very reason the particular class of speech is unprotected.*

   Example: The state may choose to criminalize just the very most dangerous "fighting words," just the very most obscene images, etc. [*R.A.V.*]

   ❑ **Penalty-enhancement statutes:** Also, a state may identify particular generally-applicable criminal proscriptions, and may then choose to punish *more severely* those criminal acts that happen to be motivated by hate than those not motivated by hate. This is called the *"penalty enhancement"* approach. [*Wisconsin v. Mitchell*]

Example: For instance, from within the overall class of acts that constitute arson (all of which are defined as crimes), the state may punish arson more seriously if it's motivated by bias against particular groups.

❑ **All intimidating acts:** Finally, a state may select a particular type of expressive act (e.g., cross-burning), and punish *all instances* where that act is done with a purpose of *intimidating or threatening* someone, even though the state doesn't punish other types of intimidating or threatening acts. [*Virginia v. Black*]

Example: A state may choose to ban all cross-burnings that are done with intent to intimidate another. That's true even if the state chooses not to criminalize other types of expressive activity that are done with intent to intimidate another (e.g., burning that other in effigy).

H. The public forum: Let's turn now to the concept of the *"public forum."*

1. Rules: Here are the rules concerning when the fact that speech occurs in a public forum makes a difference, and how:

a. Content-based: If a regulation is *content-based*, it makes no difference whether the expression is or is not in a public forum: strict scrutiny will be given to the regulation, and it will almost never be upheld.

b. Neutral "time, place and manner": It's where a regulation is *content-neutral* that the existence of a public forum makes a difference; especially regulations on "time, place and manner" are less likely to be upheld where the expression takes place in a public forum.

i. Non-public forum: When expression takes place in a *non-public forum*, the regulation merely has to be *rationally related* to some *legitimate governmental objective*, as long as equally effective alternative channels for the expression are available.

ii. Public forum: When the expression takes place in a *public forum*, by contrast, the regulation has to be *narrowly drawn* to achieve a *significant governmental interest* (roughly *intermediate-level* review). It is necessary, but not sufficient, that the government also leaves alternative channels available.

Example 1 (public forum speech): A city says, "No political campaign messages may be presented in handbills distributed on city streets." Since this rule impairs communications in a public forum (city streets), the city will have to show that its ordinance is necessary to achieve a significant governmental interest, which it probably can't do (anti-littering won't be enough, for instance). The city can't say, "Well, TV or radio ads will let the same message be given" — the existence of alternative channels for the communication is necessary, but is not enough, when the expression takes place in a public forum.

Example 2 (non-public forum speech): A city says, "No political campaign messages may be displayed on privately-owned billboards, even with the consent of the owner." Here, no public forum is involved. Therefore, as long as adequate alternative channels are available (which they probably are, e.g., radio and TV ads), the city only has to show that its regulation is rationally related to some legitimate governmental objective. The city can probably meet this burden (e.g., by pointing to the objective of beautifying the city).

2. What are public forums: What places, then, are public forums?

a. "True" or "traditional" public forums: First, there are *"true"* or *"traditional"* public forums. These are areas that are public forums by custom and tradition, not by virtue of any particular government policy. The classic examples are: (1) *streets;* (2) *sidewalks*; and (3) *parks*.

b. **"Designated" public forums:** There's a second type of public forum: places that the government has *decided to open up* to a broad range of expressive conduct ("designated" public forums).

Some possible examples:

- ❑ places where *government meetings* take place that the government has decided to open to the public at large (e.g., a school board meeting held in a school auditorium);
- ❑ places that government has decided may be used by a broad range of people or groups (e.g., school *classrooms* after hours, under a policy that lets pretty much any group use them, or a municipal theater that any group may rent).

These are called *"designated"* public forums.

i. **Same rules:** The *same rules* apply to designated public forums as apply to true public forums, except that government can *change its mind* and remove the designation (in which case the place becomes a non-public forum that can be subjected to much broader viewpoint-neutral regulation, as described below).

ii. **MBE tip:** When the MBE examiners want to test you on time, place and manner regulations for public forums, they're much *more likely* to pick *"traditional"* public forums than "designated" public forums.

c. **Non-public-forums:** Still other public places are not at all associated with expression traditionally, so they can be treated as *non-public forums. Here, the government regulation just has to be rationally related* to some *legitimate governmental objective*, as long as the interference with speech is not "substantial." And if alternative channels are available, then this fact alone usually *makes* the interference "insubstantial." So we basically use "mere rationality" review for content-neutral "time, place and manner" regulations of non-public-forum expression that leave open alternative channels of communication.

i. **All expression banned:** Often, even a regulation that completely *bans* expression in a particular non-public forum will be found to satisfy this "mere rationality" test. Or, the government can choose to forbid discussion of certain subjects (but *not certain viewpoints*).

Example: A publicly-owned airport terminal is not a public forum. Therefore, the government may ban face-to-face solicitation of funds in the terminal, because such a ban is rationally related to the legitimate governmental objectives of reducing congestion and combatting fraud. (However, a total ban even on literature distribution will not be upheld, because this ban does not even satisfy the "mere rationality" standard.) [*Int'l Soc. for Krishna Consciousness v. Lee*]

ii. **Illustrations of non-public-forums:** Here are some illustrations of facilities that, even though they are owned by the government, are not public forums: *airport terminals*, *jails*, *military bases*, the insides of *courthouses*, and *governmental office buildings*.

I. **Access to private property:** In general, a speaker does not have a First Amendment right of *access* to another person's *private property* to deliver his message. Most significantly, a person does not have a First Amendment right to speak in *shopping centers*. [*Hudgens v. NLRB*]

Example: State trespass laws may be used to prevent a person from conducting an anti-war demonstration or a religious proselytizing campaign at her local privately-owned shopping center.

IV. REGULATION OF SYMBOLIC EXPRESSION

A. **Symbolic expression:** Let's consider *"symbolic expression,"* i.e., expression that consists solely of *non-verbal* actions.

1. **Standard:** We use essentially the same rules to analyze restrictions on symbolic expression as we do for restrictions that apply to verbal speech, or to verbal speech coupled with conduct. Thus: (1) any attempt by government to restrict symbolic expression because of the *content* of the message will be strictly scrutinized and almost certainly struck down; (2) any restriction on the *time, place or manner* of symbolic expression will have to be *narrowly tailored* to a *significant governmental objective* and will have to *leave open alternative channels*.

   Example: The Ds (high school students) wear armbands to school, in the face of a school policy forbidding students from wearing such armbands. Because school officials were motivated by a desire to suppress particular messages — anti-war messages — the ban must be strictly scrutinized, and is struck down. [*Tinker v. Des Moines Schl. Dist.*]

2. **Flag desecration:** The most interesting example of government regulation of symbolic expression is *flag desecration* statutes. The main thing to remember is that if a statute bans flag desecration or mutilation, and either on the statute's face or as it is applied, the statute is directed only at particular *messages*, it will be invalid.

   Example: A federal statute bans flag burning. *Held*, Congress was trying to preserve the flag as a "symbol of national unity." The statute was therefore content-based, so it must be strictly scrutinized (and will be struck down). [*U.S. v. Eichman*]

V. DEFAMATION AND INVASION OF PRIVACY

A. **Defamation:** The First Amendment places limits on the extent to which a plaintiff may recover tort damages for *defamation*.

1. ***New York Times v. Sullivan* test:** Most importantly, under the rule of *New York Times v. Sullivan*, 376 U.S. 254 (1964), where P is a *public official*, he may only win a defamation suit against D for a statement relating to P's official conduct if P can prove that D's statement was made either "with *knowledge* that it was false" or with *"reckless disregard"* of whether it was true or false. These two mental states are usually collectively referred to as the *"actual malice"* requirement.

   Example: The *New York Times* runs an ad saying that P — the Montgomery, Alabama police commissioner — has terrorized Dr. Martin Luther King by repeatedly arresting him. Even if these statements are false, P cannot recover for libel unless he can show that the *Times* knew its statements were false or acted with reckless disregard of whether the statements were true or false. [*N.Y. Times v. Sullivan, supra*].

   a. **Meaning of "actual malice":** "Actual malice" does *not* require what is commonly called "malice" — a statement made with knowledge of its falsity or with reckless disregard of whether it is true meets the actual-malice requirement even if the speaker feels *no ill will* at all towards the public official being defamed.

2. **Public figures:** This rule of *Times v. Sullivan* — that P can only recover for defamation if he shows intentional falsity or recklessness about truth — applies not only to public "officials" but also to public *"figures"*. Thus a well known college football coach, and a prominent retired Army general, were public figures who had to show that the defendant acted with actual malice. [*Assoc. Press v. Walker*]

a. **Partial public figure:** Someone who voluntarily *injects himself* into a public controversy will be a public figure for *just that controversy* — thus an anti-abortion activist might be a public figure for any news story concerning abortion, but not for stories about, say, his private life unrelated to abortion.

b. **Involuntary public figure:** Also, some people may be *"involuntary"* public figures.

Example: A *criminal defendant* is an involuntary public figure, so he cannot sue or recover for a news report about his crime or trial unless he can prove actual malice.

3. **Private figure:** If the plaintiff is a *"private"* (rather than "public") figure, he does *not* have to meet the *New York Times v. Sullivan* "actual malice" rule. [*Gertz v. Robert Welch, Inc.*] On the other hand, the First Amendment requires that he show at least *negligence* by the defendant — the states may not impose strict liability for defamation, even for a private-figure plaintiff. *Id.*

a. **No punitive damages:** Also, a private-figure plaintiff who shows only negligence cannot recover *punitive* damages — he must show actual malice to get punitive damages. *Id.*

B. **Other state-law tort claims:** Apart from defamation, state law often gives a person the right to sue for other state-defined torts, such as "*invasion of privacy*" and "*misappropriation of publicity.*" But the Supreme Court recognizes a First Amendment *"newsworthiness privilege"* that may conflict with such suits. So, for instance, if D publishes or broadcasts information about P that would constitute an invasion of privacy under state law, as a constitutional matter P cannot recover if D's publication of the item is protected by the newsworthiness privilege.

Example: D publishes a newsletter stating truthfully that P was recently convicted of theft, and that D helped bring P to justice. P sues for "misappropriation of identity," a form of invasion-of-privacy tort law recognized under state law. A court would likely hold that P cannot recover because the information here was newsworthy (a matter of public concern), and therefore D's First Amendment right to publish it trumped P's right to recover for misappropriation.

1. **Can't take whole performance:** But the First-Amendment-based newsworthiness privilege does not entitle the defendant to publish or broadcast the *entirety of a performance or copyrighted work* belonging to P, where this would deprive P of the ability to receive the commercial value of his intellectual property.

Example: D, a TV station, secretly films and broadcasts P's entire 15-second circus act, in which P, a "human cannonball," is shot from a cannon and lands safely in a net 200 feet away. P sues for "misappropriation of publicity," a tort recognized under state law. D defends on the grounds that it had a First Amendment right to report on this newsworthy event. *Held*, for P: however newsworthy the event, the First Amendment does not protect the media's right to "broadcast a performer's entire act without his consent." [*Zacchini v. Scripps-Howard Broadcasting Co.*]

C. **Intentional infliction of emotional distress:** The *Times v. Sullivan* rule applies to actions for intentional infliction of *emotional distress* as well as ones for defamation. Thus a public-figure plaintiff cannot recover for any intentional infliction of emotional distress unless he shows that the defendant acted with actual malice.

Example: *Hustler* Magazine satirizes religious leader Jerry Falwell as a drunken hypocrite who has sex with his mother. *Held*, Falwell cannot recover for intentional infliction of emotional distress unless he shows that *Hustler* made a false statement with knowledge of falsity or with reckless disregard of falsity. [*Hustler Magazine v. Falwell*]

D. **Falsity:** The First Amendment also probably requires that the plaintiff (whether or not she is a public figure) must show that the statement was *false*.

VI. OBSCENITY

A. Obscenity: Another of our "unprotected categories" is *obscenity*. Expression that is obscene is simply *unprotected* by the First Amendment, so the states can ban it, punish it, or do whatever else they want without worrying about the First Amendment.

B. Three-part test: For a work to be "obscene," all three parts of the following test must be met:

1. **Prurient interest:** First, the average person, applying today's community standards, must find that the work as a whole appeals to the *"prurient"* interest;

2. **Sexual conduct:** Second, the work must depict or describe in a "patently offensive way" particular types of *sexual conduct* defined by state law; and

3. **Lacks value:** Finally, the work taken as a whole, must lack "serious literary, artistic, political or scientific value."

   [*Miller v. Calif.*]

C. Significance: So something will not be "obscene" unless it depicts or describes *"hard core sex."* (For instance, mere *nudity*, by itself, is not obscene.)

1. **Abandonment of "redeeming social value" test:** Don't be fooled on the MBE by a choice that says that something is obscene only if it lacks "the slightest redeeming social importance." This was once a requirement — which made it harder to get obscenity convictions — but was replaced in 1973 by the *Miller* "lacks serious literary, artistic, political or scientific value" requirement mentioned above.

D. Materials addressed to minors: It will be much easier for the state to keep erotic materials out of the hands of *minors*. Probably even minors have some First Amendment interest in receiving sexually explicit materials, but this is typically *outweighed* by the state's compelling interest in protecting minors against such material. So the distribution of non-obscene but sexually explicit materials may basically be forbidden to minors (provided that the regulations do not substantially impair the access of adults to these materials).

1. **Adults' rights impaired:** But if a measure aimed at minors *does* substantially impair the access of adults to material that's "indecent" but not obscene, the measure will be struck down.

   Example: If Congress outright bans all "indecent" material on the Internet (as it has done), out of a fear that the material will be seen by minors, the measure will be found to violate the First Amendment rights of adults. [*Reno v. ACLU*]

E. "Pandering": The issue of whether the material appeals primarily to prurient interests may be influenced by the manner in which the material is *advertised* — if the publisher or distributor plays up the prurient nature of the materials in the advertising, this will make it more likely that the materials will be found to appeal mostly to prurient interests and thus to be obscene. The advertisement itself, and expert testimony about the likely effect of the advertising, may be admitted into evidence to aid the determination on obscenity. (The marketing of materials by emphasizing their sexually provocative nature is often called *"pandering."*)

F. Private possession by adults: The mere *private possession* of obscene material by an adult may *not* be made criminal. [*Stanley v. Georgia*].

Example: While police are lawfully arresting D at his house on a robbery charge, they spot obscene magazines on his shelf. D may not be criminally charged with possession of pornography, because one has both a First Amendment right and a privacy right to see or read what one wants in the privacy of one's own home.

1. **Child pornography:** However, the states *may* criminalize even private possession of *child pornography*. [*Osborne v. Ohio*]

2. **No right to supply to consenting adults:** Also, the state may punish a person who *supplies* pornography even to consenting adults. In other words, there is a right to *have* pornography for one's own home use, but not a right to supply it to others for their home use.

G. **Regulating secondary effects of adult speech:** Suppose conduct or speech is "sexually explicit" but does not rise to the level of obscenity (e.g., because it has some serious artistic value). Even though such *"adult" content* is not obscene, the government may *regulate its "secondary effects"* without having to face strict scrutiny.

1. **Regulation of red-light districts:** For instance, local governments may impose tight zoning restrictions on "adult" activities like *live nude dancing*, as long as there's some evidence that such activities increase crime, lower property values, etc., and that zoning restrictions make some headway against the problem. These kind of zoning-oriented regulations are deemed to be *content-neutral* (because they're directed at the "secondary effects" of the expression, not at the "content" of the expression) and therefore do not face strict scrutiny.

VII. COMMERCIAL SPEECH

A. **Commercial speech generally:** Speech that is *"commercial"* — that is, speech advertising a product or proposing some commercial transaction — gets First Amendment protection. But this protection is in some ways *more limited* than the protection given to non-commercial (e.g., political) speech.

1. **Truthful speech:** *Truthful* commercial speech gets a pretty fair degree of First Amendment protection. The government may restrict truthful commercial speech only if the regulation:

   [1] *directly advances*

   [2] a *substantial governmental interest*

   [3] in a way that is *reasonably tailored* to achieve the government's objective.

   [*Central Hudson Gas v. Public Serv. Comm.; Edenfeld v. Fane.*] So basically, we apply *mid-level review* to government restrictions based on the content of commercial speech (whereas we apply strict scrutiny to content-based restrictions on non-commercial speech).

   Example: Virginia forbids a pharmacist from advertising his prices for prescription drugs. Virginia must show that it is pursuing a "substantial" governmental interest, and that materially-less-restrictive alternatives are not available. Here, the state's desire to prevent price-cutting that will lead to shoddy service is not strong enough to qualify as "substantial," so the measure must be struck down on First Amendment grounds. [*Virginia Pharmacy Board v. Virginia Consumer Council*]

2. **False, deceptive or illegal:** On the other hand, *false or deceptive* commercial speech may be *forbidden* by the government. Similarly, speech which proposes an *illegal transaction* may be forbidden (e.g., advertisements for cocaine).

   Example: Congress makes it a crime to disseminate by means of the Internet any deceptive advertisement for any product. The statute does not violate anyone's First Amendment rights, because false or deceptive speech is not protected at all by the First Amendment.

   a. **Harmful:** But if the product or service is *harmful* but *lawful*, the state *may not limit* advertising about it any more than the state may limit advertising about a non-harmful product — the right to ban product X does not necessarily include the "lesser" right to regulate speech about product X.

Example: Congress is free to ban casino gambling entirely. But if Congress allows such gambling, it may not limit advertising of casino gambling unless the limitation passes the mid-level review standard, summarized above, that applies to regulation of truthful commercial speech. [*Greater New Orleans Broadcasting v. U.S.*]

3. **No overbreadth:** The *overbreadth* doctrine does *not apply* in commercial speech cases, because advertisers are thought not likely to be "chilled" by overly broad governmental regulation of speech. Therefore, a commercial enterprise that is protesting a regulation of speech must show that the regulation infringes the enterprise's own speech, not merely that the regulation would curtail speech not now before the court.

B. **Advertising of lawful but harmful products:** Sellers of products that are *lawful* but *harmful* receive the *same protection as any other commercial speaker*. That is, the fact that government could completely *ban* the product does *not* mean that government can automatically curtail truthful advertising about the product. Therefore, regulation of advertising about the product must be substantially related to an important governmental objective, and the court will require a fairly tight fit between means and end.

Example: A state bans all outdoor tobacco advertising, on the theory that this will help minors be less attracted to tobacco products. (Tobacco cannot legally be sold to minors in the state.) *Held*, the regulation is invalid — it unduly interferes with the rights of tobacco vendors, and their adult customers, to exchange truth information about tobacco. [*Lorillard Tobacco v. Reilly*]

C. **Lawyers:** The qualified First Amendment protection given to commercial speech means that *lawyers* have a limited right to advertise. Thus a state may not ban all advertising by lawyers or even ban advertising directed to a particular problem. See, e.g., *Bates v. State Bar of Ariz.*

Example: A lawyer can has a First Amendment right to advertise, "If you've been injured by the Phen-fen diet drug, I may be able to help you."

1. **In-person solicitation:** On the other hand, the states may ban certain types of *in-person solicitation* by lawyers seeking clients (e.g., solicitation of accident victims in person by tort lawyers who want to obtain a contingent-fee agreement. [*Ohralik v. Ohio St. Bar Ass'n.*])

2. **Direct mail:** Similarly, the states may ban lawyers from *direct-mail* solicitation of accident victims, at least for a 30-day period following the accident. [*Florida Bar v. Went For It*]

VIII. SOME SPECIAL CONTEXTS

A. **Special contexts:** Here are two special contexts raising First Amendment issues: the operation of public schools, and the regulation of political campaigns.

B. **Public school students:** Students in *public schools* have a limited right of free speech. The student's right to speak freely has to be *balanced* against the administration's right to carry out its educational mission and to maintain discipline.

1. **Allowable regulation:** Thus a school may ban profanity. It may also ban the school newspaper from running stories that would disturb the school's *educational mission* (e.g., stories about sex and birth control that the principal reasonably believes are inappropriate for younger students at the school). [*Hazelwood Sch. Dist. v. Kuhlmeier*]

2. **Non-allowable regulation:** But school officials may not suppress students' speech merely because they disagree with that speech on ideological or political grounds.

Example: School officials may not ban the wearing of anti-war armbands.

C. Campaign spending: The state or federal governments can regulate *campaign spending* to some extent, but other campaign regulations would violate the First Amendment.

1. **Contributions:** Contributions made by individuals or groups to candidates, political parties, or Political Action Committees may be limited.

   Example 1: Congress may constitutionally prevent anyone from contributing more than $1,000 to a candidate for federal office, in order to curb actual or apparent corruption. [*Buckley v. Valeo*]

   Example 2: Congress may prevent national political parties from receiving more than $2,000 from any donor, thus outlawing unregulated "soft money" donations. That's because such donations give the appearance that large donors get special access to office-holders, a type of corruption that Congress may constitutionally combat. [*McConnell v. F.E.C.*]

   a. **Lower limit:** But contribution limits may not be made *so low* that they substantially interfere with candidates' and parties' ability to *run a competitive election campaign.*

      Example: Vermont prevents any individual or political party from contributing more than $400 to the campaign of any candidate for governor during any two-year period. *Held*, this limit is so low that it violates the free speech and free association rights of individuals and parties (though no majority of the Court can agree on the precise test for "how low is too low"). *Randall v. Sorrell.*

2. **Expenditures:** But an individual's *independent* campaign-related *expenditures* (whether he's a candidate or not) may *not* be limited at all.

   Example 1: A candidate may not be prevented from spending as much of his own money on getting elected as he wishes. [*Buckley v. Valeo; Randall v. Sorrell*]

   Example 2: Similarly, private citizen X may spend as much money to try to get Y elected as he wishes, as long as X spends the money in a truly independent manner rather than contributing it to Y or coordinating with Y on how it should be spent. [*Buckley v. Valeo*]

3. **Ballot measure:** A person has a First Amendment right to spend as much as he wants and however he wants in connection with a *ballot measure.*

   Example: The insurance industry can spend as many millions as it wants, and organize those expenditures however it wants, in order to defeat a proposal that would roll back car insurance rates.

IX. FREEDOM OF ASSOCIATION, AND DENIAL OF PUBLIC BENEFITS OR JOBS

A. Freedom of association generally: First Amendment case law recognizes the concept of *"freedom of association."* In general, the idea is that if an individual has a First Amendment right to engage in a particular expressive activity, then a *group* has a "freedom of association" right to engage in that same activity as a group.

Example: Groups have the right to get together to bring law suits, or to conduct non-violent economic boycotts. Therefore, they cannot be prevented from doing these things by state rules against fomenting litigation or conducting boycotts. [*NAACP v. Button*]

1. **Trick:** Remember that freedom of association is protected by the First Amendment, not some other provision. The MBE examiners will sometimes try to trick you by referring to the "Fourteenth Amendment freedom of association," or some other non-First Amendment basis for freedom of association.

2. **Right not to associate:** Individuals and groups also have a well-protected *"right not to associate."* Thus any government attempt to make an individual give *financial support* to a cause she dislikes, or to make a group *take members* whose presence would interfere with the group's expressive activities, will be *strictly scrutinized.*

    Example 1: Where public school teachers are required to pay union dues, a teacher has a freedom-of-association right not to have the dues used to support ideological causes the teacher dislikes. [*Abood v. Detroit Bd. of Ed.*]

    Example 2: The Boy Scouts can't be forced (by a state anti-discrimination law) to accept an openly-gay male as a scoutmaster, because this would significantly interfere with the Scouts' First Amendment-protected message that homosexuality is immoral. [*Boy Scouts of America v. Dale*]

B. Illegal membership: The freedom of association means that *mere membership in a group or association may not be made illegal*. Membership in a group may only be made part of an offense if: (1) the group is *actively engaged in unlawful activity*, or *incites others* to *imminent lawless action*; and (2) the individual *knows* of the group's illegal activity, and specifically intends to further the group's illegal goals.

Example: Congress cannot make it a crime simply to be a member of the American Communist Party. On the other hand, Congress can make it a crime to be a member of a party that advocates imminent overthrow of the government, if the member knows that the party so advocates and the member intends to help bring about that overthrow.

C. Denial of public benefit or job: Freedom of expression also prevents the government from *denying a public benefit or job* based on a person's association.

1. **Non-illegal activities:** If a person's activities with a group could not be made *illegal*, then those activities may generally not be made the basis for denying the person the government job or benefit.

    Example 1: A state may not refuse to hire a person as a teacher merely because he is a member of the American Communist Party, since the state could not make it illegal to be a member of the ACP.

    Example 2: At a time when Republicans are in power, a state may not refuse to hire Democrats for non-policy-making jobs like police officer or clerk. [*Rutan v. Republican Party of Illinois*]

    a. **Licenses:** This rule that "if it can't be made illegal, it can't be the basis for denial of a job or benefit," applies to government-issued *licenses*. Such licenses are often the focus of MBE questions — a license-holder wants to exercise some First Amendment right that the government couldn't directly forbid her from exercising, but tries to "regulate" her by saying she'll lose her license if she exercises the right. Government will lose in this scenario.

    Example: Muni, a city, requires any barber to receive a license from the city. The licenses are available to any graduate of a one-year program in barbering who is of good moral character. After controversy in Muni about the appropriateness of the U.S.'s involvement in a war in the Middle East, the Muni city council passes an ordinance prohibiting any barber from publicly displaying, in his or her place of business, any poster opposing or supporting the U.S.'s involvement in any foreign war.

    The ordinance is a content-based restriction on core political speech, and cannot survive strict scrutiny. Muni would not be permitted to simply ban all citizens from displaying pro-war or anti-war messages in their places of business (that would be a content-based restriction on core political speech, which would be strictly scrutinized, and struck down because no compelling governmental interest has been shown). What the government cannot do directly, it cannot do indirectly by conditioning a government benefit (a barber's license) on the licensee's agreement not to exercise the speech right in question. And nothing about the barbershop-licensing process changes the fact that the restriction cannot survive strict scrutiny: there is no indication of any meaningful risk that members of the public might incorrectly think that the slogans were attributable to council members, and even if there were such risk, avoiding it would hardly risk to the level of a "compelling" interest.

2. **No right/privilege distinction:** There is no constitutional distinction between a *"right"* and a *"privilege."* Even if, say, a particular public benefit or job is defined by the state to be a "privilege" (i.e., something that does not rise to the level of a "property" interest under the Fourteenth Amendment) the state may not deny that job or benefit on the basis of the applicant's constitutionally-protected membership in a group or organization.

   Example: Consider the above barbershop Example. Muni could not defend its ban on the displaying of messages opposing or supporting foreign wars on the basis that "a barbershop license is a privilege and not a right" so that such displays are not protected by the First Amendment. Since the display of political messages in one's place of business is generally protected by the First Amendment, as described above, Muni cannot condition a government-bestowed "privilege" (a barber's license) on the licensee's willingness to forgo the right to make such a display.

3. **Loyalty oath:** Government may generally not require an applicant to sign a *loyalty oath*, unless the things that the applicant is promising in the loyalty oath not to do are things which, if he did them, would be grounds for punishing him or denying him the job.

   Example: A person cannot be required to sign a loyalty oath that he is not a member of the Communist Party in order to get a teaching job. But he can be required to sign an oath that he will not advocate the forcible overthrow of our government.

4. **Compulsory disclosure:** Similarly, the government may not force you to *disclose* your membership activities (or require a group to disclose who its members are), unless it could make that membership illegal.

   Example: The state cannot require the Communist Party to furnish a list of its members.

5. **Some exceptions:** There are some *exceptions* to the general rule that associational activities that couldn't be outlawed directly also can't be made the basis for public hiring or benefits decisions. In general, these exceptions are for conduct which, although it includes protected expression, directly (and negatively) relates to *performance of the job.*

   a. **Partisan political activities:** For instance, civil servants can constitutionally be forced to choose between their jobs and engaging in *partisan political activities*, since there's a very strong government interest in making sure that civil servants can do their jobs without being coerced into campaigning for or contributing to their elected bosses. [*CSC v. Letter Carriers*].

   b. **Patronage hirings:** Similarly, some public jobs may be awarded as *patronage appointments*, ones the performance of which is *reasonably related to a person's politics.*

      Example: Even though I have a First Amendment right to be a Democrat, the Republican Congressman representing my district doesn't violate my rights when, on the basis of my political beliefs, he declines to hire me as, say, a speech writer, a high advisor, or some other post with a *heavy political content.*

On the other hand, if I'm a Democrat, and there's a Republican governor in power, he can't block me from getting a government job as a clerk or secretary or police officer — the old-fashioned "patronage" system whereby all public jobs could be restricted to supporters of the party in power has been outlawed as a violation of freedom of association, and only jobs with a heavy political content, like speech writer, say, or Chief of Staff, can be based on party membership.

i. **Independent contractors:** The same rule — that party affiliation may be used if and only if the performance is reasonably related to one's politics — applies to people and companies doing work for government on an *independent-contractor* basis.

Example: P has a contract to haul trash for City. Even if the contract is at-will, City can't decline to renew it on the grounds that P belongs to the wrong political party or has supported the Mayor's opponent.

c. **Speech critical of superiors or otherwise inappropriate:** An employee gets limited protection for speech or associational activities that are *critical of superiors*, or that the employer believes are *inappropriate for the workplace*. Where such speech involves a matter of *"public concern,"* the court will *balance* the speech rights of the employee and the government's interest as employer in promoting efficiency on the job. [*Connick v. Myers*]

i. **Non-policy-making role:** This means that if the worker has a relatively *non-public* and *non-policy-making* role, the court is *less likely* to find that the speech on a matter of public concern justified dismissal.

Example: P works as a clerk in the back office of the State Department of Motor Vehicles, and has no policy-making role and minimal contact with the public. P hears on the radio that someone has just tried and failed to assassinate the President. P remarks to a co-worker, "Good — I hope they get him next time." The D.M.V. attempts to fire P for this remarking, claiming that the remark indicates that P reflects poorly on the D.M.V.

P may not be fired, because his remark was on a matter of public concern, and his non-public and non-policy-making role prevented the remark from signalling any significant job unfitness that would outweigh his right to comment on such public matters. [Cf. *Rankin v. McPherson* (1987).]

ii. **Interferes with job:** Conversely, if the employee's speech, or the attitudes it reveals, *significantly* interfere with the employee's *performance* of her duties, this will make it far more likely that the employee may be discharged were disciplined for the speech, even if it was on a topic of public concern.

Example: P, a middle-school teacher for School, a public school, says at a public meeting, "Society shouldn't make it a crime for an adult to have sex with a minor over the age of 12 — these kinds of laws are archaic and reflect outmoded paternalistic ideas. I would have sex with my 13-year-old student if it weren't illegal." School fires P for this remark.

A court would likely conclude that the firing did not violate P's First Amendment rights. Even where First Amendment expression by a public employee is made on matters of public concern or policy, the remark can be grounds for dismissal if the content of the speech significantly interferes with the speaker's proper performance of his job, or indicates that the speaker has underlying attitudes that would interfere with job performance. Here, between the fact that the remark indicates a significant danger that P will sleep with a student, and the fact that P's ability to teach will likely be undermined by public perceptions of that danger, this standard is satisfied.

iii. **Not a matter of public concern:** Where the speech does *not* involve a matter of public concern, *Connick* and *Rankin*, *supra*, p. 91, do *not* apply, and the court gives great *deference* to the employer's judgment.

iv. **Must not be part of employee's job function:** Also, even the limited protection given to employee speech on matters of public concern doesn't apply where the speech occurs as *part of the employee's job functions* — here, the employee gets no First Amendment protection at all, no matter how important the issue on which the employee is speaking.

Example: P, a supervising lawyer in a District Attorney's Office (D), is called on to investigate whether an affidavit prepared by a deputy sheriff to obtain a search warrant was properly done. P writes a memo to his supervisor concluding that the affidavit was improperly done. The supervisor retaliates against him for what he says in the memo.

Held, for D. "[W]hen public employees make statements *pursuant to their official duties,* the employees are *not speaking as citizens* for First Amendment purposes, and *the Constitution does not insulate their communications from employer discipline."* Here, because P's investigation and the ensuing memorandum were part of his job responsibilities, D had the right to regulate the content and manner of P's speech. [*Garcetti v. Ceballos*]

X. SPECIAL PROBLEMS OF THE MEDIA

A. **The media (and its special problems):** Here is a brief review of some special problems related to the *media*:

1. **Prior restraint:** In general, the government will not be able to obtain a *prior restraint* against broadcasters or publishers (or for that matter against any other speaker). In other words, only in exceptionally rare circumstances may the government obtain an *injunction* against the printing or airing of a story, and the government will almost never be allowed to require that a publisher or broadcaster obtain a *permit* before it runs a story.

Example: The *New York Times* may not constitutionally be enjoined from publishing part of the Pentagon Papers, even though these government-prepared materials might contain information that is useful to our enemies or that would embarrass the U.S. [*N.Y. Times v. U.S.*]

a. **Gag order:** This means that a judge may generally not impose a *gag order* on the media ordering it not to disclose a certain fact about a pending trial.

i. **Participants:** But the judge may usually order the *participants* not to speak to the press. For instance, a state may prevent a lawyer from making any statement which would have a "substantial likelihood of materially prejudicing" a trial or other court proceeding. [*Gentile v. State Bar of Nevada*]

2. **Subpoenas by government:** The press does not get any special protection from government demands that the press *furnish information* which other citizens would have to furnish. In particular, if a reporter has information that is of interest to a *grand jury*, the reporter may be required by subpoena to disclose that information to the grand jury even though this would cause him to violate a promise of confidentiality to a source. [*Branzburg v. Hayes*] (But the state is always free to enact a "shield law" making such subpoenas illegal under some or all circumstances.)

3. **Right of access:** The press has never been held to have a general First Amendment *right of access* to information held by the government.

a. **No right to compel disclosure of government information:** Indeed, the Supreme Court has never squarely held that *any* person — whether a reporter or a private citizen — has a First Amendment right to cause government to release information in the government's possession.

   i. **Right to publish information held in private hands:** On the other hand, the media (and for that matter private citizens) generally *do* have the right to publish secret information that is in *private hands,* unless government is pursuing a compelling need (see *infra*, p. 93). And that's true even if the information originally came from government (as long as the media didn't commit wrongdoing in getting the information). So distinguish between (a) cases where government is refusing to disclose to the press secrets held by the government (no First Amendment problem); and (b) cases where government is trying to prevent the media from disclosing government secrets that have already come into the media's hands without media wrongdoing (potential First Amendment problem).

b. **Right to attend trials:** As we've just seen, the media does not have a general First Amendment right to information within government's possession. However, there seems to be one narrow exception to this no-right-of-access rule: the media (and the public) do have a constitutionally protected right to *attend criminal trials*. But this right is not absolute — the government can close the media (and the public) out of a trial if it shows that there is an "overriding" government interest being served by a closed trial, and that that interest cannot be served by less restrictive means. [*Richmond Newspapers v. Virginia*]

   i. **Showing rarely made:** But this showing will rarely be made, so that as a practical matter the press is usually entitled to attend a criminal trial.

   Example: A state statute automatically bars the press from hearing any trial testimony by a minor who was allegedly the victim of a sex crime. *Held*, the statute unduly interferes with the public's right of access to criminal trials. [*Globe Newspapers v. Sup. Ct.*]

   ii. **Other proceedings:** Probably the media also has a qualified constitutional right to attend other proceedings, like *civil trials* and *pre-trial proceedings*. [*Gannett Co. v. DePasquale*]

4. **Disclosure of confidential or illegally-obtained information:** Government may generally *not* prohibit the media from disclosing information that government believes ought to be *secret*. If a media member *lawfully* obtains information about a matter of public significance, government may punish disclosure of the information only if government has "a *need* of the *highest order*," which it will rarely be found to have. [*Smith v. Daily Mail*]

   Example: A broadcaster may not be held civilly liable for *publishing the name of a rape victim*, if the broadcaster learns the name from reading a publicly-filed indictment. [*Cox Broadcasting v. Cohn*]

   a. **Where publisher has acted illegally:** If the *publisher itself* has *acted illegally* in obtaining the information, then government *may make it a crime* to punish the information, no matter how newsworthy it is.

   Example: A newspaper reporter breaks into a private home to steal an audiotape, then publishes a transcript of the tape. The newspaper may constitutionally be punished for the publication.

   b. **Where private party has acted illegally but publisher has not:** On the other hand, the fact that the secret information was originally *obtained illegally* by a person *acting inde-*

pendently of the eventual publisher is *not* enough to allow publication to be made criminal, at least where the material has significant newsworthiness.

CHAPTER 11

FREEDOM OF RELIGION

I. INTRODUCTION

A. Two clauses: There are two quite distinct clauses in the First Amendment pertaining to religion.

1. **Establishment Clause:** First, we have the *Establishment* Clause. That clause prohibits any law "respecting an establishment of religion." The main purpose of the Establishment Clause is to prevent government from *endorsing* or *supporting* religion.

2. **Free Exercise:** The second clause is the *Free Exercise* Clause. That clause bars any law "prohibiting the free exercise of religion." The main purpose of the Free Exercise Clause is to prevent the government from *outlawing* or seriously *burdening* a person's pursuit of whatever religion (and whatever religious practices) he chooses.

B. Applicable to states: Both the Establishment and the Free Exercise Clauses by their terms only restrict legislative action by *Congress*. However, both clauses have been interpreted to apply also to the *states*, by means of the Fourteenth Amendment's Due Process Clause. Therefore, you don't have to worry whether the government action in question is federal or state — the same standards apply to each.

C. Conflict: Occasionally, the Establishment and Free Exercises Clauses seem to *conflict* on particular facts. That is, a religious group may be asking for some government benefit; if the benefit is given, there may be an Establishment Clause problem. Yet if the benefit is not given, this may be a burdening of religion. When the two clauses seem to conflict, the *Free Exercise* Clause dominates. In other words, if a particular benefit or accommodation to religion is arguably required by the Free Exercise Clause, then when government grants that accommodation or benefit it is not violating the Establishment Clause.

Example: A public university makes meeting rooms available to all sorts of student groups. If the university allows religious groups to use the room, there might be an Establishment Clause problem. But if it doesn't allow religious groups to use the rooms, while allowing non-religious groups to do so, there might be a Free Exercise Clause problem. Consequently, it will not be an Establishment Clause violation for the university to allow the religious groups to use the rooms.

II. THE ESTABLISHMENT CLAUSE

A. General rule: The overall purpose of the Establishment Clause is to *separate government from the practice of religion*. That is, the Clause attempts to keep the government from sponsoring religious observances, from preferring one religion over another, or even from preferring religious beliefs in general over non-religious beliefs.

1. **Some examples:** Here are some things that would clearly be forbidden by the Establishment clause:

   a. **Official church:** Congress cannot establish an "official religion of the United States." In fact, Congress probably couldn't even declare that "the American people believe in God," because the Establishment Clause means that government may not prefer or endorse religion over non-religion.

b. **Go to church:** The government cannot force people to worship. In fact, the state can't even intentionally *encourage* people to worship — for example, it cannot decide that it wants to promote church attendance, and then give people a special tax deduction that applies to church donations but not to other charitable donations. (But it could, as Congress does, give a *general* tax deduction for charitable contributions, and let contributions to churches be eligible. This would be allowable because the government is treating religion the same as non-religion, not preferring religion over non-religion.)

c. **Preference of one religion over another:** The government cannot intentionally *prefer one religion over another religion.* For instance, a state may not decide that since Christians are in the majority, it will allow tax deductions for contribution to Christian churches but not for contributions made, say, to synagogues.

d. **Participate:** Government may not actively *participate* in religious affairs, or allow religious organizations to have a special participation in government affairs. For instance, Congress probably could not constitutionally use public officials and public polling places to run an election to determine the next head of the American Presbyterian Church — this would be an undue governmental entanglement in religious affairs.

B. **Three-part test:** Government action that has some relationship to religion will violate the Establishment Clause unless it satisfies *all three parts* of the following test (known as the "*Lemon*" test, from *Lemon v. Kurtzman*):

[1] **Purpose:** First, the government action must have a *secular legislative purpose*. In other words, there must be some governmental purpose that has nothing to do with religion. (If there is both a religious and a non-religious purpose, then this prong is probably satisfied.)

Example: Alabama passes a statute saying, "Every public school student shall have the opportunity to engage in silent prayer or meditation for at least two minutes at the start of every school day." If there is evidence that the legislature was *motivated* solely by a desire to help students pray, then the statute will be struck down (and in fact such an Alabama statute was struck down. [*Wallace v. Jaffree*]) This is true even if many of the students who take advantage of the statute engage in non-religious meditation — if the sole purpose was to aid religion, that's enough to make the government action void.

[2] **Primary effect:** Second, the governmental action's principal or *primary effect* must *not be to advance* religion. (But *incidental effects* that help religion do not violate this prong.)

[3] **Entanglement:** Finally, the governmental action must not foster an *excessive governmental entanglement* with religion.

Example: Massachusetts lets a church veto the issuance of a liquor license to any premises located within 500 feet of the church. *Held*, this statute violates the Establishment Clause, because it entangles churches in the exercise of governmental powers. [*Larkin v. Grendel's Den*]

1. **Incidental benefit not fatal:** Government action that gives some *incidental benefit* to religion, but that is designed to benefit a *wide variety of parties* some of whom are religiously-oriented and others not, will typically *not run afoul* of the *Lemon v. Kurtzman* test.

Example: A state enacts a tuition-voucher plan, under which anyone who sends a child to a private school — parochial or secular — can receive money in partial reimbursement of the tuition cost. The state acts primarily to reimburse the parents of private-school students for the savings the public-school system has reaped from not having to educate those children, not out of any special desire to help parents of parochial-school students in particular. The plan would be held to meet all three prongs of the *Lemon* test, and thus not to constitute a violation of the Establishment Clause. [*Zelman v. Simmons-Harris*]

C. **Religion and the public schools:** If the government tries to introduce religion into the *public schools*, it is probably violating the Establishment Clause.

1. **Instruction:** Thus the government may, of course, not conduct religious instruction in the public schools. In fact, it can't even allow privately-employed religious teachers to conduct classes on the public schools' premises during school hours.

   a. **Accommodation:** However, it's probably allowable for the government to allow students to *leave school early* to attend religious instruction somewhere else. It's also probably acceptable for government to let religious groups have access to school facilities, as long as non-religious groups are given equal access. Remember our example of the university that lets all kinds of student groups, including religious groups, use meeting rooms — that's permissible.

2. **Prayer reading:** The official *reading of prayers* in the public schools will virtually always be unconstitutional. (See, e.g., *Engel v. Vitale.*) That is, it will almost always turn out to be the case that either the sole purpose, or the primary effect, of the prayer reading is to advance religion.

   a. **Moment of silence:** Even the setting aside of a *"moment of silence"* at the beginning of the school day will generally violate the Establishment Clause, since a moment-of-silence statute will usually turn out to have been solely motivated by the legislators' intent to advance religion, or will at least have the primary effect of advancing religion. (But this will always turn on the actual purpose and effect of the particular statute — there's no absolute *per se* rule against moments of silence.) [*Wallace v. Jaffree*]

   b. **Prayer reading at graduation:** Similarly, the school may not conduct a prayer as part of a *graduation ceremony*, at least where school officials can fairly be said to be *sponsoring the religious message.* [*Lee v. Weisman*]

   c. **Student-selected speakers don't solve problem:** The school can't easily get around prayer-reading problems by having the student body *elect a student speaker,* and then having that speaker decide whether to give a prayer. As long as the school's process can be reasonably viewed as supporting school prayer, the fact that a student-body election intervenes is irrelevant. [*Santa Fe Indep. Sch. Dist. v. Doe*]

3. **Curriculum:** The state may not design or modify the *curriculum* of its schools in order to further religion at the expense of non-religion, or to further one set of religious beliefs over others.

   Example: A state may not forbid the teaching of evolution. [*Epperson v. Ark.*] Similarly, it probably may not demand that "creationism" be taught in addition to evolution, since "creationism" is mainly a religious doctrine the teaching of which would have the primary effect of advancing religion. [*Edwards v. Aguillard*]

4. **Equal treatment of religion and non-religion:** But it's not a violation of the Establishment Clause for government to treat religion and non-religion *equally* in the schools (and government may in fact be *required* to do this because of free-speech principles).

   Example: If a public university funds non-religion-oriented student publications, it must fund an evangelical Christian publication on the same terms. [*Rosenberger v. Univ. of Virginia*]

D. **Sunday closing laws:** Laws requiring *merchants* to be *closed on Sundays* generally do *not* violate the Establishment Clause. The reason is that these "blue laws" have a primarily secular effect and purpose — they permit everyone (Christian, non-Christian and atheist alike) to have a uniform day of rest. [*McGowan v. Md.*]

E. Tax exemption for religious groups: *Tax laws* that *single out religious institutions* for an *exemption* from a generally-applicable tax typically *violate* the Establishment Clause, because they manifest a purpose (and probably also show an effect) of advancing religion. But broader tax laws that exempt, say, a *wide variety of non-profits* — including but not limited to religious organizations — probably *don't* violate the Establishment Clause. [*Texas Monthly, Inc. v. Bullock*]

F. Ceremonies and displays: Governmentally-sponsored *ceremonies* or *displays* may violate the Establishment Clause.

1. Ceremonies: Thus a *ceremony* put on by the government may not have the sole purpose or primary effect of advancing religion. (For instance, as noted above, the government may not normally conduct a prayer as part of a high school graduation ceremony.)

a. Long-standing tradition: However, if a particular ceremony has a *long historical tradition* going back to the time when the Constitution was enacted, then it will probably be allowable, especially outside of the public-school context.

Example: The practice of opening a session of the legislature with a prayer by the legislative chaplain dates back to colonial days, so presumably the authors of the Bill of Rights thought that it did not violate the Establishment Clause. Therefore, the practice will be upheld. [*Marsh v. Chambers*]

b. Incidental references: Similarly, the Establishment Clause probably is not violated when the ceremony has an *incidental reference* to God or to a religious theme.

Example: The Pledge of Allegiance, with the phrase "One nation, under God," is probably allowable.

2. Religious displays: Where a *display* with religious themes is either put on by the government, or put on by private groups using government property, there is a potential Establishment Clause problem. The problem usually arises where there is a "Christmas" display, "Easter" display, etc. Ask yourself this question: Would a reasonable observer seeing the display conclude that the government was *endorsing* religion? If so, there is a violation of the Establishment Clause.

a. Context: *Context* is very important. If there is one religious symbol, but it is surrounded by primarily-secular symbols, then the display would be taken as a whole and probably does not violate the Establishment Clause.

Example: For instance, if a nativity scene is surrounded by reindeer, Santa Claus, "Season's Greetings" banners, etc., then as a whole the display would seem to be primarily secular, and the nativity scene won't be a violation of the Establishment Clause. [*Lynch v. Donnelly*]. But if the nativity scene or other primarily-religious symbol stands by itself, then that display probably will have a primarily religious effect, and thus violate the Establishment Clause.

b. History: The *history* behind the display is also very important. The longer the display has been around without objection or controversy, the less likely it is to be an Establishment Clause violation.

Example: In Case 1, a display of the text of the Ten Commandments has existed for 40 years without objection, before the present suit, and was originally donated as part of an anti-juvenile-delinquency campaign. *Held*, no Establishment Clause violation. [*Van Orden v. Perry*] In Case 2, a display of the text of the Ten Commandments is recent, and has replaced two other recent displays that were from the beginning criticized on Establishment Clause grounds. *Held*, an Establishment Clause violation. [*McCreary County v. ACLU of Kentucky*]

G. Intentional preferences between denominations: The government may not intentionally *prefer one religion over another*, or one sect over another. That's true even if government thinks that it's merely trying to "accommodate" a particular religion.

Example: The New York legislature creates a special school district whose residents consist solely of members of a particular orthodox Jewish sect, the Satmar Hassidim. The purpose and effect of the special district is to let the Satmars get public funding for a public school in their village to educate their handicapped children. *Held*, the district violates the Establishment Clause, because it was created in a way that singled out the Satmars for a special preference not made available to other groups (and also because it amounted to a delegation of state authority to a group chosen according to a religious criterion). [*Bd. of Educ. of Kiryas Joel Village v. Grumet*]

1. **Unintended effect:** But a regulation that has the incidental unintended *effect* of helping one religion or sect more than another, or hurting one more than another, does not generally violate the Establishment Clause.

2. **Preference of religion over non-religion:** In theory, government can't even "accommodate" *religion generally*, by giving religion in general a preference over non-religion. But in practice, the Court is *less likely to object* to a special accommodation of religion generally than to an accommodation of a particular sect.

   Example: In a federal statute, the Religious Land Use and Institutionalized Persons Act (RLUIPA), the federal government orders prison officials to go out of their way to accommodate the religious needs of all prisoners (e.g., by giving them opportunities for group worship and the right to adhere to the dress mandates of their religion). *Held*, even though comparable accommodations are not given to similar needs/desires that are not mandated by religious belief, RLUIPA (at least on its face) does not violate the Establishment Clause. [*Cutter v. Wilkinson*]

H. Aid to religious schools: Whenever your fact pattern shows that the government is giving some sort of *financial aid* to religious schools, you must immediately think "Establishment Clause." And, of course, you must apply the three-part test.

1. **General principles:** In general, here are some things to look for when you analyze aid to religious schools:

   a. **Benefit to all students:** A government program that benefits *all students*, at public, private non-parochial and parochial schools alike, is much more likely to pass muster than aid which goes overwhelmingly to parochial-school students;

   b. **Colleges:** Aid to religious *colleges* is easier to justify than aid to high schools or, especially, elementary schools; and

   c. **Aid to parents:** Aid given to *parents* in a way that permits them to choose what school to use the aid at is more likely to be sustained than aid given directly to the *school.*

2. **Transportation:** Programs by which parents may have their children *transported* free to religious schools are probably constitutional, as long as the transport program also covers public and private non-parochial students. [*Everson v. Bd. of Ed.*]

3. **Textbooks and equipment:** Similarly, *textbooks* and *equipment* (e.g., computers) may be loaned to parochial school students as long as loans on the same basis are made to public school and pri-

vate non-parochial students. But only books and materials that are *strictly secular* may be used (e.g., Bibles can't be lent out). [*Bd. of Ed. v. Allen; Mitchell v. Helms*]

4. **Teachers:** The state *may* send *public school teachers* into parochial schools, even to teach basic academic subjects, as long as what's taught is free of: (1) religious content and (2) influence from the parochial school's administration. [*Agostini v. Felton*]

5. **Tuition vouchers:** The state may give *tuition vouchers* to parents to enable them to pay religious-school tuition, if the vouchers may also be used in non-religious private schools. That's true even if the tuition is used to cover the costs of educating the children in core religious doctrine, and even if the benefits overwhelmingly go to the parents of religious school students. [*Zelman v. Simmons-Harris*]

III. THE FREE EXERCISE CLAUSE

A. **Free Exercise generally:** The second clause relating to religion is the *Free Exercise* Clause. Under this clause, the government is barred from making any law "prohibiting the free exercise" of religion. The Free Exercise Clause prevents the government from getting in the way of people's ability to practice their religions.

1. **Conduct vs. belief:** The Free Exercise Clause of course prevents the government from unduly burdening a person's abstract "beliefs." (*Example:* Congress cannot ban the religion of voodooism merely because it disapproves of voodooism or thinks that voodooism is irrational.) But the Clause also relates to *conduct.*

a. **Non-religious objectives:** Free Exercise Clause problems most typically arise when government, acting in pursuit of *non-religious objectives*, either: (1) forbids or burdens conduct which happens to be *required* by someone's religious belief; or conversely, (2) compels or encourages conduct which happens to be *forbidden* by someone's religious beliefs.

Example (government forbids conduct dictated by belief): The military prohibits any soldier from wearing a hat (other than a regular military cap) while on duty. This order prevents orthodox Jewish soldiers from wearing yarmulkes, which their religion requires them to wear at all times. (On these facts, the Supreme Court held that the Jewish officer-plaintiffs had a free exercise right that was being burdened, but that this right was outweighed by the need to defer to the military's judgment that discipline and uniformity require the ban on all non-standard headgear. [*Goldman v. Weinberger*])

Example (government compels or encourages conduct forbidden by the belief): The state awards unemployment compensation only to jobless workers who make themselves available for work Monday through Saturday. This rule has a non-religious purpose (making sure that only those whose employment is truly involuntary collect). But the statute strongly encourages conduct that violates the religious beliefs of some persons (e.g., Seventh Day Adventists, for whom Saturday is the Sabbath). Therefore, the rule raises significant free exercise problems. (In fact, the statute was held to violate the Free Exercise Clause as applied to Seventh Day Adventists. [*Sherbert v. Verner*])

B. **Intentional vs. unintentional burdens:** The Free Exercise Clause prevents the government from unduly interfering with religion whether the government does so *intentionally* or *unintentionally.*

1. **Intent:** If the interference with religion is *intentional* on government's part, then the interference is subjected to the *most strict scrutiny*, and will virtually never survive.

Example 1: The Ps practice Santeria, a religion involving animal sacrifice. D (the local city council), motivated by the citizenry's dislike of this religion and of the sacrifices, outlaws all animal sacrifice (but exempts Kosher slaughter). *Held*, the Ps' free exercise rights have been violated. D has acted with the purpose of outlawing a practice precisely because the practice is motivated by religion, so D's act must be most strictly scrutinized. Because there is no compelling state objective here, and because any state objective that the state is pursuing (e.g., maintenance of public health) could be achieved by less discriminatory means, the law fails this strictest scrutiny. [*Church of the Lukumi Babalu Aye v. Hialeah*]

Example 2: Muni has a number of Christian churches, and has always permitted them to ring their bells, or play a recording of bells, to announce when a service is starting. Recently, an Islamic mosque opened up in town, catering to recent immigrants from the Middle East. The mosque plays a recorded "call to prayer" of a singer backed by an instrumentalist. This recording is no louder than the typical recorded bellringing sounds from the churches. After complaints by Christian citizens about the "loud and strange sounds coming from the mosque," the City Council amended its zoning regulation to forbid any public outdoor playing by any house of worship of a recording, except for "recordings of traditional church bells."

A court will strictly scrutinize the amended ordinance, because it's clear that the City Council acted to disfavor the exercise of a particular religion. The ordinance will not survive that strict scrutiny, because the Council could easily have pursued the objective of maintaining quiet by setting a decibel limit rather than forbidding a particular type of sound — in other words, the means chosen wasn't a "necessary" means of achieving that goal.

a. **Perhaps limited to "punishments":** However, this rule of strict scrutiny probably applies only to criminal or civil *"sanctions"* — in essence *punishments* or rules forbidding conduct — that are imposed for the purpose of disfavoring religious practices, not to government conduct that merely *withholds some generally-applicable benefit* so the benefit cannot be used in connection with a religiously-motivated activity.

Example: A state gives merit scholarships to college-bound student with a certain G.P.A., but excludes anyone who wants to use the scholarship to study for the ministry. *Held*, this exclusion doesn't violate the Free Exercise Clause, because it doesn't involve a criminal or civil sanction, merely a refusal by government to grant an affirmative benefit to subsidize an "essentially religious endeavor." [*Locke v. Davey*]

2. **Unintentional burden:** If government *unintentionally burdens* religion, the Free Exercise Clause is still applied. Here, however, the government action is not *per se* illegal. Instead, the Court traditionally uses a somewhat less stringent form of strict scrutiny. (But there are signs that the Court is cutting back on this strict scrutiny for unintentional burdens on religion. For instance, if the government makes certain conduct a *crime*, and this unintentionally burdens the exercise of religion, the Court does not use strict scrutiny, and instead uses "mere rationality" review. See "Generally-applicable laws," *infra*, p. 101.)

C. **Coercion required:** The Free Exercise Clause only gets triggered where government in some sense *"coerces"* an individual to do something (or not to do something) against the dictates of his religion. If the government takes an action that *unintentionally happens to make it harder for a person to practice his religion* — but without coercing him into taking or not taking some action as an individual — the Free Exercise Clause *does not apply.*

Example: The federal government, without intending to affect any religious practice, wants to build a road. The effect will be to destroy Native American ritual grounds.

Held, there is no impairment of free exercise rights, because the Native American plaintiffs are not being coerced into doing or not doing anything — external reality is simply being changed in a way that makes it harder for them to practice their religion. (But if government *forbade* the Native Americans from using existing grounds to pray on, this *might* conceivably be a violation, because the Native Americans would be coerced into not taking some action of their own.) [*Lyng v. Northwest Indian Cemetery Ass'n*]

D. Denial of benefits: One way the government may be found to have interfered with a person's free exercise of religion is if the government *denies the person a benefit* solely because of that person's religious beliefs or practices.

Example: A state may not forbid practicing members of the clergy from holding elective state office, because this imposes a burden on the exercise of a religious belief. [*McDaniel v. Paty*]

E. Generally-applicable laws: The single most important thing to remember about the Free Exercise Clause as tested on the MBE is this:

A valid and neutral *generally applicable law* is *automatically enforceable*, regardless of how much *burden it causes* to an individual's religious beliefs (assuming that the government did not *intend* to disadvantage a particular religion when it enacted its law), as long as the government is *advancing important public interests.* [*Employment Div. v. Smith*]

1. **Criminal prohibitions:** This rule applies to *criminal prohibitions* — a *generally-applicable, nondiscriminatory criminal prohibition* is *enforceable* even as against *a person whose religious expression is burdened by it,* as long as the prohibition *directly advances important governmental interests.*

   Example: Oregon makes it a crime to possess the drug peyote. An Indian tribe uses peyote as a central part of their religious rites. *Held*, Oregon need not give an exemption from its ban for the tribe. As long as the ban is generally applicable, and not motivated by a governmental desire to affect religion, the law is enforceable against the tribe. [*Employment Div. v. Smith*]

2. **No serious impairment required:** Also, even where no criminal prohibition is involved, government does *not* have to tolerate a *serious impairment* of some *important* governmental goal — here, no exemption needs to be given, because strict scrutiny is satisfied.

   Example: A religiously-affiliated university honestly believes that its religion bars African Americans and whites from studying together. Government need not tolerate interference with its compelling goal of eliminating racial discrimination, so government does not need to exempt the university from anti-discrimination laws.

3. **No serious impairment involved:** On the other hand, if no criminal prohibition is involved, and the granting of an exemption on account of religion would *not impair any important governmental interest,* then an exemption probably *is* required by the Free Exercise Clause.

   Example: A public high school routinely lets students make up missed tests when the student is ill or has a family emergency. However, the school refuses to allow a student to make up a test when the student missed school because of a religious holiday. A court would likely hold that (1) the availability of a make-up test for absences caused by illness and family emergency demonstrates that no major governmental interest is compromised by such tests; and (2) the Free Exercise clause therefore requires the school to allow the student to make up the exam.

F. Conscientious objection: Probably Congress *must* (as it does) give an exemption for military service for *conscientious objectors* (i.e., those who believe that all war is evil).

1. **Selective c.o.'s:** But Congress need not give an exemption to "selective" c.o.'s (i.e., those who do not believe that all war is evil, but who believe that the particular war in which they are being asked to fight is evil). [*Gillette v. U.S.*]

G. **Public health:** Government may have to sacrifice its interest in the *health* of its citizenry, if individuals' religious dictates so require.

1. **Competent adult:** Where the case involves a *competent adult*, and only that adult's own health is at stake, government may probably not force treatment on the individual over his religious objection.

   Example: A state probably can't force a Jehovah's Witness to accept a blood transfusion or other life-saving medical care over that person's religious objections.

2. **Child:** However, where the patient is a *child* whose parents object on religious grounds, the state may probably compel the treatment.

3. **Danger to others:** Also, if the case involves not only a health danger to the person asserting a religious belief, but also a health danger to *others*, then government probably does not have to give an exemption.

   Example: P may be forced to undergo a vaccination over his religious objections. [*Jacobsen v. Mass.*]

H. **What constitutes a religious belief:** Only *bona fide* "religious beliefs" are protected by the Free Exercise Clause. But "religious beliefs" are defined very *broadly*.

1. **Non-theistic:** For instance, *non-theistic* beliefs are protected. That is, the belief need not recognize the existence of a supreme being.

   Example: Public officials cannot be forced to take an oath in which they say that they believe that God exists. [*Torcaso v. Watkins*]

2. **Unorganized religions:** Similarly, *unorganized* or obscure religions get the same protection as the major religions. In fact, even if a person's religious beliefs are followed *only by him*, he's still entitled to free exercise protection.

3. **Sincerity:** A court will not sustain a free exercise claim unless it is convinced that the religious belief is *"genuine"* or *"sincere."* (The fact that the belief or practice has been observed by a religious group for a long period of time may be considered in measuring sincerity. But the converse — absence of a long-standing practice — does not mean that the belief is insincere.)

   a. **Unreasonableness:** The court will *not* consider whether the belief is "true" or *"reasonable."* Even a very "unreasonable" belief (that is, a belief that most people might consider unreasonable) is not deprived of protection, so long as it is *genuine*. [*U.S. v. Ballard*]

   Example: The practice of voodoo, including sticking pins into dolls representing one's enemies, might be considered by most of us to be "unreasonable." But as long as such a practice is part of a person's genuine set of beliefs and religious practices, it will not be deprived of protection merely because most find it unreasonable.

CHAPTER 12
JUSTICIABILITY

I. JUSTICIABILITY GENERALLY

A. List: In order for a case to be heard by the federal courts, the plaintiff must get past a series of procedural obstacles which we collectively call requirements for *"justiciability"*:

[1] the case must not require the giving of an *advisory opinion*;

[2] the plaintiff must have *standing*;

[3] the case must not be *moot*;

[4] the case must be *ripe* for decision; and

[5] the case must not involve a non-justiciable *political question*.

II. ADVISORY OPINIONS

A. Constitutional "case or controversy" requirement: Article III, Sec. 2, of the Constitution gives the federal courts jurisdiction only over "cases" and "controversies." The federal courts are therefore prevented from issuing opinions on *abstract* or *hypothetical* questions. This means that the federal courts may not give *"advisory opinions."* In other words, the federal courts may not render opinions which answer a legal question when no party is before the court who has suffered or faces specific injury.

Example: Suppose that both houses of Congress approve a bill, but the President has doubts about the bill's constitutionality. The President may *not* go to a federal court and ask the federal court whether the bill is constitutional, so that he may decide whether to veto it. If the federal court were to give its opinion about whether the bill was constitutional, at a time when no party who had been or might soon be injured by the unconstitutionality was before the court, this would be an "advisory opinion" that would violate the constitutional "case or controversy" requirement.

1. Declaratory judgments sometimes allowed: But *declaratory judgments* are sometimes allowed, and are not forbidden by the rule against advisory opinions. A declaratory judgment is a judicial decision in which the court is not requested to award damages or an injunction, but is instead requested to state what the legal effect would be of proposed conduct by one or both of the parties.

a. Requirements: But the plaintiff is not entitled to get a declaratory judgment on just any question about what the legal consequence of the particular conduct would be. If the declaratory judgment action raises only questions that are very *hypothetical* or *abstract*, the federal court is likely to conclude that what's sought here is an illegal advisory opinion, because no specific, concrete controversy exists.

III. STANDING

A. Function of a standing requirement: The federal courts may hear a case only when the plaintiff has *"standing"* to assert his claim. This means that the plaintiff must have a significant *stake* in the controversy.

Example: Suppose that during the Vietnam War, P, a federal taxpayer, becomes convinced that, since Congress has never formally declared war, P's tax dollars are being used to support an unconstitutional war. If P were to sue the federal government in federal court to have the war effort enjoined on this ground, the court would not hear his claim — he would be found to lack "standing," since (as we'll see in detail later) a person whose only connection with the controversy is that he is a taxpayer will almost never be deemed to have standing to claim that tax dollars are being used illegally.

B. Requirement of "injury in fact": The key concept behind the law of standing is simple: the litigant must show that he has suffered an *"injury in fact."* At its broadest level, the standing requirement means that the plaintiff must show that *he has himself been injured* in some way by the conduct that he complains of.

C. Taxpayer and citizen suits: Here is the single most important context in which standing problems get tested on the MBE: suits that are brought by federal *"citizens"* or *"taxpayers"* arguing that their general rights as citizens or taxpayers are violated by governmental action.

1. **Taxpayer suits:** Suppose that the plaintiff contends that: (1) he is a federal *taxpayer*; and (2) his tax dollars are being spent by the government in some illegal way. May the plaintiff pursue this suit in federal court? In general, the answer will be *"no."* The fact that a person's federal taxes are used to fund an unconstitutional or illegal government program is simply not a sufficient connection with the governmental action to confer standing on the plaintiff. [*Frothingham v. Mellon*]

   a. **One exception:** There is one very narrow exception: a federal taxpayer has standing to sue to overturn a congressionally-funded *tax or spending program* that violates the *Establishment Clause*. [*Flast v. Cohen*]

   b. **State taxpayers:** A *state* taxpayer, like a federal taxpayer, does *not* have federal-court standing to litigate the legality of the state's expenditures. [*DaimlerChrysler Corp. v. Cuno*]

   c. **Municipal taxpayer:** But a *municipal* taxpayer definitely *does* have standing to litigate the legality of his city's expenditures.

   d. **Not a rule of state-court standing:** At the risk of stating the obvious, notice that the taxpayer-suit rules (like all the rules we're discussing here) are limits on *federal*-court, *not state-court,* standing. The MBE examiners will sometimes give you a state-court suit, and try to trick you into thinking that the federal-court standing limitations apply.

2. **Citizen suits:** Suppose now that plaintiff argues that he is a federal *"citizen,"* and that as such he has the right to have his government act in accordance with the Constitution. Assume that P has no direct connection with the governmental act he's complaining about (he's merely claiming that, like every other citizen, he has the right to have the federal government obey the Constitution). In this "citizen suit" situation, P will *not have standing*. The Court has always held that one federal citizen's interest in lawful government is no different from the interest of any other citizen, and that an individual litigant relying on citizenship has not shown the *"individualized"* injury-in-fact that is required for standing.

D. Cases not based on taxpayer or citizen status: Now suppose that the plaintiff is not arguing that his standing derives from his status as citizen or taxpayer. In other words, we're now talking about the vast bulk of ordinary law suits.

1. **Three requirements:** Here, there are *three standing requirements* that the plaintiff must meet:

   [a] he must show that he has suffered (or is likely to suffer) an *"injury in fact"*;

   [b] the injury he is suffering must be *concrete* and *"individuated"*; and

   [c] the action being challenged must be the *"cause in fact"* of the injury.

2. **"Injury in fact":** The plaintiff must show that he either *has suffered*, or *will probably suffer*, some concrete *"injury in fact."*

   a. **Non-economic harm:** This "injury in fact" requirement is pretty loosely applied. For instance, the harm does not have to be *economic* in nature.

      Example: A group of people who use a national forest claim that the construction of a recreation area in the forest will violate federal laws. To get standing, the plaintiffs point to the injury to their "esthetic and environmental well-being" that would result from the construction. *Held*, this esthetic and environmental injury satisfies the "injury in fact" requirement, even though the harm is non-economic and in fact very intangible. [*Sierra Club v. Morton*]

   b. **Imminent harm:** If P has not *already* suffered the injury in fact, he must show that the future injury is not only probable but *"concrete"* and *"imminent."* In other words, a vague sort of harm that may come about in the indefinite future will not suffice.

      Example: The Ps challenge a federal regulatory action that they say will endanger certain species abroad. The Ps say that they have in the past, and will in the future, travel abroad to visit the habitats of these species. *Held*, the Ps lack standing, because the lack of specific information about their future plans means the harm to them is not sufficiently concrete or imminent. [*Lujan v. Defenders of Wildlife*]

      i. **P hasn't made relevant decision:** One way the requirement of concrete and imminent harm is often tested on the MBE is by a fact pattern in which P would clearly be harmed if she took a particular action, but she has *not decided yet* whether to take that action — here, the fact that P may never in fact take the action probably means that the "injury in fact" requirement has not been met, so there is no Article III case or controversy. Cases in which P challenges some sort of ballot restriction, but has not yet decided whether to be a candidate, fall into this category.

         Example: P sues in federal court on a claim that a particular ballot requirement imposed by City for City Council candidates violates his substantive due process right as a potential candidate. P has not yet decided whether to run for Council in the next election, which is almost two years away. A court would likely decide that P does not yet meet the "injury in fact" requirement, because he may never decide to run.

3. **Individuated harm:** The harm that has been or will be suffered by the plaintiff has to be *"individuated."* That is, it can't be the same harm as suffered by every citizen, or every taxpayer.

   a. **Large number:** But the harm may still be found to be "individuated" even though there are a *large number* of people suffering the harm.

      i. **Same harm:** But remember that if the harm complained of by the plaintiff is truly the same harm as suffered by every citizen or every taxpayer in the country, the harm will not be sufficiently "individuated," and the plaintiffs won't have standing.

b. **Organizations and associations:** What about organizations and associations — does the organization itself have to suffer the harm, or can it merely assert that its *members* will suffer or have suffered the required harm? In general, the answer is that organizations and associations will be able to sue on behalf of their members. However:

(1) the members have to be people who would have *standing in their own right* (so that an organization of citizens or taxpayers could not complain of harm that is suffered by all citizens or taxpayers);

(2) the interests being asserted by the organization in the lawsuit must be *related to the organization's purpose* (so that an environmental group could probably not try to pursue its members' interests in, say, an effective criminal justice system); and

(3) the case cannot be one which requires the *participation of individual members.*

[*Hunt v. Wash. Apple Advt'g. Comm.*] But these three requirements are pretty liberally interpreted (i.e., they're pretty *easy to satisfy*).

4. **Causation:** Finally, the action that the plaintiff is complaining about must be the *"cause in fact"* of his injury. Actually, this causation requirement breaks down into two sub-requirements:

(1) P has to show that the challenged action was a *"but for"* cause of his injury, that is, that the injury would not have occurred unless the challenged action had taken place; and

(2) More subtly, P must show that a favorable decision in the suit will probably *redress the injury* to him.

Example: The bar of state Red (a governmental agency) has enacted a rule that no applicant to the Red bar may be admitted unless the applicant proves that, in addition to passing the bar exam, he graduated from an ABA-approved law school. Applicant, who has passed the Red bar, submits an application without the required proof of graduation from an ABA-approved law school (which he cannot submit because he graduated from a law school located in and accredited by state Blue but not accredited by the ABA). The agency summarily denies the application, without offering Applicant a live hearing at which he can call witnesses or cross-examine agency officials. Applicant asserts that the agency's refusal to grant him a live judicial-type hearing violates his right to procedural due process.

A court would almost certainly dismiss the suit on the standing-related grounds that the lack of the requested live hearing was not a but-for cause of the underlying injury to Applicant, namely, his failure to be admitted to the bar. The court would likely reason that: (1) the substantive rule that persons who have not graduated from an ABA-approved law school may not be admitted is itself not a violation of substantive due process (it is rationally related to a legitimate objective of maintaining minimum standards for legal education); and (2) since the substantive rule is constitutional, the denial of a live hearing to Applicant *did not make any difference to the outcome* — that is, providing a live hearing could not have "redressed the injury," i.e., changed the outcome by leading to Applicant's admission.

5. **Claimed violation need not be directed at P:** A plaintiff may well have standing even though the challenged governmental action is not in any way *directed at P*. In other words, if P has been, in a practical sense, injured by the unintended *consequences* of a governmental action, the fact that the action was intended by government solely to affect *some third person* rather than P won't prevent P from having standing.

Example: The FCC operates under a statute providing that no person may own a newspaper and a television station in the same city. The FCC licenses X, a newspaper owner in Metro City, to operate a new TV station in Metro. P, the owner of a different TV station in Metro, sues the FCC to have the license to X ruled a violation of the federal statute. P has standing, since he will suffer economic damage as a result of the claimed violation of the statute (extra competition). Therefore, the fact that the FCC wasn't trying to affect him in any way is irrelevant to the standing issue.

E. Third-party standing: One of the key functions of the standing doctrine is that this is how courts apply the general rule that a litigant normally may *not assert the constitutional rights of persons not before the court.*

Example: Zoning laws enacted by the city of Penfield, N.Y., intentionally exclude the building of low-income housing. The Ps are residents of nearby Rochester, who claim that because Penfield has refused to allow low- and middle-income housing, the taxes of these Rochester residents have risen, since Rochester has to subsidize or build more low-income housing than it would have to build than had Penfield not practiced exclusionary zoning.

Held, these Rochester residents lack standing. It is true that their higher taxes are an "injury in fact" to them. But Penfield's zoning laws do not apply to these Rochester residents, and therefore do not violate *their* rights. And the Rochester residents may not claim that the rights of *other people not before the court* have been violated (e.g., people who would have moved to Penfield had exclusionary zoning not been practiced). [*Warth v. Seldin*]

1. Exceptions: Here are two important clarifications or exceptions to the general rule that a litigant will not normally be entitled to assert the rights of third parties who are not before the court:

a. Associations: One exception is that an *association* will normally be allowed to raise the rights of its *members*. For instance, if a group of people would be injured by damage to the air they breathe and the water they drink, an organization of which they are members (e.g., the Sierra Club) would typically be allowed to sue on their behalf.

b. Overbreadth: Another sort of exception to the rule against third-party standing is the *First Amendment overbreadth* doctrine, which we covered earlier in our discussion of freedom of expression (see *supra*, p. 75). Remember that the basic idea behind overbreadth is that even where a statute could constitutionally be applied to the plaintiff's conduct, if he can show that the statute would unconstitutionally restrict the expression of *some other person not before the court,* the court may hear the lawsuit and strike down the statute. Courts allow overbreadth in the *First Amendment area* but not elsewhere because statutes that purport to restrict expression in an overbroad manner will have a *"chilling effect"* on citizens' general willingness to exercise their freedom of speech.

IV. MOOTNESS

A. General rule: A case may not be heard by the federal courts if it is *"moot."* A case is moot if it raised a live controversy at the time the complaint was filed, but *events occurring after the filing* have deprived the litigant of an ongoing stake in the controversy.

Example: P sues D, a state university, claiming that the university's law school admissions program is racially discriminatory. P is permitted to attend the law school while the case is being litigated. By the time the case arrives at the Supreme Court for review, P is in his final year of law school, and the university says that he will be allowed to graduate regardless of how the case is decided. *Held*, the case is moot. Therefore, the appeal will not be decided. [*DeFunis v. Odegaard*]

1. Constitutional basis for: The rule that the federal courts may not decide "moot" cases is *required* by the Constitution. That is, deciding a case when the parties no longer have a live controversy would amount to issuing an advisory opinion, in violation of Article III's "case or controversy" requirement.

B. Exceptions: Nonetheless, the courts recognize a few situations where a case that would appear to be "moot" will nonetheless be heard.

1. **"Capable of repetition, yet evading review":** For instance, a case will not be treated as moot if the issue it raises is *"capable of repetition, yet evading review."* This "capable of repetition, yet evading review" doctrine takes care of situations in which, if the case were to be declared moot, a *different person* might be injured in the *same way* by the same defendant, and his claim, too, would become moot before review could be had.

   Example: P, a pregnant woman, attacks the constitutionality of Texas' anti-abortion law. She brings the suit as a class action, in which she is the named plaintiff and other pregnant women who want abortions are unnamed members. By the time the case reaches the Supreme Court, P is no longer pregnant.

   Held, the case should not be dismissed as moot. A pregnancy will almost always be over before the usual appellate process is complete. Therefore, if the Court insisted that the named plaintiff who starts the suit must still be pregnant by the time the suit gets to the Supreme Court, no plaintiff could ever get to that Court. So the constitutionality of the Texas anti-abortion law is "capable of repetition, yet evading review." [*Roe v. Wade*]

2. **Voluntary cessation by defendant:** The case will generally not be treated as moot if the defendant *voluntarily ceases* the conduct that the plaintiff is complaining about.

   a. **Injunction:** So if the plaintiff is seeking an *injunction*, the defendant can't usually get the case dismissed on mootness grounds merely by saying that he has *voluntarily stopped* the conduct that the plaintiff is trying to get an injunction against — unless the defendant shows that there is *no strong likelihood* that he will return to his old ways (i.e., that he will *resume* the challenged conduct), the court will let the action go forward.

      i. **No reasonable likelihood of revival of conduct:** On the other hand, in an injunction proceeding, if the defendant *can* show that there is no strong likelihood that the defendant will resume the challenged conduct — for instance, because the defendant's *underlying motive for that conduct has disappeared* — then the court will treat the injunction request as moot.

      Example: A federal judge issues a "gag order" in a criminal case against X, barring any participant in the trial from discussing the case with any member of the media while the case is going on. P, a newspaper, sues for an injunction against the continuation of the gag order, on the grounds that it is a violation of the paper's First Amendment rights. Before the case comes to trial, X pleads guilty, is sentenced, and gives up any right to appeal. A court would likely dismiss the case as moot, because the subject matter of the suit (the gag order) has ceased to exist, and it is very unlikely to be revived.

3. **Collateral consequences:** Finally, a case will not be moot even if it is mostly decided, if there are still *collateral consequences* that might be adverse to the defendant. For instance, suppose that a criminal defendant has already served his sentence by the time his attack on the constitutionality of his conviction comes before the federal court. The case will not be moot, because there will probably be future collateral consequences to the defendant from his conviction (e.g., he will lose the right to vote, his reputation or employability will be damaged, etc.).

V. RIPENESS

A. Ripeness problem generally: You can think of the problem of ripeness as being the opposite of mootness. A case is moot, as we've just seen, because it *no longer* involves an actual controversy. By contrast, a case is not yet ripe (and therefore not yet decidable by a federal court) if it has *not yet become sufficiently concrete* to be easily adjudicated.

Example: The federal Hatch Act prohibits federal executive-branch employees from getting involved in "political management or ... political campaigns." The plaintiffs are federal civil servants who want to attack the constitutionality of the Hatch Act. The plaintiffs claim that they want to engage in prohibited political activities. But they concede that they have not yet engaged in such activities.

Held, the plaintiffs' claims are not yet ripe. The problem is not that the Ps have not yet violated the statute. Rather, the problem is that the plaintiffs have not been adequately specific about the *precise acts* that they wish to carry out. (If the Ps would specify in detail what they want to do, their suit might not be unripe even though they haven't yet violated the act.) [*United Public Workers v. Mitchell*]

1. **Remedy is dismissal:** When the federal court determines that the action is unripe, it must *dismiss the action entirely*. It may *not* merely *stay* (suspend) the action until such time as the action becomes ripe. So a new action will have to be filed when/if the action becomes ripe.

B. Uncertain enforcement of criminal statute: One common ripeness problem arises where the plaintiff attacks the constitutionality of a statute and says that he has violated the statute, but it is clear that the statute is *rarely enforced* and probably will not be enforced in this particular situation. Here, the rules are pretty blurry — suffice it to say that if the court believes that it is *very unlikely* that the statute will be enforced against the plaintiff either for the activity he has already done or similar activity he is likely to do in the future, the court will probably treat the case as being not ripe.

Example: Connecticut forbids the distribution of contraceptives. Two married couples and a physician challenge the law's constitutionality, and allege that they have violated the law. *Held*, the case is not ripe, because the statute has been on the books for 80 years with only one reported prosecution, so there does not exist the required "clear" threat that the plaintiffs will be prosecuted. [*Poe v. Ullman*]

C. Reasonable probability of harm required: For a case to be ripe, it is not necessary that the litigant have *already suffered* harm. It will be enough that there is a *reasonable probability* of harm.

1. **Specificity required:** However, the anticipated harm has to be fairly *specific*, both as to the type of harm, and as to *when and how* it will occur. Where it is far from clear when the harm will occur (or whether it will occur at all), the court is likely to dismiss the matter as unripe.

Example: P is a student at a state-owned university. When P is a freshman, the university announces that, contrary to previous policy in which tuition never rose at faster than a 3% annual rate, the university might at some point in the next several years increase tuition by more than 5 percent annually. The university also announces that the increase will be applicable to those already attending the school, and that the increase may be made effective on less than 90 days notice. P sues for a declaration that such an increase would violate his Contract Clause rights in that when the University accepted him it impliedly contracted not to vary its tuition-increase policies from past practices.

A court would probably hold that the case is not ripe — it is not sufficiently clear when or whether the anticipated harm to P will occur. For instance, the university may decide not to increase rates more than 3% at all while P is at the school, or it may do this so late in P's school career that no substantial damage to him occurs.

VI. THE ELEVENTH AMENDMENT AND SUITS AGAINST THE STATES

A. The Eleventh Amendment generally: The *Eleventh Amendment* specifically bars any federal suit "against any one of the *states* by citizens of another state, or by citizens or subjects of any foreign state."

1. **Damage suits against states:** The Eleventh Amendment has been held to bar most types of *damage suits* against a state.

   a. **Plaintiff not a citizen of defendant state:** By its own terms, the Amendment clearly applies to suits against a state brought by citizens of a *different state* or by foreigners.

   Example: A citizen of Missouri may not bring a damage suit against the state of Illinois. Nor may a British subject bring a damage suit against the state of Illinois.

   b. **Suit by citizen of defendant state:** But the Eleventh Amendment has been *interpreted* to apply *also* to bar a damage suit where the plaintiff is a *citizen of the defendant state*. [*Hans v. Louisiana*]

   Example: Suppose P is an employee of the Delmarva state legislature and a Delmarva citizen. He is then fired, in apparent violation of his employment contract. P brings a suit for contract damages against Delmarva in federal court. This suit would be a violation of the Eleventh Amendment, as interpreted by the Supreme Court.

2. **Suits by states or federal government:** The Eleventh Amendment does *not* bar federal suits brought by *one state* against another state, or by the *federal government* against a state.

3. **No counties or cities protected:** Only the *state itself*, not its *subdivisions*, such as *counties* or *cities*, is protected by the Eleventh Amendment.

   Example: P, a county worker, is fired. He brings a federal suit for contract damages against the county. Since the suit is not against the state *per se*, the Eleventh Amendment does not apply, even though the county is in essence a subdivision of the state.

4. **No bar against injunctions:** The Eleventh Amendment essentially bars only suits for *damages*. That is, it does not bar most suits for *injunctions*. For instance, if a private litigant sues a state official to enjoin him from taking acts which would violate the plaintiff's *constitutional* or *federal-law* rights, the Eleventh Amendment does not apply and the suit may proceed. [*Ex parte Young*]

5. **No bar against state-court suits:** The Eleventh Amendment does not bar suits against states that *occur in state court,* only (certain) suits occurring in federal court. The MBE examiners will sometimes try to trick you into thinking that the Amendment can apply in a suit brought against a state in state court.

   a. **Sovereign immunity:** But beware — principles of *state sovereign immunity*, apart from the Eleventh Amendment, *do* prevent the federal government from authorizing money-damage-suits against states to be brought in state courts. See *infra*, p. 111.

6. **Congress can't override:** *Congress* generally *can't change* the "no federal-court suits against the states" principle behind the Eleventh Amendment, even if it wants to and expressly says it's doing so. [*Seminole Tribe v. Florida*]

Example: Congress passes a statute saying any state *can* be sued in federal court by private citizens for violating, say, federal patent or environmental laws. This statute won't have any effect — a federal court still can't hear a private suit against a state for damages for violating the federal law. [*Florida Prepaid v. Coll. Sav. Bank*]

a. **Commerce regulation:** So even if Commerce purports to act under its power to regulate commerce, it cannot use that power to subject a state to federal damage suits. [*Seminole Tribe of Florida v. Florida*]

b. **Exception for remedial powers:** But there's an important *exception* — if Congress is acting properly pursuant to its *remedial powers* under the Thirteenth, Fourteenth or Fifteenth Amendments (p. 70 *supra*), it may *abrogate* the states' Eleventh Amendment immunity. The MBE examiners sometimes seize on this one tricky exception to the Eleventh Amendment.

Example: Congress passes a statute allowing anyone fired from his job as a state employee on the grounds of his race or ethnicity to sue the state for damages. P, alleging that he was fired by the State of Blue on account of his race, sues Blue for damages in federal court. P's suit will be allowed to go forward notwithstanding the Eleventh Amendment, because P's right to sue was given by Congress pursuant to its power to enforce the Fourteenth Amendment, and in this limited situation Congress is permitted to abrogate the state's Eleventh Amendment immunity.

B. **Sovereign immunity of states:** The states have a constitutionally-guaranteed *sovereign immunity* from certain proceedings brought by private parties.

1. **Suit in states' own courts:** Thus the states have constitutional sovereign immunity from private damage suits brought against the state in the *state's own courts.* This is true even if the suit is based on a *congressionally-granted federal right.*

Example: Congress passes a valid statute saying that state employees must receive premium pay for overtime just as private-sector employees do. Employees of Maine sue the state in Maine courts on this right. *Held*, the Constitution's structure incorporates the doctrine of sovereign immunity, and that doctrine allows Maine to avoid hearing the employees' suit, even if Congress has expressly said that the states must hear such suits. [*Alden v. Maine*]

2. **Proceeding before federal administrative agency:** Similarly, the states have sovereign immunity from being required to respond to a private complaint before a *federal administrative agency*. [*Federal Maritime Comm. v. So. Car. St. Ports Auth.*]

VII. POLITICAL QUESTIONS

A. **The doctrine generally:** The final aspect of justiciability is the requirement is that the case not involve the decision of a *"political question."* This rule is even more vague than the other justiciability rules we've talked about already. The doctrine does *not* mean that federal courts will not decide a case that involves politics. It doesn't even mean that courts will refuse to decide cases where political issues are right at the heart of the controversy. Instead, the court will decline to hear a case on political question grounds only if it thinks that the doctrine of *separation of powers* requires this, or if it thinks that deciding the case would be unwise as a policy matter.

1. **Two of the factors used:** Two of the factors that seem to be very important in whether a case will be found to involve a non-justiciable political question are:

a. **Commitment to another branch:** First, the fact that the case presents an issue which has been committed by the Constitution to *another branch of the federal government*, i.e., to Congress or to the President instead of the courts.

b. **Lack of standards:** Second, the fact that there are no manageable *standards* by which a court could resolve the issue.

B. "Commitment to other branches" strand: The courts will refuse to decide a case on political-question grounds if the case raises an issue the determination of which is clearly committed by the Constitution to *another branch of the federal government.*

1. **Impeachment:** This "commitment to another branch" rationale has been used in cases about *impeachment* procedures.

Example: D, a federal judge, claims that the Senate has used improper procedures in convicting him following his impeachment, because the case was heard before a committee of Senators rather than the full Senate (though the full Senate voted, after receiving a transcript of the committee proceedings). D claims that this violates the Impeachment Clause, which says that "the Senate shall have sole Power to try all Impeachments." *Held*, the case presents a nonjusticiable political question, because the Constitution has given the Senate, not the courts, the power to decide what constitutes a "trial." [*Nixon v. U.S.*]

a. **Other impeachment issues:** The same principle probably applies to *all* aspects of the impeachment process. Thus if the House voted to impeach the President and the Senate voted to convict, the Supreme Court would probably refuse to review either of these decisions on "commitment to other branches" political-question grounds (so that if the President tried to get the Supreme Court to hear his argument that the crime for which he was impeached and convicted was not within the constitutionally-defined category of "high crimes and misdemeanors," the Court would probably refuse to consider the merits of this argument).

2. **Ratification of amendments:** Another type of case that will be nonjusticiable because committed to another branch of government is where the issue is *whether a particular state has ratified a proposed constitutional amendment.* The Court has held that under Article V (governing ratification of amendments), questions about whether a particular state has ratified an amendment are solely the province of Congress, not the federal judiciary. [*Coleman v. Miller*]

3. **Rare:** Outside of the impeachment and ratification-of-amendments scenarios, it is quite rare for a case to be declined on the grounds that it involves a question committed to some other branch of government.

C. "Lack of judicially manageable standards": The second major factor that may lead the court to decide that there is a non-justiciable political question, is that there are no *manageable standards* by which the courts can resolve the issue.

Example: Article IV, Sec. 4 provides that "the United States shall guarantee to every state in this union a republican form of government." Some unhappy Rhode Island citizens stage a rebellion. Ultimately, various Rhode Islanders ask the federal courts to decide which of two competing factions is the lawful government of the state.

Held, the Court cannot decide this question, because it presents a political question. There are no criteria by which a court could determine whether a particular "government" was "Republican." [*Luther v. Borden*]

D. Reapportionment: Let's now look in some detail at the federal cases on *legislative reapportionment.*

1. **One person, one vote rule:** The landmark case of *Baker v. Carr,* and cases following it, establish the so-called *"one person, one vote"* principle: any governmental body, whether it's a federal one (like congressional districts) or a state one (like a state legislature) must be apportioned on a *population* basis, so that *all voters have essentially the same voting power.* If a governmental electoral scheme does not comply with this "one person, one vote" principle, it violates the *equal protection* rights of the under-represented voters. [*Reynolds v. Sims*].

    a. **Justiciable:** Such cases raising the "one person, one vote" argument are *justiciable.* The Court has rejected the argument that these cases raise non-justiciable political questions. [*Baker v. Carr*]

    b. **Both houses of state legislature:** One of the consequences of the "one person, one vote" principle is that if a state has a bicameral (two-house) legislature, *both* houses must be elected based on population. Thus, paradoxically, the U.S. Constitution prohibits a state from having one body that awards seats without reference to population (e.g., a house that gives the same number of votes to each county), even though the U.S. Senate is built upon exactly this kind of non-population-based scheme!

2. **How much equality is required:** The rules for *how much equality is required* vary depending on whether we're talking about a congressional districting scheme or, instead, a state or local districting scheme.

    a. **Congressional:** For *congressional districts*, the districts have to be *almost precisely equal.* Even a scheme where one congressional district within a state was only 1% more populous than another has been struck down. States must make a "good-faith effort to achieve *precise mathematical equality*" in the drawing of congressional districts. [*Kirkpatrick v. Preisler*]

    b. **State and local:** *Much greater deviation* from mathematical equality is allowed where what is being apportioned is *state legislatures* or *local governmental bodies*. So for example, a *10%* or smaller deviation between the voting power of a voter in one district versus a voter in another will generally be *upheld.* [*White v. Regester*] Even greater disparities will be allowed if there are good reasons for them. (For instance, suppose a state wants not to have to redraw its county boundaries, and wants to have each county elect its own representative to the state Assembly. This desire to "respect pre-existing political boundaries" will probably justify, say, a 15% or even 20% disparity in per-person voting power.)

3. **Gerrymandering:** Consider *gerrymandering*, that is, the process by which the strength of a particular voting bloc is curtailed by restricting its members to carefully and artificially-constructed districts.

    a. **"Partisan gerrymandering" cases hard to win:** First, consider *"partisan gerrymandering"* cases, i.e., cases arguing that a group is being disadvantaged based on its *political* rather than racial status. These cases are almost impossible for the plaintiffs to win. See p. 55 *supra*.

    b. **Racial minority:** But if a *racial or ethnic minority* can show that the gerrymandering scheme was intentionally designed to hurt, and did hurt, that minority, the plaintiffs' case *will* be justiciable, and probably winnable. For instance, if the state legislature draws districts for the state senate in a way that intentionally gives African Americans control of 5% of the districts when African Americans constitute 10% of the state population, African American voters have a good chance of winning an equal protection suit.

MBE-STYLE QUESTIONS ON CONSTITUTIONAL LAW

CONSTITUTIONAL LAW QUESTIONS

These questions are the Constitutional Law questions from the Self-Assessment Test. They are presented here in approximately the order in which the main topic or theme of the question is treated in the substantive outline earlier in this book. Thus questions focusing on Federal Judicial Power come first, followed by questions on Federalism and Federal Power, etc.

1. Plaintiff challenged the constitutionality of a state tax law, alleging that it violated the Equal Protection Clauses of both the United States Constitution and the state constitution. The state supreme court agreed and held the tax law to be invalid. It said: "We hold that this state tax law violates the Equal Protection Clause of the United States Constitution and also the Equal Protection Clause of the state constitution because we interpret that provision of the state constitution to contain exactly the same prohibition against discriminatory legislation as is contained in the Equal Protection Clause of the Fourteenth Amendment to the United States Constitution."

   The state sought review of this decision in the United States Supreme Court, alleging that the state supreme court's determination of the federal constitutional issue was incorrect.

   How should the United States Supreme Court dispose of the case if it believes that this interpretation of the federal Constitution by the state supreme court raises an important federal question and is incorrect on the merits?

   (A) Reverse the state supreme court decision, because the Equal Protection Clause of a state constitution must be construed by the state supreme court in a manner that is congruent with the meaning of the Equal Protection Clause of the federal Constitution.

   (B) Reverse the state supreme court decision with respect to the Equal Protection Clause of the federal Constitution and remand the case to the state supreme court for further proceedings, because the state and federal constitutional issues are so intertwined that the federal issue must be decided so that this case may be disposed of properly.

   (C) Refuse to review the decision of the state supreme court, because it is based on an adequate and independent ground of state law.

   (D) Refuse to review the decision of the state supreme court, because a state government may not seek review of decisions of its own courts in the United States Supreme Court.

   [Q1010]

2. Which of the following acts by the United States Senate would be constitutionally IMPROPER?

   (A) The Senate decides, with the House of Representatives, that a disputed state ratification of a proposed constitutional amendment is valid.

   (B) The Senate determines the eligibility of a person to serve as a senator.

   (C) The Senate appoints a commission to adjudicate finally a boundary dispute between two states.

   (D) The Senate passes a resolution calling on the President to pursue a certain foreign policy.

   [Q1087]

3. The National Ecological Balance Act prohibits the destruction or removal of any wild animals located on lands owned by the United States without express permission from the Federal Bureau of Land Management. Violators are subject to fines of up to $1,000 per offense.

   After substantial property damage was inflicted on residents of a state by hungry coyotes, the state legislature passed the Coyote Bounty Bill, which offers $25 for each coyote killed or captured within the state. A National Forest, owned by the federal government, is located entirely within that state. Many coyotes live in the National Forest.

   Without seeking permission from the Bureau of Land Management, a hunter shot several coyotes in the National Forest and collected the bounty from the state. As a result, he was subsequently tried in federal district court, convicted, and fined $1,000 for violating the National Ecological Balance Act. The hunter appealed his conviction to the United States Court of Appeals.

   On appeal, the Court of Appeals should hold the National Ecological Balance Act, as applied to the hunter, to be

   (A) constitutional, because the property clause of Article IV, Section 3, of the Constitution authorizes such federal statutory controls and sanctions.

   (B) constitutional, because Article I, Section 8, of the Constitution authorizes Congress to enact all laws necessary and proper to advance the general welfare.

   (C) unconstitutional, because Congress may not use its delegated powers to override the Tenth Amendment right of the state to legislate in areas of traditional state governmental functions, such as the protection of the property of its residents.

   (D) unconstitutional, because Congress violates the full faith and credit clause of Article IV when it punishes conduct that has been authorized by state action.

   [Q2079]

4. A federal statute prohibits the sale or resale, in any place in this country, of any product intended for human consumption or ingestion into the human body that contains designated chemicals known to cause cancer, unless the product is clearly labeled as dangerous.

   The constitutionality of this federal statute may most easily be justified on the basis of the power of Congress to

   (A) regulate commerce among the states.

   (B) enforce the Fourteenth Amendment.

   (C) provide for the general welfare.

   (D) promote science and the useful arts.

   [Q1026]

5. A newly enacted federal statute appropriates $100 million in federal funds to support basic research by universities located in the United States. The statute provides that “the ten best universities in the United States” will each receive $10 million. It also provides that “the ten best universities” shall be “determined by a poll of the presidents of all the universities in the nation, to be conducted by the United States Department of Education.” In responding to that poll, each university president is required to apply the well-recognized and generally accepted standards of academic quality that are specified in the statute. The provisions of the statute are inseverable.

   Which of the following statements about this statute is correct?

   (A) The statute is unconstitutional, because the reliance by Congress on a poll of individuals who are not federal officials to determine the recipients of its appropriated funds is an unconstitutional delegation of legislative power.

   (B) The statute is unconstitutional, because the

limitation on recipients to the ten best universities is arbitrary and capricious and denies other high- quality universities the equal protection of the laws.

(C) The statute is constitutional, because Congress has plenary authority to determine the objects of its spending and the methods used to achieve them, so long as they may reasonably be deemed to serve the general welfare and do not violate any prohibitory language in the Constitution.

(D) The validity of the statute is nonjusticiable, because the use by Congress of its spending power necessarily involves political considerations that must be resolved finally by those branches of the government that are closest to the political process.

[Q2145]

6. Congress passed a statute directing the United States Forest Service, a federal agency, to issue regulations to control campfires on federal public lands and to establish a schedule of penalties for those who violate the new regulations. The statute provided that the Forest Service regulations should "reduce, to the maximum extent feasible, all potential hazards that arise from campfires on Forest Service lands." The Forest Service issued the regulations and the schedule of penalties directed by Congress. The regulations include a rule that provides for the doubling of the fine for any negligent or prohibited use of fire if the user is intoxicated by alcohol or drugs.

Which of the following is the best argument for sustaining the constitutionality of the Forest Service's rule providing for the fines?

(A) The executive branch of government, of which the Forest Service is part, has inherent rule-making authority over public lands.

(B) The rule is issued pursuant to a valid exercise of Congress's power to delegate rule-making authority to federal agencies.

(C) The rule is justified by a compelling governmental interest in safeguarding forest resources.

(D) The rule relates directly to law enforcement, which is an executive rather than legislative function, and hence it does not need specific congressional authorization.

[Q7036]

GO ON TO THE NEXT PAGE

7. The vaccination of children against childhood contagious diseases (such as measles, diphtheria, and whooping cough) has traditionally been a function of private doctors and local and state health departments. Because vaccination rates have declined in recent years, especially in urban areas, the President proposes to appoint a Presidential Advisory Commission on Vaccination which would be charged with conducting a national publicity campaign to encourage vaccination as a public health measure. No federal statute authorizes or prohibits this action by the President. The activities of the Presidential Advisory Commission on Vaccination would be financed entirely from funds appropriated by Congress to the Office of the President for "such other purposes as the President may think appropriate."

   May the President constitutionally create such a commission for this purpose?

   (A) Yes, because the President has plenary authority to provide for the health, safety, and welfare of the people of the United States.

   (B) Yes, because this action is within the scope of executive authority vested in the President by the Constitution, and no federal statute prohibits it.

   (C) No, because the protection of children against common diseases by vaccination is a traditional state function and, therefore, is reserved to the states by the Tenth Amendment.

   (D) No, because Congress has not specifically authorized the creation and support of such a new federal agency.

   [Q3109]

8. Small retailers located in the state of Yellow are concerned about the loss of business to certain large retailers located nearby in bordering states. In an effort to deal with this concern, the legislature of Yellow enacted a statute requiring all manufacturers and wholesalers who sell goods to retailers in Yellow to do so at prices that are no higher than the lowest prices at which they sell them to retailers in any of the states that border Yellow. Several manufacturers and wholesalers who are located in states bordering Yellow and who sell their goods to retailers in those states and in Yellow bring an action in federal court to challenge the constitutionality of this statute.

   Which of the following arguments offered by these plaintiffs is likely to be most persuasive in light of applicable precedent?

   The state statute

   (A) deprives them of their property or liberty without due process of law.

   (B) imposes an unreasonable burden on interstate commerce.

   (C) deprives them of a privilege or immunity of national citizenship.

   (D) denies them the equal protection of the laws.

   [Q1190]

9. Central City in the state of Green is a center for businesses that assemble personal computers. Components for these computers are manufactured elsewhere in Green and in other states, then shipped to Central City, where the computers are assembled. An ordinance of Central City imposes a special license tax on all of the many companies engaged in the business of assembling computers in that city. The tax payable by each such company is a percentage of the company's gross receipts.

   The Green statute that authorizes municipalities to impose this license tax has a "Green content" provision. To comply with this provision of state law, the Central City license tax ordinance provides that the tax paid by any assembler of computers subject to this tax ordinance will be reduced by a percentage equal to the proportion of computer components manufactured in Green.

The plaintiff is a company that assembles computers in Central City and sells them from its offices in Central City to buyers throughout the United States. All of the components of its computers come from outside the state of Green. Therefore, the plaintiff must pay the Central City license tax in full without receiving any refund. Other Central City computer assemblers use components manufactured in Green in varying proportions and, therefore, are entitled to partial reductions of their Central City license tax payments.

Following prescribed procedure, the plaintiff brings an action in a proper court asking to have Central City's special license tax declared unconstitutional on the grounds that it is inconsistent with the negative implications of the Commerce Clause.

In this case, the court should rule

(A) against the plaintiff, because the tax falls only on companies resident in Central City and, therefore, does not discriminate against or otherwise adversely affect interstate commerce.

(B) against the plaintiff, because the Commerce Clause does not interfere with the right of a state to foster and support businesses located within its borders by encouraging its residents to purchase the products of those businesses.

(C) for the plaintiff, because any tax on a company engaged in interstate commerce, measured in whole or in part by its gross receipts, is a per se violation of the negative implications of the Commerce Clause.

(D) for the plaintiff, because the tax improperly discriminates against interstate commerce by treating in-state products more favorably than out-of-state products.

[Q3114]

10. The United States Congress enacted a federal statute providing that any state may "require labeling to show the state or other geographic origin of citrus fruit that is imported into the receiving state." Pursuant to the federal statute, a state that produced large quantities of citrus fruit enacted a law requiring all citrus fruit imported into the state to be stamped with a two-letter postal abbreviation signifying the state of the fruit's origin. The law did not impose any such requirement for citrus fruit grown within the state. When it adopted the law, the state legislature declared that its purpose was to reduce the risks of infection of local citrus crops by itinerant diseases that have been found to attack citrus fruit. A national association of citrus growers sued to have the state law declared unconstitutional. The association claims that the law is prohibited by the negative implications of the Commerce Clause of the Constitution.

Which of the following is the best argument in favor of the state's effort to have this lawsuit dismissed?

(A) Any burden on interstate commerce imposed by the state law is outweighed by a legitimate state interest.

(B) Congress has the authority to authorize specified state regulations that would otherwise be prohibited by the negative implications of the Commerce Clause, and it has done so in this situation.

(C) The state law does not discriminate against out-of-state citrus growers or producers.

(D) The state law furthers a legitimate state interest, the burden it imposes on interstate commerce is only incidental, and the state's interest cannot be satisfied by other means that are less burdensome to interstate commerce.

[Q7084]

11. The United States Department of the Interior granted the plaintiff the food and drink concession in a federal park located in the state of Purple. The plaintiff operated his concession out of federally owned facilities in the park. The federal statute authorizing the Interior Department to grant such concessions provided that the grantees would pay only a nominal rental for use of these federal facilities because of the great benefit their concessions would provide to the people of the United States.

    The legislature of the state of Purple enacted a statute imposing an occupancy tax on the occupants of real estate within that state that is not subject to state real estate taxes. The statute was intended to equalize the state tax burden on such occupants with that on people occupying real estate that is subject to state real estate taxes. Pursuant to that statute, the Purple Department of Revenue attempted to collect the state occupancy tax from the plaintiff because the federal facilities occupied by the plaintiff were not subject to state real estate taxes. The plaintiff sued to invalidate the state occupancy tax as applied to him.

    The strongest ground upon which the plaintiff could challenge the occupancy tax is that it violates the

    (A) Commerce Clause by unduly burdening the interstate tourist trade.

    (B) Privileges and Immunities Clause of the Fourteenth Amendment by interfering with the fundamental right to do business on federal property.

    (C) Equal Protection Clause of the Fourteenth Amendment because the tax treats him less favorably than federal concessionaires in other states who do not have to pay such occupancy taxes.

    (D) Supremacy Clause of Article VI and the federal statute authorizing such concessions.

    [Q2150]

12. A federally owned and operated office building in the state of Red is heated with a new, pollution-free heating system. However, in the coldest season of the year, this new system is sometimes insufficient to supply adequate heat to the building. The appropriation statute providing the money for construction of the new heating system permitted use of the old, pollution-generating system when necessary to supply additional heat. When the old heating system operates (only about two days in any year), the smokestack of the building emits smoke that exceeds the state of Red's pollution-control standards.

    May the operators of the federal office building be prosecuted successfully by Red authorities for violating that state's pollution control standards?

    (A) Yes, because the regulation of pollution is a legitimate state police power concern.

    (B) Yes, because the regulation of pollution is a joint concern of the federal government and the state and, therefore, both of them may regulate conduct causing pollution.

    (C) No, because the operations of the federal government are immune from state regulation in the absence of federal consent.

    (D) No, because the violations of the state pollution-control standards involved here are so *de minimis* that they are beyond the legitimate reach of state law.

    [Q1195]

13. A doctor, a resident of the city of Greenville in the state of Green, is a physician licensed to practice in both Green and the neighboring state of Red. The doctor finds that the most convenient place to treat her patients who need hospital care is in the publicly owned and operated municipal hospital of the city of Redville in the state of Red, which is located just across the state line from Greenville. For many years the doctor had successfully treated

her patients in that hospital. Early this year she was notified that she could no longer treat patients in the Redville hospital because she was not a resident of Red, and a newly adopted rule of the Redville hospital, which was adopted in conformance with all required procedures, stated that every physician who practices in that hospital must be a resident of Red.

Which of the following constitutional provisions would be most helpful to the doctor in an action to challenge her exclusion from the Redville hospital solely on the basis of this hospital rule?

(A) The bill of attainder clause.

(B) The privileges and immunities clause of Article IV.

(C) The due process clause of the Fourteenth Amendment.

(D) The ex post facto clause.

[Q3190]

14. A man bought an antique car from a car dealer in State A. Under State A law, a person who buys from such a dealer acquires good title, even if the property was stolen from a previous owner. The man showed the car at an antique car show in State B. A woman recognized the car as having been stolen from her. Under State B law, a person whose property is stolen may reclaim it, even if the current possessor is an innocent purchaser. The woman sued the man in a State B court to reclaim the car. The man defended, claiming that he had good title under the law of State A. Nevertheless, the State B court applied State B law, and the woman prevailed. The man did not appeal. The sheriff gave the woman possession of the car. Several months later, the woman drove the car to State A. The man brought a new suit against the woman, claiming that the State B court in the prior suit should have applied the State A law, which protected innocent purchasers. The woman appeared and moved to dismiss the suit.

What should the State A court do?

(A) Apply the federal law of sale of goods, because the car has moved in interstate commerce.

(B) Apply the State A law, because the car is currently located in State A.

(C) Dismiss the suit, because the State A court must give full faith and credit to the State B judgment.

(D) Remove the case to federal court, because the car has moved in interstate commerce, and therefore the case raises a federal question.

[Q7051]

GO ON TO THE NEXT PAGE

15. A state statute requires each insurance company that offers burglary insurance policies in the state to charge a uniform rate for such insurance to all of its customers residing within the same county in that state. So long as it complies with this requirement, a company is free to charge whatever rate the market will bear for its burglary insurance policies.

    An insurance company located in the state files suit in federal district court against appropriate state officials to challenge this statute on constitutional grounds. The insurance company wishes to charge customers residing within the same county in the state rates for burglary insurance policies that will vary because they would be based on the specific nature of the customer's business, on its precise location, and on its past claims record.

    In this suit, the court should

    (A) hold the statute unconstitutional, because the statute deprives the insurance company of its liberty or property without due process of law.

    (B) hold the statute unconstitutional, because the statute imposes an undue burden on interstate commerce.

    (C) hold the statute constitutional, because the statute is a reasonable exercise of the state's police power.

    (D) abstain from ruling on the merits of this case until the state courts have had an opportunity to pass on the constitutionality of this state statute.

    [Q2008]

16. A state statute prohibits the use of state-owned or state-operated facilities for the performance of abortions that are not "necessary to save the life of the mother." That statute also prohibits state employees from performing any such abortions during the hours they are employed by the state.

    A woman was in her second month of pregnancy. She sought an abortion at a state-owned and state-operated hospital. The woman did not claim that the requested abortion was necessary to save her life. The officials in charge of the hospital refused to perform the requested abortion solely on the basis of the state statute. The woman immediately filed suit against those officials in an appropriate federal district court. She challenged the constitutionality of the state statute and requested the court to order the hospital to perform the abortion she sought. In this case, the court will probably hold that the state statute is

    (A) unconstitutional, because a limit on the availability of abortions performed by state employees or in state-owned or state-operated facilities to situations in which it is necessary to save the life of the mother impermissibly interferes with the fundamental right of the woman to decide whether to have a child.

    (B) unconstitutional, because it impermissibly discriminates against poor persons who cannot afford to pay for abortions in privately owned and operated facilities and against persons who live far away from privately owned and operated abortion clinics.

    (C) constitutional, because it does not prohibit a woman from having an abortion or penalize her for doing so, it is rationally related to the legitimate governmental goal of encouraging childbirth, and it does not unduly burden the voluntary performance of abortions by private physicians in private facilities.

    (D) constitutional, because the use of state-owned or state-operated facilities and access to the services of state employees are privileges and not rights and, therefore, a state may condition them on any basis it chooses.

    [Q2162]

17. A state statute declares that after five years of continuous service in their positions all state employees, including faculty members at the state university, are entitled to retain their positions during "good behavior." The statute also contains a number of procedural provisions. Any state employee who is dismissed after that five-year period must be given reasons for the dismissal before it takes effect. In addition, such an employee must, upon request, be granted a post-dismissal hearing before an administrative board to seek reinstatement and back pay. The statute precludes any other hearing or opportunity to respond to the charges. That post-dismissal hearing must occur within six months after the dismissal takes effect. The burden of proof at such a hearing is on the state, and the board may uphold the dismissal only if it is supported by a preponderance of the evidence. An employee who is dissatisfied with a decision of the board after a hearing may appeal its decision to the state courts. The provisions of this statute are inseverable.

    A teacher who had been employed continuously for seven years as a faculty member at the state university was dismissed. A week before the dismissal took effect, she was informed that she was being dismissed because of a charge that she accepted a bribe from a student in return for raising the student's final grade in her course. At that time she requested an immediate hearing to contest the propriety of her dismissal.

    Three months after her dismissal, she was granted a hearing before the state administrative board. The board upheld her dismissal, finding that the charge against her was supported by a preponderance of the evidence presented at the hearing.

    The faculty member did not appeal the decision of the state administrative board to the state courts. Instead, she sought a declaratory judgment in federal district court to the effect that the state statute prescribing the procedures for her dismissal is unconstitutional.

    In this case, the federal district court should

    (A) dismiss the suit, because a claim that a state statute is unconstitutional is not ripe for adjudication by a federal court until all judicial remedies in state courts provided for by state law have been exhausted.

    (B) hold the statute unconstitutional, because the due process clause of the Fourteenth Amendment requires a state to demonstrate beyond a reasonable doubt the facts constituting good cause for termination of a state employee.

    (C) hold the statute unconstitutional, because a state may not ordinarily deprive an employee of a property interest in a job without giving the employee an opportunity for some kind of predismissal hearing to respond to the charges against that employee.

    (D) hold the statute constitutional, because the due process clause of the Fourteenth Amendment entitles state employees who have a right to their jobs during good behavior only to a statement of reasons for their dismissal and an opportunity for a post-dismissal hearing.

    [Q1152]

GO ON TO THE NEXT PAGE

18. A city has had a severe traffic problem on its streets. As a result, it enacted an ordinance prohibiting all sales to the public of food or other items by persons selling directly from trucks, cars, or other vehicles located on city streets. The ordinance included an inseverable grandfather provision exempting from its prohibition vendors who, for 20 years or more, have continuously sold food or other items from such vehicles located on the streets of the city.

    A retail ice cream vendor qualifies for this exemption and is the only food vendor that does. A yogurt company is a business similar to the ice cream company, but the yogurt company has been selling to the public directly from trucks located on the streets of the city only for the past ten years. The yogurt company filed suit in an appropriate federal district court to enjoin enforcement of this ordinance on the ground that it denies the yogurt company the equal protection of the laws.

    In this case, the court will probably rule that the ordinance is

    (A) constitutional, because it is narrowly tailored to implement the city's compelling interest in reducing traffic congestion and, therefore, satisfies the strict scrutiny test applicable to such cases.

    (B) constitutional, because its validity is governed by the rational basis test, and the courts consistently defer to economic choices embodied in such legislation if they are even plausibly justifiable.

    (C) unconstitutional, because the nexus between the legitimate purpose of the ordinance and the conduct it prohibits is so tenuous and its provisions are so underinclusive that the ordinance fails to satisfy the substantial relationship test applicable to such cases.

    (D) unconstitutional, because economic benefits or burdens imposed by legislatures on the basis of grandfather provisions have consistently been declared invalid by courts as per se violations of the Equal Protection Clause of the Fourteenth Amendment.

[Q1021]

19. A public high school has had a very high rate of pregnancy among its students. In order to assist students who keep their babies to complete high school, the high school has established an infant day-care center for children of its students, and also offers classes in child care. Because the child-care classes are always overcrowded, the school limits admission to those classes solely to students at the high school who are the mothers of babies in the infant day-care center.

    A male student at the high school has legal custody of his infant son. The school provides care for his son in the infant day-care center, but will not allow the male student to enroll in the child-care classes. He brings suit against the school challenging, on constitutional grounds, his exclusion from the child-care classes.

    Which of the following best states the burden of persuasion in this case?

    (A) The student must demonstrate that the admission requirement is not rationally related to a legitimate governmental interest.

    (B) The student must demonstrate that the admission requirement is not as narrowly drawn as possible to achieve a substantial governmental interest.

    (C) The school must demonstrate that the admission policy is the least restrictive means by which to achieve a compelling governmental interest.

    (D) The school must demonstrate that the admission policy is substantially related to an important governmental interest.

[Q2155]

20. A state has a statute providing that an unsuccessful candidate in a primary election for a party's nomination for elected public office may not become a candidate for the same office at the following general election by nominating petition or by write-in votes.

    A woman sought her party's nomination for governor in the May primary election. After losing in the primary, the woman filed nominating petitions containing the requisite number of signatures to become a candidate for the office of governor in the following general election. The chief elections officer of the state refused to certify the woman's petitions solely because of the above statute. The woman then filed suit in federal district court challenging the constitutionality of this state statute.

    As a matter of constitutional law, which of the following is the proper burden of persuasion in this suit?

    (A) The woman must demonstrate that the statute is not necessary to achieve a compelling state interest.

    (B) The woman must demonstrate that the statute is not rationally related to a legitimate state interest.

    (C) The state must demonstrate that the statute is the least restrictive means of achieving a compelling state interest.

    (D) The state must demonstrate that the statute is rationally related to a legitimate state interest.

    [Q1122]

GO ON TO THE NEXT PAGE

21. Public schools in a state are financed, in large part, by revenue derived from real estate taxes imposed by each school district on the taxable real property located in that district. Public schools also receive other revenue from private gifts, federal grants, student fees, and local sales taxes. For many years, the state has distributed additional funds, which come from the state treasury, to local school districts in order to equalize the funds available on a per-student basis for each public school district. These additional funds are distributed on the basis of a state statutory formula that considers only the number of students in each public school district and the real estate tax revenue raised by that district. The formula does not consider other revenue received by a school district from different sources.

    The school boards of two school districts, together with parents and schoolchildren in those districts, bring suit in federal court to enjoin the state from allocating the additional funds from the state treasury to individual districts pursuant to this formula. They allege that the failure of the state, in allocating this additional money, to take into account a school district's sources of revenue other than revenue derived from taxes levied on real estate located there violates the Equal Protection Clause of the Fourteenth Amendment. The complaint does not allege that the allocation of the additional state funds based on the current statutory formula has resulted in a failure to provide minimally adequate education to any child.

    Which of the following best describes the appropriate standard by which the court should review the constitutionality of the state statutory funding formula?

    (A) Because classifications based on wealth are inherently suspect, the state must demonstrate that the statutory formula is necessary to vindicate a compelling slate interest.

    (B) Because the statutory funding formula burdens the fundamental right to education, the state must demonstrate that the formula is necessary to vindicate a compelling state interest.

    (C) Because no fundamental right or suspect classification is implicated in this case, the plaintiffs must demonstrate that the funding allocation formula bears no rational relationship to any legitimate state interest.

    (D) Because the funding formula inevitably leads to disparities among the school districts in their levels of total funding, the plaintiffs must only demonstrate that the funding formula is not substantially related to the furtherance of an important state interest.

    [Q1073]

22. A company wanted to expand the size of the building it owned that housed the company's supermarket by adding space for a coffeehouse. The company's building was located in the center of five acres of land owned by the company and devoted wholly to parking for its supermarket customers.

    City officials refused to grant a required building permit for the coffeehouse addition unless the company established in its store a child care center that would take up space at least equal to the size of the proposed coffeehouse addition, which was to be 20% of the existing building. This action of city officials was authorized by provisions of the applicable zoning ordinance.

    In a suit filed in state court against appropriate officials of the city, the company challenged this child care center requirement solely on constitutional grounds. The lower court upheld the requirement even though city officials presented no evidence and made no findings to justify it other than a general assertion that there was a shortage of child care facilities in the city. The company appealed.

The court hearing the appeal should hold that the requirement imposed by the city on the issuance of this building permit is

(A) constitutional, because the burden was on the company to demonstrate that there was no rational relationship between this requirement and a legitimate governmental interest, and the company could not do so because the requirement is reasonably related to improving the lives of families and children residing in the city.

(B) constitutional, because the burden was on the company to demonstrate that this requirement was not necessary to vindicate a compelling governmental interest, and the company could not do so on these facts.

(C) unconstitutional, because the burden was on the city to demonstrate that this requirement was necessary to vindicate a compelling governmental interest, and the city failed to meet its burden under that standard.

(D) unconstitutional, because the burden was on the city to demonstrate a rough proportionality between this requirement and the impact of the company's proposed action on the community, and the city failed to do so.

[Q3162]

23. Insurance is provided in a particular state only by private companies. Although the state insurance commissioner inspects insurance companies for solvency, the state does not regulate their rates or policies. A particular insurance company charges higher rates for burglary insurance to residents of one part of a county in the state than to residents of another section of the same county because of the different crime rates in those areas.

A resident of that county was charged the higher rate by the insurance company because of the location of her residence. The resident sues the insurance company, alleging that the differential in insurance rates unconstitutionally denies her the equal protection of the laws.

Will the resident's suit succeed?

(A) Yes, because the higher crime rate in the resident's neighborhood demonstrates that the county police are not giving persons who reside there the equal protection of the laws.

(B) Yes, because the insurance rate differential is inherently discriminatory.

(C) No, because the constitutional guarantee of equal protection of the laws is not applicable to the actions of these insurance companies.

(D) No, because there is a rational basis for the differential in insurance rates.

[Q1114]

GO ON TO THE NEXT PAGE

24. A proposed federal statute would prohibit all types of discrimination against black persons on the basis of their race in every business transaction executed anywhere in the United States by any person or entity, governmental or private.

    Is this proposed federal statute likely to be constitutional?

    (A) Yes, because it could reasonably be viewed as an exercise of Congress's authority to enact laws for the general welfare.

    (B) Yes, because it could reasonably be viewed as a means of enforcing the provisions of the Thirteenth Amendment.

    (C) No, because it would regulate purely local transactions that are not in interstate commerce.

    (D) No, because it would invade the powers reserved to the states by the Tenth Amendment.

    [Q2101]

25. A man intensely disliked his neighbors, who were of a different race. One night, intending to frighten his neighbors, he spray-painted their house with racial epithets and threats that they would be lynched. The man was arrested and prosecuted under a state law providing that "any person who threatens violence against another person with the intent to cause that person to fear for his or her life or safety may be imprisoned for up to five years." In defense, the man claimed that he did not intend to lynch his neighbors, but only to scare them so that they would move away.

    Can the man constitutionally be convicted under this law?

    (A) No, because he was only communicating his views and had not commenced any overt action against the neighbors.

    (B) Yes, because he was engaged in trespass when he painted the words on his neighbors' house.

    (C) Yes, because his communication was a threat by which he intended to intimidate his neighbors.

    (D) Yes, because his communication was racially motivated and thus violated the protections of the Thirteenth Amendment.

    [Q7095]

26. A city has an ordinance that prohibits the location of "adult theaters and bookstores" (theaters and bookstores presenting sexually explicit performances or materials) in residential or commercial zones within the city. The ordinance was intended to protect surrounding property from the likely adverse secondary effects of such establishments. "Adult theaters and bookstores" are freely permitted in the areas of the city zoned industrial, where those adverse secondary effects are not as likely. A storekeeper is denied a zoning permit to open an adult theater and bookstore in a building owned by him in an area zoned commercial. As a result, the storekeeper brings suit in an appropriate court challenging the constitutionality of the zoning ordinance.

    Which of the following statements regarding the constitutionality of this city ordinance is most accurate?

    (A) The ordinance is valid, because a city may enforce zoning restrictions on speech-related businesses to ensure that the messages they disseminate are acceptable to the residents of adjacent property.

    (B) The ordinance is valid, because a city may enforce this type of time, place, and manner regulation on speech-related businesses, so long as this type of regulation is designed to serve a substantial governmental interest and does not unreasonably limit alternative avenues of communication.

(C) The ordinance is invalid, because a city may not enforce zoning regulations that deprive potential operators of adult theaters and bookstores of their freedom to choose the location of their businesses.

(D) The ordinance is invalid, because a city may not zone property in a manner calculated to protect property from the likely adverse secondary effects of adult theaters and bookstores.

[Q2193]

27. A clerical worker has been employed for the past two years in a permanent position in the Public Records Office of a county. The clerk has been responsible for copying and filing records of real estate transactions in that office. The clerk works in a nonpublic part of the office and has no contact with members of the public. However, state law provides that all real estate records in that office are to be made available for public inspection.

On the day an attempted assassination of the governor of the state was reported on the radio, the clerk remarked to a coworker, "Our governor is such an evil man, I am sorry they did not get him." The clerk's coworker reported this remark to the clerk's employer, the county recorder. After the clerk admitted making the remark, the county recorder dismissed him stating that "there is no room in this office for a person who hates the governor so much."

The clerk sued for reinstatement and back pay. His only claim is that the dismissal violated his constitutional rights.

In this case, the court should hold that the county recorder's dismissal of the clerk was

(A) unconstitutional, because it constitutes a taking without just compensation of the clerk's property interest in his permanent position with the county.

(B) unconstitutional, because in light of the clerk's particular employment duties his right to express himself on a matter of public concern outweighed any legitimate interest the state might have had in discharging him.

(C) constitutional, because the compelling interest of the state in having loyal and supportive employees outweighs the interest of any state employee in his or her job or in free speech on a matter of public concern.

(D) nonjusticiable, because public employment is a privilege rather than a right and, therefore, the clerk lacked standing to bring this suit.

[Q2184]

GO ON TO THE NEXT PAGE

28. A city operates a cemetery pursuant to a city ordinance. The ordinance requires the operation of the city cemetery to be supported primarily by revenues derived from the sale of cemetery lots to individuals. The ordinance further provides that the purchase of a cemetery lot entitles the owner to perpetual care of the lot, and entitles the owner to erect on the lot, at the owner's expense, a memorial monument or marker of the owner's choice, subject to certain size restrictions. The ordinance requires the city to maintain the cemetery, including mowing the grass, watering flowers, and plowing snow, and provides for the expenditure of city tax funds for such maintenance if revenues from the sale of cemetery lots are insufficient. Although cemetery lots are sold at full fair market value, which includes the current value of perpetual care, the revenue from the sale of such lots has been insufficient in recent years to maintain the cemetery. As a result, a small amount of city tax funds has also been used for that purpose.

A group of city taxpayers brings suit against the city challenging the constitutionality of the city ordinance insofar as it permits the owner of a cemetery lot to erect a religious memorial monument or marker on his or her lot.

Is this suit likely to be successful?

(A) No, because only a small amount of city tax funds has been used to maintain the cemetery.

(B) No, because the purpose of the ordinance is entirely secular, its primary effect neither advances nor inhibits religion, and it does not foster an excessive government entanglement with religion.

(C) Yes, because city maintenance of any religious object is a violation of the establishment clause of the First Amendment as incorporated into the Fourteenth Amendment.

(D) Yes, because no compelling governmental interest justifies authorizing private persons to erect religious monuments or markers in a city-operated cemetery.

[Q1138]

29. The governor of a state proposes to place a Christmas nativity scene, the components of which would be permanently donated to the state by private citizens, in the state Capitol Building rotunda where the state legislature meets annually. The governor further proposes to display this state-owned nativity scene annually from December 1 to December 31, next to permanent displays that depict the various products manufactured in the state. The governor's proposal is supported by all members of both houses of the legislature.

If challenged in a lawsuit on establishment clause grounds, the proposed nativity scene display would be held

(A) unconstitutional, because the components of the nativity scene would be owned by the state rather than by private persons.

(B) unconstitutional, because the nativity scene would not be displayed in a context that appeared to depict and commemorate the Christmas season as a primarily secular holiday.

(C) constitutional, because the components of the nativity scene would be donated to the state by private citizens rather than purchased with state funds.

(D) constitutional, because the nativity scene would be displayed alongside an exhibit of various products manufactured in the state.

[Q3165]

30. Members of a religious group believe in Lucifer as their Supreme Being. The members of this group meet once a year on top of Mt. Snow, located in a U.S. National Park, to hold an overnight encampment and a midnight dance around a large campfire. They believe this overnight encampment and all of its rituals

are required by Lucifer to be held on the top of Mt. Snow. U.S. National Park Service rules that have been consistently enforced prohibit all overnight camping and all campfires on Mt. Snow because of the very great dangers overnight camping and campfires would pose in that particular location. As a result, the park Superintendent denied a request by the group for a permit to conduct these activities on top of Mt. Snow. The park Superintendent, who was known to be violently opposed to cults and other unconventional groups had, in the past, issued permits to conventional religious groups to conduct sunrise services in other areas of that U.S. National Park.

The group brought suit in Federal Court against the U.S. National Park Service and the Superintendent of the park to compel issuance of the requested permit.

As a matter of constitutional law, the most appropriate result in this suit would be a decision that denial of the permit was

(A) invalid, because the free exercise clause of the First Amendment prohibits the Park Service from knowingly interfering with religious conduct.

(B) invalid, because these facts demonstrate that the action of the Park Service purposefully and invidiously discriminated against the group.

(C) valid, because the establishment clause of the First Amendment prohibits the holding of religious ceremonies on federal land.

(D) valid, because religiously motivated conduct may be subjected to nondiscriminatory time, place, and manner restrictions that advance important public interests.

[Q2112]

31. An ordinance of a city requires that its mayor must have been continuously a resident of the city for at least five years at the time he or she takes office. The plaintiff, who is thinking about running for mayor in an election that will take place next year, will have been a resident of the city for only four and one-half years at the time the mayor elected then takes office. Before he decides whether to run for the position of mayor, the plaintiff wants to know whether he could lawfully assume that position if he were elected. As a result, the plaintiff files suit in the local federal district court for a declaratory judgment that the five-year-residence requirement is unconstitutional and that he is entitled to a place on his political party's primary election ballot for mayor. He names the chairman of his political party as the sole defendant but does not join any election official. The chairman responds by joining the plaintiff in requesting the court to declare the residence requirement invalid.

In this case, the court should

(A) refuse to determine the merits of this suit, because there is no case or controversy.

(B) refuse to issue such a declaratory judgment, because an issue of this kind involving only a local election does not present a substantial federal constitutional question.

(C) issue the declaratory judgment, because a residency requirement of this type is a denial of the equal protection of the laws.

(D) issue the declaratory judgment, because the plaintiff will have substantially complied with the residency requirement.

[Q2153]

GO ON TO THE NEXT PAGE

32. City police officers shot and killed the plaintiff's friend as he attempted to escape arrest for an armed robbery he had committed. The plaintiff brought suit in federal district court against the city police department and the city police officers involved, seeking only a judgment declaring unconstitutional the state statute under which the police acted. That newly enacted statute authorized the police to use deadly force when necessary to apprehend a person who has committed a felony. In his suit, the plaintiff alleged that the police would not have killed his friend if the use of deadly force had not been authorized by the statute.

    The federal district court should

    (A) decide the case on its merits, because it raises a substantial federal question.

    (B) dismiss the action, because it involves a nonjusticiable political question.

    (C) dismiss the action, because it does not present a case or controversy.

    (D) dismiss the action, because the Eleventh Amendment prohibits federal courts from deciding cases of this type.

    [Q1133]

33. A federal statute enacted pursuant to the power of Congress to enforce the Fourteenth Amendment prohibits any state from requiring any of its employees to retire from state employment solely because of their age. The statute expressly authorizes employees required by a state to retire from state employment solely because of their age to sue the state government in federal district court for any damages resulting from that state action. On the basis of this federal statute, a retiree who had worked for State X sues the state in federal district court. State X moves to dismiss the suit on the ground that Congress lacks authority to authorize such suits against a state.

    Which of the following is the strongest argument that the retiree can offer in opposition to the state's motion to dismiss this suit?

    (A) When Congress exercises power vested in it by the Fourteenth Amendment, Congress may enact appropriate remedial legislation expressly subjecting the states to private suits for damages in federal court.

    (B) When Congress exercises power vested in it by any provision of the Constitution, Congress has unlimited authority to authorize private actions for damages against a state.

    (C) While the Eleventh Amendment restrains the federal judiciary, that amendment does not limit the power of Congress to modify the sovereign immunity of the states.

    (D) While the Eleventh Amendment applies to suits in federal court by citizens of one state against another state, it does not apply to such suits by citizens against their own states.

    [Q1027]

ANSWERS TO CONSTITUTIONAL LAW QUESTIONS

1. **B** Although the state supreme court made a finding about what the state constitution required, this decision was not truly "independent" of federal constitutional law, because the facts make it clear that the state court was first determining what the federal constitution required, and only then concluding that the state constitution required the same thing. Therefore, the Supreme Court can and should correct the state court's error in federal constitutional law. Once the Supreme Court has done this, it should then remand in order to give the state court the opportunity to conclude, after further reflection, that the state constitution's ban on discriminatory legislation goes further than the federal ban.

   (A) is wrong as a pure matter of law: even where provisions of a state and the federal constitution contain identical language, the state court is always free to interpret the state constitution as imposing different requirements than the apparently-identical federal provision.

   (C) is wrong because, for the reasons described above, the state court's decision was not in fact based on an adequate and independent state ground.

   (D) is wrong as a pure matter of law: nothing prevents a state government from seeking review of the decisions of its own courts in the U.S. Supreme Court, as long as the decision poses some serious question of federal law.

   [Q1010]

2. **C** Article III, Sec. 2 says that the federal judicial power extends "to controversies between two or more States." Article III, Sec. 3 then says that "in all cases ... in which a State shall be a Party, the Supreme Court shall have original jurisdiction." That same article says that the Supreme Court's "appellate jurisdiction" shall be "with such exceptions, and under such regulations as the Congress shall make." There is no similar provision allowing Congress to make exceptions to (i.e., restrictions on) the Supreme Court's original jurisdiction, so Congress can't restrict the Supreme Court's original jurisdiction. Since a boundary dispute between two states is a dispute in which "a State shall be a party," since the Supreme Court has original jurisdiction over cases involving a party, and since Congress is not authorized to limit the Supreme Court's original jurisdiction, it follows that Congress cannot "adjudicate finally" (i.e., remove the Supreme Court's right to adjudicate) the boundary dispute.

   (A) is wrong because, under *Coleman v. Miller* (1939), the House and Senate together *do* have the right (indeed, the exclusive right) to determine whether a disputed state ratification of an amendment is valid.

   (B) is incorrect because the Senate *does* have the power to determine the eligibility of its members — Art. I, Sec. 5, Cl. 1 says that "each House shall be the judge of the Elections, Returns, and *Qualifications* of its own Members."

   (D) is wrong because Art. I, Sec. 7, Cl. 3 says that "Every Order, *Resolution*, or Vote to which the Concurrence of the Senate and House of Representatives may be necessary ... shall be presented to the President of the United States[.]" This clause implicitly gives each house the power to adopt resolutions; a resolution will not become law unless signed by the President, but the clause means that either house's adoption of a resolution is proper.

   [Q1087]

3. **A** Art. IV, Sec. 3, Cl. 2 gives Congress the power to "make all needful Rules and Regulations respecting the Territory or other Property belonging to the United States[.]" Since the National Forest is federally-owned property, this clause gives Congress the power to pass regulations governing it.

Under the Supremacy Clause, those regulations would take precedence over any conflicting state regulations, such as the right to kill coyotes implied by the state bounty bill.

(B) is wrong because it suggests that there is an independent congressional power to act to advance "the general welfare." This is not so — there's a power to "*tax and spend* ... for the general welfare," but that's not what's at issue here (because Congress is doing pure regulating, not taxing or spending).

(C) is wrong because if Congress has been given an explicit power in a certain area (here, the power to regulate on federal lands), Congress can indeed override whatever right the state might otherwise have to legislate in areas of traditional state governmental functions.

(D) is wrong because the Full Faith and Credit clause does not block Congress from punishing conduct that has been authorized by a state; the clause merely requires one state to enforce every other state's judgments.

[Q2079]

4. **A** The key point is that Congress can use its commerce powers to regulate even entirely *intrastate* transactions, on the theory that such transactions are being regulated as part of a broader regulation of interstate transactions, and excluding purely intrastate transactions from the overall scheme would be unwieldy. So, for instance, Congress here can forbid a farmer's sale, at a roadside stand adjacent to his farm, of a tomato that he had raised, where the farmer sprayed a cancer-causing substance produced inside that same state onto the tomato — even though this is an entirely intrastate transaction, it is still a "commercial" transaction, and can be regulated pursuant to Congress's broader interstate-commerce regulatory scheme.

(B) is wrong for several reasons; most importantly, the Fourteenth Amendment protects only against various conduct (e.g., denials of equal protection and due process) involving "state action," and while Congress has the power to enforce that Amendment by appropriate legislation, Congress here is not focused on attempting to prohibit any state from violating the Amendment.

(C) is wrong because there is no general congressional power to "provide for the general welfare"; there is only a power to *tax and spend* for the general welfare.

(D) is similarly incorrect because there is no general congressional power to "promote science and the useful arts"; there is only the limited power in Article I, Sec. 8, Cl. 8 to "promote the progress of science and useful arts" by "securing for limited times to authors and inventors the exclusive right to their respective writings and discoveries" (i.e., the power to issue *patents* and *copyrights*).

[Q1026]

5. **C** Although Congress, when it spends, must spend "for the general welfare," this test is extremely easy to satisfy — as the choice correctly states, all that is required is that the spending be "reasonably deemed to serve the general welfare," and that it not violate some specific constitutional ban (e.g., the Establishment Clause's ban on spending for the purpose of advancing religion). Since Congress could rationally have believed that rewarding the "best universities" would promote the country's general welfare, and that determining the "ten best" by this kind of vote was a rational way to go about attaining that end, the spending is constitutional.

(A) is wrong because the statute here is an acceptable exercise of legislative delegation: Congress has made it reasonably clear to the Dept. of Education what they are to do, and how they are to do it, so there is no "unconstitutional delegation" despite the fact that non-federal officials will be somehow involved in the process.

(B) is wrong, because when a governmental classification does not involve a suspect or semi-suspect class or fundamental right, equal protection requires only a rational relation between the means chosen and a legitimate governmental objective, and the means and end here meet this easy-to-satisfy standard. (To put it another way, limiting the money to the "top ten," and picking the top ten this way, are *not* "arbitrary and capricious" methods.)

(D) is wrong because the mere fact that Congress's use of its spending power is being challenged does not make the matter a nonjusticiable political question.

[Q2145]

6. **B** Congress can only delegate powers it possesses, so you first have to determine whether Congress itself has power to regulate federal lands. The answer is "yes," because Article I, Sec. 8, Cl. 17 gives Congress power to regulate federal lands. Next, you have to determine whether Congress validly delegated this power that it possesses. Here, too, the answer is "yes." Congress may delegate rule-making authority to federal agencies through statutes that set concrete objectives for the agency, and that list adequate criteria for carrying out those objectives. The Supreme Court has been very deferential in applying these "concrete objectives" and "adequate criteria" requirements. The objective being pursued here (control of campfires on federal lands) is quite concrete, and the criteria specified by Congress for achieving that objective (use of a penalty schedule for rule violators) seem quite adequate. Therefore, the statute's provision of authority to the Forest Service would likely be held to satisfy the requirements.

(A) is incorrect, because the executive branch does not have inherent rule-making authority over public lands. The only source of federal power to regulate public lands is the grant in Article I, Sec. 8, Cl. 17, to *Congress* to regulate such lands, as discussed above. So the executive's rule-making authority over public lands comes from delegation by Congress, not from any inherent authority.

(C) is wrong because the compelling nature of the government's regulatory interest is neither necessary nor sufficient to justify the Forest Service's regulation. The constitutional requirement is merely that the regulation be pursuant to a valid act of Congress, and that it not violate any specific constitutional prohibition. Since the act is a valid exercise of Congress's power to regulate federal lands, and since the delegation was validly done (as described in (B) above), that's the end of the matter, and the strength of the federal interest never becomes relevant.

(D) is wrong because, although law enforcement is an executive function, the constitutional exercise of that function requires that the executive act pursuant to congressional authorization provided by law.

[Q7036]

7. **B** The setting up of a presidential advisory commission, such as the one here, falls within the President's executive powers — nothing in the facts indicates that the commission will have legislative or judicial powers, so the commission is a proper delegation by the President of his executive power. As to funding: Congress has the right to earmark specified federal monies to be spent as the President shall determine. Therefore, nothing about this arrangement violates any constitutional provision.

(A) is wrong, because the President does *not* have "plenary power to provide for the health, safety, and welfare of the people..." For instance, the President does not have power to spend federal money for what he determines to be the health needs of "the people." This answer ignores both the source of the President's authority (which is limited to the executive power, that is, the power to see that the laws are carried out) and the need for all funding to be appropriated by Congress.

(C) is wrong because it incorrectly states the effect of the Tenth Amendment. The Tenth Amendment states that the powers not delegated to the federal government by the Constitution, and not prohibited to the states, are reserved to the states. The Tenth Amendment has relatively little force today as a limit on federal power. (About the only force it has as a limit on federal powers is to prevent Congress from directly forcing the states to enact or enforce federal policies.) The Amendment does not mean that the federal government may not exercise power over a "traditional state function." So the fact that vaccination has traditionally been a function handled by the states does not mean that the Tenth Amendment bars the federal government from taking action with respect to vaccinations.

(D) is wrong, because Congress does not need to authorize the creation of a temporary commission. An Advisory Commission on Vaccination is not a new federal agency — it is an advisory group, set up for a specific purpose and having a temporary existence. The President does not need congressional approval to create such an organization. Nor has Congress prohibited its creation (which if it had happened might bar creation of the Commission), because as the facts state no federal statute authorizes or prohibits this action.

[Q3109]

8. **B** This is a classic case of protectionism: the in-state retailers have persuaded the legislature to strengthen the in-staters' economic position vis-á-vis out-of-state retailers (since small in-state retailers now get an advantage that small out-of-state retailers don't get, and get an unearned cost-equality with large out-of-state retailers). So out-of-state retailers are being discriminated against (treated less favorably by virtue of their out-of-state status). This sort of protectionism is virtually a per se violation of the dormant Commerce Clause, and is certainly an undue burden on commerce.

(A) is wrong because economic regulation that does not involve a suspect class or fundamental right (and the regulation here involves neither) will receive only mere-rationality review under the due process clause, and the measure here would pass that review.

(C) is wrong because the privileges and immunities of "national" (as opposed to state) citizenship are guaranteed by the Fourteenth Amendment, Sec. 1; that P&I clause would not protect the plaintiffs because only a few rights have been recognized as rights of national citizenship for purposes of the clause (e.g., the right to travel physically from state to state, to move from state to state, and to vote in national elections), and the right of an out-of-stater to be free of economic discrimination is not one of them. (The plaintiffs might win with an argument based on Article *IV*'s P&I clause, which protects against discrimination by a state against out-of-staters; however, that clause doesn't protect the rights of "national citizenship," but rather, the rights of state citizenship.)

(D) is wrong because economic regulations that do not involve a suspect or semi-suspect class or fundamental right receive only easy-to-satisfy mere-rationality review under the Equal Protection Clause, and the statute here would pass that review (since the legislature could reasonably have believed that its citizens would fare better, overall, if small local retailers were not at a disadvantage to large out-of-state retailers).

[Q1190]

9. **D** When a state or local government uses its taxing powers (just as when it regulates), the state violates the dormant Commerce Clause if the tax: (1) intentionally discriminates against (i.e., treats less favorably) out-of-state competition to the benefit of local economic interests; or (2) unduly burdens interstate commerce. By reducing the amount of taxes paid by assemblers of computers in an amount equal to the portion of computer components manufactured in Green, Central City is discriminating against out-of-state component-makers to benefit local component-makers (the in-state makers get an effective price advantage). This discrimination causes the tax measure to violate test (1) above.

(A) is not the best response, because the ordinance has the effect of making parts manufactured outside of Green more expensive. It is true that the tax directly falls only on companies resident in Central City. But the *effect* of the tax is to make components manufactured in Green less expensive than those manufactured outside of Green, making this intentional discrimination against out-of-staters, even though the out-of-staters aren't being directly taxed.

(B) is not the best response, because the dormant Commerce Clause *does* place some limits on a state's right to foster resident corporations. Although a state may sometimes foster local businesses by encouraging its residents to "buy local," some methods of encouragement violate the dormant Commerce Clause. Where a state uses its tax system to confer a direct financial benefit to those who buy locally-manufactured goods, at the expense of out-of-state makers, the state crosses the line into forbidden "economic protectionism," and violates the dormant Commerce Clause. That's what the tax here does.

(C) is not the best response, because taxes based on gross receipts are not a per se violation of dormant Commerce Clause principles. Some tax schemes violate the dormant Commerce Clause because they either discriminate against, or unduly burden, interstate commerce. But the mere fact that a tax is "measured in whole or in part by [the taxpayer's] gross receipts" does not automatically mean that either forbidden discrimination or an undue burden on commerce is present. It's true that if a state enacted a tax on a multi-state taxpayer's gross receipts, and made no distinction between receipts from in-state activities and those from out-of-state activities, that tax might well be found to be an undue burden on commerce, and thus a violation of the dormant Commerce Clause. But Choice (C) goes way beyond this principle, and doesn't tie in to the problem with the tax here (which is that it intentionally discriminates against out-of-state component makers).

[Q3114]

10. **B** In the absence of congressional action, the state rule here probably would be a violation of the dormant Commerce Clause (what the question calls the "negative implications of the Commerce Clause"), because it discriminates against out-of-state growers. But Congress may use its commerce power to permit states to discriminate against interstate commerce. The federal statute here explicitly authorizes states to enact state-of-origin labeling requirements on imported citrus fruit.

(A) is incorrect, because the balancing argument would work only if: (1) Congress had not enacted a statute authorizing the state regulation at issue; and (2) the state law did not discriminate against interstate commerce. In this case, however, neither of these conditions is satisfied: Congress *has* authorized state-of-origin labeling requirements on imported citrus fruit, and the state law *is* discriminatory.

(C) is incorrect, because the state law *does* discriminate against out-of-state citrus growers, in that the law requires that all citrus fruit "imported" into the state be stamped with the state of origin, while the law imposes no such requirement on citrus fruit grown within the state.

(D) is incorrect, because although this argument correctly paraphrases the burden on the state to justify a law that discriminates against interstate commerce, the argument would be less likely to succeed than the "Congress authorized it" argument: in the absence of congressional authorization, the burden on a state to justify its discriminatory regulation is a heavy one, and states only rarely succeed in carrying it. Here, the availability of less-discriminatory alternatives (e.g., requiring in-state growers, not just out-of-staters, to stamp the state's two-letter code on the fruit) makes it unlikely that the state would win with this argument.

[Q7084]

11. **D** The federal concession statute, by requiring a nominal rental on account of the great public benefit from concessions, shows a federal intent to keep the total occupancy costs for concessionaires low. The state occupancy tax has the effect (and purpose) of making occupancy costs higher for the affected taxpayers than it would otherwise be. This fact is coupled with the fact that the state is singling out taxpayers on non-state-taxed property, including federally-owned property, so the interference with federal interests is especially acute. Therefore, a court might well hold that the state law so undermines the federal purposes as to be invalid under the Supremacy Clause. The court

would not *necessarily* reach this conclusion, but this is the most powerful of the four arguments.

(A) is wrong because the occupancy tax does not discriminate against interstate commerce (since the effect on tourists from inside Purple is the same as on out-of-state tourists), and it is unlikely that subjecting the plaintiff to the same overall level of overall taxation as businesses located in state-taxable facilities would be found to be an "undue burden."

(B) is wrong because the Fourteenth Amendment's P&I Clause protects only certain very limited rights of "national citizenship" (mostly the right to travel from state to state), and the Clause has never been interpreted to protect a "fundamental right to do business on federal property." (It's true that the P&I Clause of Article *IV* protects the fundamental right to pursue one's business or profession, but the examiners have tried to trick you here by using the Fourteenth Amendment's P&I Clause, not the Article IV Clause.)

(C) is wrong because the Fourteenth Amendment Equal Protection Clause protects only against a given state's unfair classification of multiple persons, not against one state's treating a person less favorably than other states treat similarly-situated persons. (Also, any classification being done by Purple here does not involve a suspect or semi-suspect class or a fundamental right, so the classification merely has to be rationally related to the achievement of a legitimate state objective, and the occupancy tax here meets this easy-to-satisfy standard.)

[Q2150]

12. **C** The operations of the federal government are indeed immune from state regulation, no matter how reasonable the state regulation, and even though the regulation is a generally-applicable one that treats the federal government no differently than anyone else. Since the office building is owned by and operated by the federal government, this regulatory immunity applies.

(A) is wrong, because even though the regulation of pollution may be a legitimate state police power concern, that regulation must give way to federal regulatory immunity.

(B) is wrong because, even if regulation of pollution is a joint concern of the federal and state governments, and even though both governments can regulate private parties (assuming that the state regulation is not inconsistent with the federal regulation), it does not follow that the state can regulate the federal government — under the principles of regulatory immunity, the state cannot do so.

(D) is wrong because there is no "de minimis" exception to the principle that states may regulate pursuant to their inherent police power. (The sole problem here is the federal immunity from regulation, which applies whether the asserted violation of the state's regulation is de minimis or not.)

[Q1195]

13. **B** When a state (or subdivision of a state, like a city and its municipally-owned operations) regulates a right that is "fundamental to national unity," and does so in a way that disadvantages out-of-staters, that regulation will essentially be subject to strict scrutiny under the Art. IV Privileges and Immunities clause. (Among other things, the state must show that the discrimination against non-residents bears a "substantial relationship" to the problem the state is attempting to solve.) Practice of one's business or profession is a right "fundamental to national unity" for P&I purposes.

The case here is on all fours with *New Hampshire v. Piper* (1985), where the Court held that New Hampshire's attempt to restrict the right to practice law to state residents violated the Art. IV P&I clause. Applying *Piper*, since there's no showing that out-of-state doctors are the peculiar source of any special problem that the hospital is trying to solve, the restriction violates the P&I Clause.

(By the way, there's no exception under the P&I Clause for activities in which the city or state is a "market participant," as there is under the dormant Commerce Clause. [*United Bldg. and Constr. Trades Counc. v. Camden* (1984)] So the fact that the city owns the hospital that's making the rule doesn't help it, as it would against a Commerce Clause attack.)

(A) is wrong because the legislature of state Red was not trying to punish the doctor. A bill of attainder is a legislative act that attempts to inflict punishment without a judicial trial upon individuals who are designated by name or in terms of past conduct. The constitutional prohibition against a bill of attainder would not be helpful to the doctor because the hospital here merely took the purely regulatory action of changing the residency requirement for practicing medicine at the hospital — no public entity named the doctor as a criminal, or attempted to punish or stigmatize him, which is what a bill of attainder would have done.

(C) is wrong because the doctor would have to show that the licensing requirement was not rationally related to a legitimate government interest, a showing the doctor probably couldn't make. The Due Process Clause of the Fourteenth Amendment provides that no state shall make or enforce any law which shall deprive any person of life, liberty, or property, without due process of law. When a fundamental right is not involved, substantive due process requires only that a law be "rationally related" to the achievement of a "legitimate government interest." So to win on due process, the doctor would have to prove that Red's new residency requirement was not rationally related to some legitimate government purpose. This standard is very lenient and easy-to-satisfy. Here, for instance, the hospital could plausibly claim that it wants to have on staff only doctors who live very nearby, and that it's entitled to use state of residence as a proxy for nearby-ness. Although the fit between means and end isn't very tight under this rationale, it's almost certainly tight enough to meet the extremely lenient rational-relation standard.

(D) is wrong because state Red was not legislating against past acts. The Ex Post Facto clauses, Article I, § 9 and § 10, prohibit both the federal government and the state, respectively, from passing legislation that retroactively alters the criminal law as to offenses or punishments, in a substantially prejudicial manner. A retroactive change in civil regulations, such as licensing requirements, cannot violate the prohibition, since the prohibition applies only to "penal," i.e., punitive, measures. Here, the facts make it clear that the hospital was not making a rule penalizing past acts, but was instead making residency a requirement to practice medicine in state Red going forward.

[Q3190]

14. **C** The Full Faith & Credit (FF&C) clause prohibits state courts from re-litigating cases in which the courts of another state have rendered final judgment. Even if the first court should have applied the second court's laws under standard conflict rules, the FF&C clause bars the second court from rehearing the case. (If the State B courts had not had jurisdiction over the man, and the jurisdiction issue had not been litigated or waived, the FF&C clause might not bar the State A courts from hearing the new suit. But the facts tell us that the man "defended" on the merits, thus waiving any claim he might have had that the State B courts lacked jurisdiction over him.) Accordingly, the court in State A was required to dismiss the suit.

(A) is incorrect, because the FF&C clause prevents the court in State A from relitigating the merits, and the fact that the woman drove the car to State A has no effect on the constitutional analysis.

(B) is, similarly, wrong because the location of the car has no effect on the constitutional analysis.

(D) is wrong because the movement of the car across state lines did not create a federal question.

[Q7051]

15. **C** This is a classic illustration of a state regulation in the economic or social-welfare area, where no fundamental right is involved. (Insurers don't have a fundamental right to adopt any particular pricing mechanism.) Since the "one price for all" scheme is rationally related to achieving one or more legitimate state objectives (e.g., promoting a sense of fairness and non-discrimination among insurance customers living in a particular county, or avoiding race-based redlining), the scheme does not violate the insurer's due process rights.

(A) is wrong for the same reason (C) is right — the company may have a due process right not to be irrationally deprived of its desired pricing mechanism, but the requirement of uniform pricing here is not irrational.

(B) is wrong, because the statute does not unduly burden interstate commerce (it only applies to policies written in-state, and it does not discriminate against out-of-state insurers).

(D) is wrong because federal courts do not have a duty to abstain from passing on the case until the state courts have had an opportunity to pass on the constitutionality of this state statute. When a litigant believes that a state statute violates the federal constitution, the litigant may sue immediately in federal court for a determination that this is so, as long as the requirements of justiciability (e.g., ripeness, actual injury to the plaintiff, etc.) are met. In other words, there is no sense in which state courts get "first shot" to determine the federal constitutionality of a state statute.

[Q2008]

16. **C** The Court held in *Webster v. Reproductive Health Services* (1989) that a state could constitutionally forbid the use of all public facilities and publicly-employed staff in abortions, without thereby violating the substantive due process right to abortion. If the state forbade all facilities in the state — public or private — from performing abortions, that would be an unconstitutional "undue burden" on abortion, but the availability of private-facility abortions here prevents an undue burden from occurring. And the fact that the state here is allowing the use of public facilities for those abortions necessary to save the life of the mother makes it even more clear that the regulation is constitutional. (Probably under *Webster* such an exception is not even required.)

(A) is wrong because the Court has held (in *Webster*, supra) that the availability of private-facility abortions means that a ban on the use of public facilities does not impermissibly interfere with the right of abortion.

(B) is wrong because the Court has held (in *Harris v. McRae* (1980)) that government's refusal to fund abortions for patients who cannot afford them does not constitute an interference with the constitutionally-protected right to abortion.

(D) is wrong because the Court no longer uses the privilege/right distinction in deciding cases involving the exercise of the important constitutional interests, and it is certainly not the case that the state may condition access to public facilities for an abortion "on any basis it chooses." (For instance, the state could not say that it will fund abortions at state-owned facilities for white women but not black women.)

[Q2162]

17. **C** Since the government had previously agreed that the teacher could only be fired if she were shown not to have had "good behavior," she had a due process "property" interest in maintaining her job. The Supreme Court has held that once a person has a property interest in a job or benefit, only the courts, not the government, may prescribe the procedures that are to be used to terminate that job or benefit. So the fact that the statute provides only for a post-discharge hearing does not mean that this is all the teacher is due. Instead, the Court has held that the job holder is entitled to a hearing before the termination (or at least before the termination of salary). [*Cleveland Bd. of Ed. v. Loudermill* (1985).] Since the statute here did not give the teacher such a pre-termination hearing, the statute was unconstitutional. And the statute did not get saved by the government's holding a hearing three months after the termination.

(A) is wrong because it is not true that a claim that a state statute is unconstitutional is not ripe until all state-court remedies have been exhausted. When a litigant believes that a state statute violates the federal constitution, the litigant may sue immediately in federal court for a determination that this is so, as long as the requirements of justiciability are met. And although it's true that one of the requirements of justiciability is that the case be "ripe," ripeness merely means that the plaintiff has already suffered, or imminently faces, actual injury.

(B) is wrong for at least two reasons: (1) not all state employees have the right not to be dismissed except for good cause (and this choice implies that all of them do); and (2) even if an employee such as the teacher here had a right not to be dismissed except for good cause, the burden of proof on the government would be just a preponderance-of-the-evidence standard, not the hard-to-satisfy "beyond a reasonable doubt" standard.

(D) is wrong because the Supreme Court has held that, where a state employee has a right to hold her job during good behavior, the employee is entitled not only to a pre-dismissal statement of reasons but a pre-dismissal hearing (and the fact that the statute provides only for a post-dismissal hearing does not change the constitutional requirement of a pre-dismissal one). [Cf. *Loudermill*, *supra*, p. 142.]

[Q1152]

18. **B** The city here is engaging in economic regulation, and no suspect class or fundamental right is involved. The "even plausibly justifiable" standard is a good summary of the extreme deference that courts give to government choices in the economic-regulatory area where no suspect class or fundamental right is at issue. Grandfather schemes in which people with longtime track records of pursuing an activity are treated more favorably than newcomers to that activity are a good illustration of classifications that are very likely to be upheld.

(A) is wrong because it incorrectly applies strict scrutiny; strict scrutiny would be appropriate for a regulation that intentionally disfavored a suspect class (e.g., persons of a particular race) or substantially impaired a fundamental right (e.g., the right to vote), but the classification here does not do either of these things.

(C) is wrong because the grandfather scheme here would not be found to be so "tenuous" or "underinclusive" as to fail the easy-to-satisfy rational-basis test.

(D) is wrong as a statement of law; so long as no suspect class or fundamental right is impaired, grandfather clauses are usually found valid, and are certainly not "per se violations" of equal protection.

[Q1021]

19. **D** The issue here is the validity of the school's gender-based classification, under which students who are mothers of an infant can use the day-care center but students who are fathers of an infant cannot. For such a gender-based classification, the court uses intermediate-level scrutiny, under which, as Choice (D) recites, the defendant (the government) bears the burden of showing that its classification is "substantially related" to the fulfillment of an "important governmental interest." [*Craig v. Boren* (1976)] Notice that the standard is the same for a male plaintiff who is disadvantaged by the classification as it would be for a female plaintiff who was disadvantaged.

(A) would be correct if the classification were one that did not involve a suspect or semi-suspect class or fundamental interest (e.g., a garden-variety economic or social-welfare regulation); but since gender is a semi-suspect category, the standard in choice (A) is insufficiently demanding.

(B) is incorrect mainly because, when the classification is based on gender, the use of semi-strict scrutiny means that the government bears the burden of persuasion. (Also, the key phrases "narrowly drawn as possible" and "substantial governmental interest" are not quite right.)

(C) is wrong because, while it correctly places the burden of persuasion on the government defendant, this choice recites the standard for strict rather than semi-strict scrutiny.

[Q2155]

20. **C** Ballot restrictions that are so severe that minor-party and independent candidates have no realistic opportunity to get on the ballot are given strict scrutiny, under both the Equal Protection Clause and the First Amendment's freedom of association clause. [*Williams v. Rhodes* (1968)] The statute

here is such a restriction, because it makes it completely impossible (not just somewhat harder) for someone who fails to get a major-party nomination to then run as an independent or minor-party candidate in the general election, no matter how much public support that person can demonstrate. Consequently, the choice here, by articulating strict scrutiny as the standard, is correct.

(A) is incorrect because, although it correctly articulates the strict-scrutiny standard, it incorrectly says that the plaintiff who is challenging the government bears the burden of persuasion; in those scenarios triggering strict scrutiny, the burden of persuasion is on the government.

(B) is wrong because it incorrectly uses the easy-to-satisfy mere-rationality standard, when what is at issue is a serious impairment of the fundamental right to be a candidate (and the right of voters to choose the best candidate).

(D) is wrong because, for the reasons stated above, the court would apply the strict scrutiny standard on these facts.

[Q1122]

21. **C** First, education is not a fundamental right for equal protection purposes. *San Antonio Sch. Dist. v. Rodriguez* (1973). Second, wealth classifications are not a suspect category. This choice therefore correctly asserts that (1) no fundamental right or suspect classification is involved in this case; and (2) where this is true, the plaintiff must bear the very difficult burden of proving that there is no rational relationship between the classification being used and any legitimate state interest. (By the way, it is very unlikely that the plaintiffs would win under this test; a school-funding scheme relying principally on local property taxes was upheld against rational-basis equal protection attack in *San Antonio v. Rodriguez, supra.*)

(A) is wrong because classifications based on wealth are not "inherently suspect" for equal protection purposes, so such classifications do not have to satisfy the strict scrutiny standard that this choice articulates.

(B) is wrong because the Court has held that education (or at least the right to have a public education that goes beyond minimally-adequate standards) is not a fundamental right for equal protection purposes; therefore, the strict scrutiny standard articulated by this choice would not apply.

(D) is wrong because it articulates an intermediate level of scrutiny, and that level is only used in cases involving semi-suspect classifications (e.g., ones based on gender).

[Q1073]

22. **D** This is the best response, because without the showing of "rough proportionality" specified in this choice, the ordinance violates the Takings clause. *Dolan v. City of Tigard* (1994) holds that when a city conditions a building permit on some "give back" by the owner, there must be a "rough proportionality" between the burdens on the public that the building permit would bring about, and the benefits to the public from the give-back. There's nothing in the facts to suggest that the city ever made the required showing here. (Indeed, the facts tell us that city officials presented no evidence of any sort, so they certainly didn't produce evidence either about the size of the public burden from allowing the coffeehouse or the size of the corresponding benefit from the new child care facility they were requiring here.)

(A), (B), and (C) are all wrong because they misstate the burden of proof and the standard. When a city demands a "give back" in return for approving construction, the city, not the owner, bears the burden of proof as to rough proportionality (and this burden is probably somewhere between the easy-to-satisfy "rational relation" test of Choice (A) and the strict scrutiny of Choice (D)).

[Q3162]

23. **C** Although the state does some regulation of the insurance industry (for solvency), the state is not sufficiently involved with the operations of the insurance company here to satisfy the requirement

— applicable to any equal protection claim — that there be "state action." Notice that the choice never uses the phrase "state action" — it's up to you to spot the state action issue and to notice that this choice's use of the phrase "not applicable to the actions of these ... companies" captures the state-action concept.

(A) is wrong for several reasons, including most basically the fact that it ignores the state-action requirement for any equal protection claim. (The fact that the *state police* are arguably failing to give equal protection is irrelevant, since the police aren't a party and aren't tightly associated with a party.)

(B) and (D) are wrong, similarly, because they too ignore the state-action requirement for equal protection claims. (If the state-action requirement were satisfied — if, for instance, the state expressly required burglary-insurance rates to be adjusted based on local crime rates — then (D) would be the best answer because it correctly expresses the idea that a governmental classification that does not involve a suspect class or fundamental right needs to be supported only by a rational basis.)

[Q1114]

24. **B** The Thirteenth Amendment permits Congress to forbid the "badges and incidents" of slavery. This power has been interpreted by the Court to include the power to forbid even private acts of racial discrimination against black people, on the theory that such discrimination is the relic of slavery.

(A) is wrong because Congress does not have any "authority to enact laws for the general welfare" (only the power to "tax and spend" for the general welfare).

(C) is wrong because this might be an explanation of why the statute couldn't be supported by Congress's commerce power, but the Thirteenth Amendment power allows Congress to forbid even purely local racial discrimination (i.e., discrimination that does not involve interstate commerce).

(D) is wrong because if Congress's action falls within a specific grant of power (here, the Thirteenth Amendment grant), the Tenth Amendment acts as a limitation only in the highly specialized case of Congress's attempt to take over state lawmaking mechanisms.

[Q2101]

25. **C** The Supreme Court has held that a threat communicated with the intent to intimidate the recipient, like the communication in this case, is not protected by the free speech clause of the First Amendment. If the state had singled out only certain types of threats (e.g., ones based on race), there might be a First Amendment problem, but the statute here bans *all* threats of violence, so it is content-neutral and thus acceptable.

(A) is incorrect, because as explained above, threats of violence with intent to intimidate are not protected by the First Amendment, and that's true even if the speaker never acted (and indeed never intended to act) on the threat.

(B) is incorrect because it misstates the legal basis for the correct conclusion that the man may be punished: intimidating threats of violence may be proscribed regardless of whether the threatener was committing a trespass.

(D) is incorrect because the Supreme Court has never held that racially motivated threats can violate the Thirteenth Amendment's prohibition of involuntary servitude.

[Q7095]

26. **B** The Supreme Court has repeatedly held that even if a city is using its zoning powers to limit or prohibit a speech-related activity, the regulation is acceptable if the city is reasonably targeting the secondary effects of that speech (e.g., crime or lower property values) rather than targeting the

expressive content of that speech. See, e.g., *Erie v. Pap's A.M.* (2004) (city may completely ban "nude dancing" to combat the bad secondary effects of such). Since the government is targeting the secondary effects rather than the message, the regulation is to be evaluated based on the test for content-neutral time, place and manner regulations, which as this choice suggests makes such regulations valid as long as they are designed to serve a substantial governmental interest and do not unreasonably limit alternative avenues of expression. Since the interest in preventing blight is "substantial," and since adult uses are permitted in alternative venues (areas zoned commercial), these requirements are easily satisfied.

(A) is wrong because it falsely asserts that the city may use its zoning powers to forbid particular messages based on their content. Such a content-based regulation would have to be strictly scrutinized, and would almost certainly be struck down.

(C) is wrong because it badly misstates the law: cities may indeed use their zoning regulations to prevent operators of adult theaters and the like from choosing their location, as long as the city is acting reasonably to combat the perceived negative secondary effects of the business, rather than out of distaste for the content of the messages transmitted by the business.

(D) is wrong because it exactly misstates present law; cities may (not "may not") "zone property in a manner calculated to protect property from the likely adverse secondary effects of adult theaters and bookstores." [*Erie v. Pap's, supra*, p. 146.]

[Q2193]

27. **B** The facts here are very similar to those of *Rankin v. McPherson* (1987), where the Court held that: (1) the clerk's statement supporting a recent assassination attempt (of Pres. Reagan) was indeed on a matter of "public concern"; and (2) the fact that the clerk had no policy-making role and that his statement had little negative impact on his job effectiveness made it unreasonable to dismiss him for that statement.

(A) is wrong because even a "permanent" public employee (i.e., one with a property right in his post) may have his job taken without just compensation, as long as procedures constituting due process are followed. In other words, what the due process clause guarantees on these facts is that the clerk's job won't be taken arbitrarily or capriciously, not that the job won't be taken "without just compensation" (a standard that would more properly be applied to the taking of tangible real or personal property rather than a job).

(C) is wrong because the Court has held (in *Rankin, supra*) that although the government has an interest in having loyal and supportive employees, this interest does not outweigh the employee's interest in commenting on matters of public concern, where the comment does not undermine the employee's effectiveness in light of the non-policy-making and limited scope of the employee's job (which, like the job here, was clerical).

(D) is wrong because: (1) the Court does not use the right/privilege distinction in First Amendment public-employment cases; and (2) even if the Court did believe that public employment was a "privilege" rather than a "right," the Court would almost certainly view the case as justiciable.

[Q2184]

28. **B** This choice correctly states the three-part *Lemon v. Kurtzman* (1970) test for government action that is alleged to benefit some religious interest. On the facts here, the statute passes all three parts: there is no evidence that the city's decision to operate the cemetery under these rules was intended to benefit religious groups; the primary effect of the cemetery operation is not to benefit those who put religious monuments on their plot; and the city's work in maintaining the religious monuments is so incidental to the overall operation of the cemetery — and so comparable to the work needed to maintain non-religious monuments — that there is no excessive entanglement between government and religion.

(A) is wrong because the amount of government funds spent is not dispositive; if the city was intending to benefit only religion (e.g., by providing a $20 reimbursement to the first 100 people who bought a piece of religious jewelry), the fact that only a "small amount" of city funds was spent would not save the expenditure from being a violation of the Establishment Clause.

(C) is wrong because it misstates the test for Establishment Clause violations; a city may maintain a "religious object" if the maintenance is part of a religiously-neutral program that is not intended to, and does not have the primary effect of, benefiting religion.

(D) is wrong because, if the government acts neutrally as to religion (as it has done here), there is no Establishment Clause violation whether the government has pursued a compelling interest or not.

[Q1138]

29. **B** In judging the constitutionality of the display of a religious symbol such as a nativity scene, the most important single factor seems to be the context in which the religious symbol is displayed: If the religious symbol is presented by itself in what is clearly a space reserved by the government for its own property and its own messages, the Court is likely to conclude that a reasonable observer would believe that the government was endorsing the religious message. Conversely, the presence of other non-religious symbols nearby, or the existence of a sign indicating that the display was furnished by private parties, may well be enough to lead a reasonable observer to the conclusion that the government was *not* endorsing religion. [*Allegheny County v. ACLU*]

On this standard, the proposed display of the nativity scene here would be unconstitutional. The nativity scene would not be surrounded by non-religious symbols having to do with the holiday season (symbols that would make it seem that the nativity scene was just part of a secular celebration of the holiday season). The whole presentation here — and the fact that the governor and legislature supported it — would create in a reasonable observer the impression that the government was endorsing a religious message. And the fact that the display components would be contributed by private citizens would not be enough to prevent the reasonable observer from believing that the government was endorsing religion.

(A) is wrong because the ownership of the display would not be dispositive on the issue of whether government seemed to be endorsing religion. If the scene here seemed to be a celebration of Christmas as a primarily secular holiday, the fact that the government owned the display would not be fatal. But, for the reasons discussed in Choice (B) above, the context of the display here would suggest to a reasonable observer that the state was endorsing religion. Consequently, the display violates the Establishment Clause.

(C) is wrong because donation would be only one element considered in the total context of the display. If the display made it clear to the public that private citizens had donated the components, this would indeed be one factor (but just one) tending to demonstrate that the display was not a forbidden government endorsement of religion. But there's no indication here that the fact of private donations would be disclosed to the public. Furthermore, this fact, even if disclosed, probably wouldn't be enough to overcome the otherwise-powerful impression that the government is endorsing a religious message.

(D) is wrong because displaying the scene next to the products would not rebut the impression that the state was endorsing the nativity scene's religious message. When a religious symbol such as a nativity scene is displayed in a public place, the issue is whether a reasonable observer would believe that the government is endorsing a religious method. Context is all-important. If the nativity scene were displayed next to other objects that pertain to December as a primarily secular holiday (e.g., a Santa Claus figure), the impression of an endorsement of religion would be rebutted. But putting the scene next to the year-round display of in-state-manufactured products would not rebut the impression of an endorsement of religion, because an observer would realize that the two displays were separate, and that the nativity scene was its own stand-alone display on an explicitly religious topic.

[Q3165]

30. **D** Government may take generally-applicable actions that advance important public interests, without giving an exemption to those whose religious beliefs are thereby burdened. The facts tell us that the rules against overnight camping and campfires are "consistently enforced" because of "very great dangers," so the "generally applicable" and "advancement of important public interests" standards are met here. The fact that the Superintendent doesn't like cults doesn't matter, because there is no indication that his decision to deny the permit here was motivated by anything other than a desire to enforce these generally-applicable rules.

(A) is wrong, for the same reason that (D) is right: government may impose a generally-applicable rule to promote an important interest, even if government knows that its enforcement of that rule will interfere with religious conduct.

(B) is wrong because the Park Service's action did not "purposely and invidiously discriminate" against the group — what was being enforced was a generally-applicable rule that was not enacted for anti-religious purposes.

(C) is wrong because it misstates the law governing the Establishment Clause as well as the facts — if non-religious groups were permitted to take the same general type of action in question (here, overnight camping and campfires), which they are not, then it would not be a violation of the Establishment Clause for the government to allow a religious group to do the same thing (and, indeed, it would probably be a violation of the Free Exercise Clause for the government *not* to allow the religious group to do the same thing that the non-religious are permitted to do).

[Q2112]

31. **A** The plaintiff does not meet the requirement of "injury in fact." He clearly has not been injured yet; the real question is whether he faces sufficiently imminent injury from the residency requirement. A court would likely hold that because the plaintiff has not yet even made the decision to run, and could not be injured unless he decided to run, any threatened injury to him is too uncertain and speculative to meet the requirement that prospective injury be reasonably concrete and imminent. The fact that the chairman has joined the suit does not change this, since the chairman (and the chairman's party) would not be injured unless some actual candidate was blocked by the residency requirement, and there is no such candidate now.

(B) is wrong because: (1) the absence of a case or controversy would prevent the court even from getting to the issue of whether there was a substantial federal constitutional question in the case; and (2) the fact that something is a local election does not prevent it from presenting a substantial federal constitutional question (for instance, an unduly long residency requirement probably *would* constitute a violation of an actual candidate's equal protection rights).

(C) is wrong because, while the residency restriction might well constitute an equal protection violation of the rights of an actual candidate, the plaintiff's lack of actual-candidate status prevents him from raising a case or controversy.

(D) is wrong because there is no basis (certainly not a federal constitutional basis) for the court to conclude that "substantially complying," rather than fully complying, with the residency requirement here would be sufficient.

[Q2153]

32. **C** Because the only person whose rights have been arguably affected by the new statute is the friend, who is not a claimant, there is no live case or controversy between the litigants, so standing rules

prevent the court from hearing it.

(A) is wrong because the lack of standing prevents the court from deciding the case on its merits even though the plaintiff is claiming that the Constitution has been violated (which would of course raise a federal question if there were a case or controversy before the court).

(B) is wrong because, if there were not any standing problem, the question of the constitutionality of the statute would not be a nonjusticiable political question (a category limited to a few special situations, none of which applies here).

(D) is wrong, because the Eleventh Amendment bars only suits seeking money damages against states, and the suit here is seeking a declaratory judgment rather than money damages.

[Q1133]

33. **A** The Eleventh Amendment generally forbids the federal courts from entertaining damage suits against states, and Congress cannot override this ban even when it is acting pursuant to some enumerated power (e.g., the Commerce Clause). But there is one exception: when Congress is using its special powers to enforce the post-Civil War amendments (the Thirteenth, Fourteenth and Fifteenth), it may authorize damage suits against the states that would otherwise be barred by the Eleventh Amendment. That is what's happening here.

(B) is wrong because it is overbroad. As a general rule Congress, even where it is acting pursuant to some power given to it by a specific provision in the Constitution, may not override the state immunity from federal-court damage suits conferred by the Eleventh Amendment; enforcement of the post-Civil War amendments represents the only exception to this rule.

(C) is wrong for essentially the same reason: the Eleventh Amendment *does* generally limit the power of Congress (not just the power of the federal judiciary) to modify the sovereign-immunity of the states, but the Supreme Court has held that in the special case in which Congress is enforcing the post-Civil War amendments this general limitation on Congress's power does not apply. [*Fitzpatrick v. Bitzer* (1976)]

(D) is wrong because it is a flat misstatement of law: the Supreme Court has held that the Eleventh Amendment protects a state from federal-court damage suits even where the suit is brought by a citizen of a different state. [*Hans v. Louisiana* (1890)]

[Q1027]